Hunter, Trader, Trapper, V69, No. 1, July,
1934

Otto Kuechler

HUNTER TRADER TRAPPER

JULY 1934
25 cents

Blank Cartridge Pistol

REVOLVER STYLE

.22 CAL. **25c 50c $1.00**

MADE IN 3 SIZES

Three new models now out **25c, 50c and $1.00.** Well made and effective. Modelled on pattern of latest type of Revolver. Appearance alone enough to scare a burglar. Takes 22 Cal. Blank Cartridges obtainable everywhere. Great protection against burglars, tramps, dogs. Have it lying around without the danger attached to other revolvers. Fine for 4th July, New Years, for stage work, starting pistol, etc. **SMALL SIZE 4 in. long 25c. MEDIUM SIZE 5 in. long 50c. LARGE SIZE 6in. long $1.00. BLANK CARTRIDGES 50c per 100. HOLSTER (Cowboy type) 50c. Shipped by Express only not prepaid.** *Big catalog of other pistols, sporting goods, etc. 10 cents.*

PRICE 10 CENTS

HOTSY TOTSY

THE FAN DANCE

HIT *of the* CENTURY *of* PROGRESS

Who will forget the famous FAN DANCE episode of the Century of Progress Exposition in Chicago? Here it is humorously, cleanly presented in vest pocket form. You flip the pages and **HOTSY TOTSY** comes to life and whirls through her dance, provoking not a sly smile, but a wholesome laugh from all, even the most fastidious. It is a most innocent fun maker that will cause you and your friends no end of fun and amusement. **HOTSY TOTSY the FAN DANCER** measures only 2 x 3 inches – 6 square inches of spicy, piquant entertainment for one and all. **PRICE 10c.** Add 3c for postage. *Big Catalog* **10c.**

Johnson Smith & Co., Dep. 720, Racine, Wis.

BOYS! THROW YOUR VOICE

[illegible] anywhere. Lots of fun fooling teacher, policeman or friends.

THE VENTRILO

a little instrument, fits in the mouth out of sight, used with above for Bird Calls, etc. Anyone can use it. **Never fails. A 16-page course on Ventriloquism together with the Ventrilo. All for 10c postpaid.**

MAKE YOUR OWN RADIO RECEIVING SET

Enjoy the concerts, baseball games, market reports, latest news, etc. This copyrighted book "EFFICIENT [illegible] shows how to make and operate inexpensive Radio Sets; the materials for which can be purchased for a mere trifle. Also tells how to build a short-wave Receiver for bringing in foreign stations, police calls, ships at sea, etc. **ONLY 15c. postpaid.**

SILENT DEFENDER

Used by police officers, detectives, sheriffs, night watchmen and others as a means of self-protection. Very effective. Easily fits the hand, the fingers being grasped in the four holes. Very useful in an emergency. Made of aluminum they are very light, weighing less than 2 ounces. Handy pocket size always ready for instant use. **PRICE 25c each, 2 for 45c postpaid.**

Electric Telegraph Set 15c

BOYS! A private Electric Telegraph Set of your own for **15c.** Lots of fun sending messages to your friends. Better still get two sets, hook them up as shown in the directions, for TWO-WAY MESSAGES (sending and re[illegible] with the simple instructions that accompany each set. Operates on any standard dry battery obtainable everywhere. With this outfit you can learn to transmit and receive by the Morse International Code, and in a very short time become an expert operator. Mounted on a wooden base measuring 4 x 3 in., first class construction throughout, complete with key, sounder, magnet miniature Western Union blanks, packed in a neat box with full illustrated instructions. **ALL FOR 15c** (without Battery) **OUR BIG catalog of novelties, jokes, puzzles, tricks, etc. 10c.**

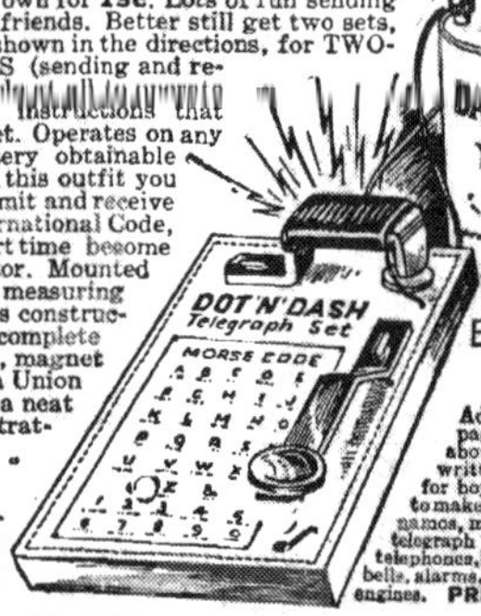

The Boy Electrician 10c

Add 10c for 64 page book all about electricity written specially for boys. Tells how to make batteries, dynamos, motors, radios, telegraph apparatus, telephones, lights, electric bells, alarms, coils, electric engines. **PRICE 10c ppd.**

CHAMELEONS

25 Cents Each. Shipped By Mail

LIVE, SAFE DELIVERY GUARANTEED

Get one of these most wonderful of all creatures. Watch it change its color. Study its habits. Wear one on the lapel of your coat as a curiosity. Watch it shoot out its tongue as it catches flies and insects for food. No trouble to keep. Can go for months without food. Measures about 4 inches in length. Shipped to any address in U. S. A. by mail. We guarantee safe arrival and live delivery. **PRICE 25 CENTS, OR 3 FOR 50 CENTS POSTPAID.**

HOW TO WIN AT POKER

Written by a card sharper. Tells how to win at draw poker. Explains different varieties of poker such as Straight Poker, Stud Poker, Whiskey Poker, Mistigris. The Freeze-out, The Widow, Buck, Jack-Pots, etc. Exposes the methods used by card sharpers and professional gamblers. 18 Chapters. This book contains a vast amount of information and may save you from being fleeced by crooked players and gamblers. **PRICE 10c Postpaid.** *Big Novelty Catalog 10 Cents*

NEW VAMPING CARD 15c

NO TEACHER NEEDED -- Surprisingly Simple System. Persons having neglected their Musical Education need not despair, for with the aid of our new VAMPING CARD (placing the card upright over the piano keys), you can Vamp away to thousands of Songs Ballads, Waltzes, Rag Time, etc. No knowledge of music is required. After using it a few times, you will be able to dispense with the aid of the Vamping Card entirely. This clever invention costs **only 15c ppd.**

MAGIC MADE EASY — 250 MAGIC TRICKS

An excellent little book containing 250 Parlor tricks, tricks with cards, coins, handkerchiefs, eggs, rings, glasses, etc. So simple that a child can perform them. Profusely illus.

Price Postpaid 10c; 3 copies 25c.

125 CARD TRICKS and sleight of hand. Contains all the latest and best card tricks as performed by celebrated magicians, with exposure of card tricks used by professional gamblers. **PRICE 25c POSTPAID.**

Novelty French Photo Ring

Here is a very great novelty in Rings, that is selling in thousands. It is a nicely made ring, finished in imitation platinum, and set with a large imitation diamond. It looks just like an ordinary ring, but in the shank of the ring is a small microscopic picture almost invisible to the naked eye, yet is magnified to an almost incredible degree and with astonishing clearness. There is quite an assortment of pictures that should suit all tastes. Some are pictures of bathing girl beauties, pretty French Actresses, etc., others are views of places of interest in France, Panama Canal and elsewhere; others show the Lord's Prayer in type, every word of which can be read by persons with normal eyesight. They are interesting without being in any way objectionable. **PRICE 25c, 3 for 65c, or $2.25 per doz. postpaid.** *BIG CATALOG* 10c

BIG ENTERTAINER 15c

326 Jokes and Riddles, 25 Magic Tricks, 10 Parlor Games, 73 Toasts, 13 Fairy Tales, 105 Money-making Secrets, 22 Monologues, 21 Puzzles and Problems, 5 Comic Recitations, 10 Funny Readings, 11 Parlor Pastimes, 13 Flirtations, 1110 Girls' and Boys' Names and their Meanings, 10 Picture Puzzles, 69 Amusing Rhymes, 37 Amusing Experiments, Deaf and Dumb Alphabet, Shadowgraphy, Gypsy Fortune Teller, How to tell Fortunes with Cards, Dice, Dominoes, Crystal, Coffee Cup, etc. Hypnotism, Ventriloquism, Cut-outs for Checkers and Chess, Dominoes, Fox and Geese, 9 Men Morris, Spanish Prison Puzzle, Game of Anagrams, 25 Card Tricks, Crystal Gazing, etc. **ALL FOR 15c.** *Novelty Catalog 10c*

Wonderful X-Ray Tube

A wonderful little instrument producing optical illusions both surprising and startling. With it you can see what is apparently the bones of your fingers; the lead in a lead pencil, the interior opening in a pipe stem, and many other similar illusions. **Price 10c, 3 for 25c.**

TELL YOUR OWN FORTUNE

With the aid of this dream book and fortune-teller. The key to your future. Will you be lucky in love? Successful in business? Will you be wealthy? Complete with dictionary of dreams with descriptions and correct interpretations, with lucky numbers, fortunate days, oracles, divination, palmistry, etc. **Price 10c postpaid.**

Learn to Hypnotize

This book tells how. Explains all about Hypnotism, how to hypnotize, how to produce sleep, how to awaken a subject, Medical hypnotism, hypnotism in diseases, how to hypnotize animals Illusions etc. 27 chapters. **ONLY 10c ppd.**

REAL LIVE PET TURTLES

25c

Sent by Mail for only 25 Cents

A FASCINATING AND INTERESTING PET

LIVE Delivery Guaranteed

If you want a fascinating and interesting little pet, just risk **25c** and we will send you a real live PET TURTLE by mail postpaid. Thousands sold at Chicago Worlds Fair. No trouble at all to keep. Just give it a little lettuce or cabbage or let it seek its own food. Extremely gentle, easily kept and live for years and years. Need less attention than any other pet. Get one or more. Study their habits. You will find them extremely interesting. **Price 25c.** SPECIAL TURTLE FOOD **10c** pkg.

Fortune Telling By Cards

Book shows how to tell fortunes with cards, dice, dominoes, crystal, etc. Tells the meaning and signification of every card. Several different methods explained and fully illustrated. Crammed full from cover to cover with complete information on fortune-telling. **PRICE 10c postpaid.** *Stamps accepted.*

Good Luck RING

Very striking, quaint and uncommon. Oxidized gunmetal finish; skull and crossbones design; two brilliant flashing imitation rubies or emeralds sparkle out of the eyes. Said to bring good luck to the wearer. **PRICE 25c Postpaid**

HOW TO PITCH Pitch the Fade-a-way, Spitter, Knuckler, Smoke Ball, etc. Lessons by leading Big League Pitchers. Clearly illustrated and described with 56 pictures. **POSTPAID 25c**

All Parts Necessary for only 10c — **Runs on No. 6 Dry Battery** — *Postage 5c Extra*

ELECTRIC MOTOR

An Electric Motor for only 10 cents. Sounds almost unbelievable but it is perfectly true. For ONLY 10 cents we send you all the parts necessary packed in a neat box with full printed and illustrated directions for assembling. No trouble at all putting the parts together. In fact it's fun.

HOME BREWED WINES BEERS

This book contains over 100 simple recipes, with full instructions, for making all kinds of wines, beers, cider, cider champagne, brandies, gin, rum, whiskey, fruit cordials and simple liqueurs, fruit syrups, various kinds of vinegars, etc., etc. Home made wines and beers are particularly good and wholesome and their manufacture is not difficult. **PRICE 10c ppd.**

Merry Widow Handkerchief

A perfect model of the most necessary lingerie garment worn by the ladies, which, when folded up and worn in the pocket, has the appearance of being a gentleman's handkerchief. A very clever and mirthful joker. **PRICE 15c ppd.**

Johnson Smith & Co. Dep. 720, Racine, Wis.

ADDRESS ORDERS FOR GOODS ON THIS PAGE TO

JOHNSON SMITH & CO.

DEPT. 720, RACINE, WISCONSIN

Our complete Catalog sent on receipt of 10c, or the De Luxe Cloth Bound Edition for 25c. Bigger and better than ever. Only book of its kind in existence. Describes thousands of all the latest tricks in magic, the newest novelties, puzzles, games, sporting goods, rubber stamps, unusual and interesting books, curiosities in seeds and plants, etc., many unprocurable elsewhere. Remit by Coin, Money Order or Postage Stamps.

You bet the public
knows good Whiskey

"Why Jack, what are you doing over here? I thought you had a liquor store in your neighborhood."

"Oh, that place got my goat by offering some inferior substitute every time I asked for Crab Orchard."

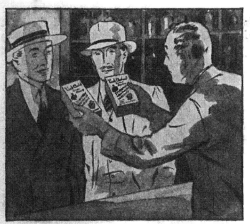

"Yes sir, Crab Orchard's our best seller. People have been waiting for a *real* straight whiskey at such a sensible price. We sell what the public calls for and make no attempt to substitute inferior goods."

It pays to insist on Crab Orchard if you want a *genuine* straight whiskey at a reasonable price. It's made the good old Kentucky way. Bottled right from the barrel — neither artificially aged nor colored. And the low price is the best news of all. *Accept no substitutes!*

Other straight whiskies
we recommend:

OLD McBRAYER
OLD GRAND DAD
OLD TAYLOR
OLD CROW
SUNNY BROOK
HILL AND HILL
MOUNT VERNON
OLD OVERHOLT
HERMITAGE

Crab Orchard

STRAIGHT KENTUCKY WHISKEY

The American Medicinal Spirits Company, Inc.

New York · Chicago · San Francisco · Baltimore · Louisville

KENTUCKY BOURBON — STRAIGHT AS A STRING

2

The Editor's Page

Fires in Fields May Menace Forests

An impression exists in the minds of most people that care in the use of fire on forest land applies only to the forest itself. This is not true because many fires are set in the open country which rapidly spread to the forest, and the same may be said of land covered with brush as well as recently reforested areas, says Dean Samuel N. Spring of the New York State College of Forestry.

The spring season is usually one of the worst in the East for forest fires. The number of fires last year, which broke all records, proved this to be true in New York, and it is now time for all persons who go afield or travel the highway to use extraordinary care in throwing away matches that have been lighted, cigarette and cigar stubs and tobacco from pipes. A few weeks of dry weather will increase the inflammability of field, brush land and forest to a vast extent causing practically all regions of the state to be in danger. Especially are the newly reforested areas in jeopardy. There is the added danger this year because precipitation has been considerably less than last year.

It does not require much of a fire to completely destroy a plantation of young trees. There is now in New York State 156,000 acres, for the most part new plantations and these plantations are often located near populous sections where automobile traffic is heavy and many persons go afield to fish, to hike and picnic and for other forms of recreation.

Smokers caused 43 per cent of the fires last year; campers caused six per cent; the burning of brush, clearing of land and burning refuse caused thirteen per cent; hunters caused ten per cent. Even children set fires; they caused two per cent of the fires last year. It is, therefore, plain that too much care cannot be used by persons who are out-of-doors and who smoke or build camp fires. Every match, after being lighted, should be broken between the fingers before throwing away, even when one is riding in an automobile or walking along the highway or a path. Lighted cigarette butts especially are dangerous as they burn with a hot fire until they are entirely consumed. Throwing away lighted cigarettes and letting them burn is a difficult habit to break but it should be stopped. Putting out cigarette butts should be practiced by every person who uses tobacco in this form, particularly when the smoker is out-of-doors.

——o——

Leave Cover For Nesting

Birds of nearly all species and small mammals are mating and beginning to look for nesting places, particularly the ground nesting species. Upon keeping intact these latter nests depends much of the game crop, both of upland game birds and waterfowl and ground nesting animals, such as rabbits. For, as "Ding" Darling, chief of the U. S. Biological Survey, says: "Ducks can't nest on picket fences." Neither can quail, pheasants, grouse or any other game bird, and only the Easter Rabbit is accredited with the ability to lay eggs anywhere.

Thus, the necessity of proper nesting cover and the assurance of not disturbing this cover until after the young birds and animals are off the nests.

Farmers, highway commissioners, county road supervisors and others are urged not to mow over where birds are nesting, if possible, until after July 15. Also farmers are asked to refrain from letting stock overgraze such areas if they want game birds.

Even where waterfowl nesting conditions are otherwise ideal, nests are destroyed by crows and other predators where cover is overgrazed by stock; the same is true of other species of ground nesting birds.

Paul L. Errington and Logan J. Bennett, both of the Iowa State College, cite the results of observations in Iowa that may be well to apply to all other parts of the country:

"A great many of the best marshes in northwest Iowa are nearly useless . . . on account of the surrounding nesting grounds having been closely grazed to the water's edge. Moderate pasturing by cattle or horses is not necessarily ruinous to nesting grounds, but overpasturing, and especially by hogs or sheep early in the season, is quite a different thing; if livestock would not be admitted before July, to be removed before the cover vegetation was cropped short, that is, while sizeable tufts of grass remained in quantities here and there, a grazing schedule might be entirely compatible with waterfowl management." They urge the fencing of shore strips a hundred yards or so back from the water's edge, leaving corners or lanes to permit stock access to parts of marshes for drinking or relief from flies. Interested sportsmen and conservation officials should aid farmers to fence off nesting cover.

——o——

Wet Hands Save Fish

Wet hands, gentle hands, and the heart of the Barefoot Boy will mean much to the nation through President Roosevelt's huge wildlife restoration program from now until ice again locks the streams and lakes in winter's grip, for some 15,000,000 Barefoot Boys and men with the heart of the Barefoot Boy will sally forth many times to try their luck at fishing.

Wet hands can be made to save millions of undersized fish so that they may grow up to be big fish. Comes now Talbott Denmead, of the U. S. Bureau of Fisheries showing just how great a savings may be made in wetting the hands and putting back undersized fish. An experiment carried on recently by the Bureau shows that practically 99 out of 100 fish so handled survive.

"Out of 288 smallmouth black bass, caught on treble hooks, and then transported in buckets and automobiles, only 4 died!" Mr. Denmead said. These fish were put in brood ponds at the Bureau's fish hatchery in West Virginia and were observed for months so there can be no dispute about that.

It seems that the only appreciable danger is not in the hooking but the handling of the fish in taking it off the hook or hooks. If the hands are dry they disturb the mucous protective sheet or "slime" on the outside of the fish, and fungi attack the disturbed places and kill the fish eventually. By wetting the hands thoroughly and handling the fish gently, preferably by grasping the fish by the under jaw rather than by the body, this danger is eliminated. Some scientists, however, are advancing a new theory with the same result, that if the slime is disturbed "salt water fish die of thirst" and that "fresh water fish drown." Whatever the real cause, the result is the same—wet hands save the fish; dry hands cause its death.

Hunter Trader Trapper

Volume LXIX   JULY, 1934   No. 1

IN THIS ISSUE

Published monthly by the HUNTER-TRADER-TRAPPER Co., at Columbus, Ohio, U. S. A.

OFFICES AND PLANT, 272 to 286 South Fourth Street.

Entered as Second Class Matter, April 5, 1905, at the Post Office
at Columbus, Ohio, under the Act of Congress of March 3, 1879.
All Rights Reserved.

$2.00 PER YEAR (RENEWAL $1.50)   **25 CENTS A COPY**
CANADIAN $3.00 A YEAR   **FOREIGN $3.00 A YEAR**

Advertising Rates and Sample Copies Will Be Sent On Application.

W. F. Heer.................Business Manager
O. Kuechler.................Managing Editor
Deshler Dickson...........Advertising Manager
W. L. Rarey.............Circulation Manager

Eastern Representative:
I. M. Hoffman, Inc......................
........420 Lexington Ave., New York City

Western Representative:
James C. Lewis Co.......................
........333 N. Michigan Ave., Chicago, Ill.

Address all communications to Hunter-Trader-Trapper, Columbus, Ohio.

RENEWALS—The date with your name on wrapper shows to what time your subscription is paid. Thus Jan. 34 shows that payment has been received up to Jan. 1934. When payment is made, the date on wrapper, which answers for a receipt, is changed; if this is not done, please write to us.

CHANGE OF ADDRESS—Subscribers wishing their address changed, must give their old

address (both postoffice and state) as well as new address.

MISSING COPIES—Should your magazine not arrive within a few days of the usual time, write. If you wait weeks we may be out of the issue wanted.

SPECIAL NOTICE—When renewing, writing about change of address or missing copies, be sure to sign your name exactly the same as it should appear on the wrapper of your H-T-T. This will prevent confusion and insure best service.

DISCONTINUATION—Your H-T-T will be promptly stopped at expiration of time paid for unless your renewal is received. Date on wrapper shows when paid to. It is best to renew a month or two in advance. However, at about the time you receive your last issue, notice will be sent you.

HOW TO REMIT—Money orders, either express or postoffice, as well as checks and drafts, are safe—can be duplicated if lost.

4

Drought and Flood; Largely Man-Made

By CAPT. PAUL MASON, "Nibowaka" to Thousands of Ohio Sportsman Readers

*D*ROUGHT is largely man-made, except in deserts; which also are man-made, as witness the great cities (including their aqueducts) dug up in recent years out of the Sahara, Arabia and northern and central Asia, from different parts of the great desert, 1500 miles wide, which extends from eastern Asia, 9000 miles to the Atlantic at the western end of the Sahara. Land surface of the Earth occupies 50,000,000 square miles (or one-fourth) of its area, and of this amount 13,500,000 square miles, or more than one fourth, is man-made desert. Much of China's 3,000,000 square miles is about to join the desert; wherefore it is germane to remark that Ohio has done as much to make a desert waste of itself in 150 years as China accomplished in two milleniums, and from the same causes. But the Chinese always were—slow!

During the period May 10-15, 0.59 of an inch of rain fell, a sharp shower of 0.11 in. on the 10th, and a 36 hour drizzle of 0.36 in. on the 13th-15th; but except for incidental benefit to growing things, all the effect was to reduce the year's deficiency of precipitation to 7.5 in. These are the central Ohio figures; but they are not far different from totals in the middle tier of Ohio counties extending from east to west—and conditions have been worse in other parts of the country. Witness the dust storms which, arising in Kansas, Nebraska and eastern Colorado, during the early part of May blanketed cities to the Atlantic coast, over a wide belt, north to south, in dense clouds taken up from the Granary of the Nation and spilled all the way to New England!

This year's conditions are the continuation of a decade of unusual dryness. Beginning in 1924, there have been only three years in which there was an excess of precipitation over normal; and those excesses were very slight. They were in 1926, '27 and '29. All the rest of these years, there was a deficiency, sometimes small, sometimes large. Years of deficient moisture mean years of excess heat; and excess heat means excessive evaporation by suspiration through trees and other vegetation, thus drawing on reserves of underground water and sapping the life-stream of the soil. During the last four years, deficiency of moisture in the central belt of Ohio was 12.87 in., and if this year's deficit to May 23 be added to it, there is a total deficiency for these counties, in four years and 143 days, amounting to 21.22 in., or 59 per cent of a normal year's rainfall in the same area! Many other sections of the country will show comparable figures.

What can be done about it? And what about floods?

Conditions that cause drought, in the end are conducive to flood. If drought is long continued, flood is inevitable. It may come at any time in the future; but come it will, for Nature is inexorable—and ruthless. She is long suffering and patient, with time to heal her own scars, whether man-made or by her own unbridled forces; but man is too impatient for her slow processes. He cuts down the forests and alters climate, destroys the mulch of thousands of years, and opens vast areas to the ravages of uncurbed run-off, when rains come. By over-drainage and deepening and straightening of streams he runs the fertility of his fields into the rivers and so to the sea—and complains that his fields are "worn out". But he did it!

Nature must restore the conditions which will minify drought; for they cannot be prevented. Only the effects can be ameliorated. When the Ohio Department of Health, in 1930-31, supplied 69 good wells to the people of 28 southern Ohio counties it did not prevent drought, but did minify its effects. And man must help to restore so much of natural conditions as may be possible in view of the complexities of modern life. He must plant trees, establish grassland strips along the streams to prevent soil erosion, put holding dams (including wing-dams) in them to retard the waters and raise ground water levels, and provide cover, food and protection for wild things of the world, by land, air and water. These are things that must engage the sportsman's interest if he would have game to hunt and fish to catch.

Floods also cannot be prevented, but they can be measurably controlled. The forces which tend to minify droughts also tend to hold flood waters to lower levels. The great sponge-like masses which Nature provides around the roots of forest trees are needed; and even the leaves of deciduous trees, in a heavy rain, hold back the first 40 per cent of it, in order that the water may reach the ground and soak into the soil slowly. Nature slows up the course of streams, with curves and obstructions, in order that as much as possible of its life-giving quality may be imparted to the soil. Man cannot be rid of it too quickly. He forgets that ONLY THE SURPLUS WATER from a rainfall should be discharged away from his fields. To this end, he should adopt contour plowing, which has been used in Europe for centuries.

But man can aid further in flood control. He can build impounding works at headwaters of his major streams; but they must be at headwaters. They will serve in moderate floods if placed elsewhere, as in the Dayton conservancy works; but there always comes a time when Nature excels all previous efforts—especially when man helps to prepare for it. Zanesville seems to be engaged on the right kind of a flood control project; for Zanesville recalls that if there had been adequate headwaters control on the Muskingum in 1913, all the water which went through the city above flood level in eight days, doing millions of damage, could have been carried through in 15 days at or below flood level, without loss.

Neither drought nor flood can be prevented; but it is in man's power to minify the one and measurably control the other; or to accelerate the power and intensify the ravages of both. It is time for Ohio to inaugurate a settled policy that will assure every possible aid to Nature to restore its safety and its prosperity through a sane and comprehensive conservation policy, wisely administered and adequately—even rigorously—enforced.

Hunting in Old Mexico

*The State of Sonora holds a hospitable welcome for
the hunter and "No Hunting" signs are never seen.*

By B. A. SWEET

*B. A. Sweet and wild hog (Javalin). When these
babies run they stick their bristles straight up.
They look plenty savage and can easily kill
hounds with their tusks.*

BELIEVING that it might be of interest to American sportsmen and particularly those of the Pacific southwest, I will try to give an authentic account of a hunting trip that was taken in December of 1933 into the State of Sonora, Mexico. I will also give a description of the state in general and of the game that can be had in different sections.

There are some regulations that must be complied with in order to enter Mexico as a tourist with arms and ammunition, camping outfit and hunting dogs to stay not longer than 60 days. The first and most important document to be obtained is a permit to take in guns and ammunition. This can be secured from the Mexican consul closest to your home town or it can be secured at Nogales, Arizona, or at any other point of entry where there is a Mexican consul located. It is always best to secure some letter of recommendation from an American official to present to the Mexican consul to show him that you are an honorable citizen of the United States in order that he may issue you a permit without any questions being asked. At present any person obtaining a gun permit may take into Mexico four arms, each must be of different caliber and 100 rounds of ammunition for each gun—duty free. This permit costs $5.00 and is good for one year from date of issue. There also must be secured a tourist permit. This is obtainable at any Mexican consul or at any point of entry. This permit costs $1.00 and is good for 60 days. Extensions can be had for this permit by applying to the Mexican officials at points of entry. A list of guns and ammuni-

tion also hunting dogs, should be left at the American customs office at point of entry so there would be no trouble when you return. You must register your car and tires at the Mexican customs office. The officials there look through all of the baggage thoroughly. The cost for your car and tire permit is five pesos, or five dollars Mexican money.

A hunting permit is obtainable at the border and costs ten pesos for ten days—thirty pesos for thirty days. This means ten days or thirty days of actual hunting. One might go into Mexico for sixty days but hunt only ten days and would need a permit for ten days only. In other words one is compelled to buy a hunting permit for only the actual time he intends to hunt.

It takes about three hours of time to go through all of the regulations at the border and you are on your way. Any party may take provisions for his trip duty free, also all kinds of wearing apparel, field glasses, cameras, etc. There are no restrictions or duty on any items of this sort. Gasoline can be secured at most all small towns but it is a good plan to take some along; duty will have to be paid on this at the rate of nine pesos for every twenty gallons.

With Mexican money at the present low rate of exchange—$3.60 pesos for every one dollar of American money—one can readily see that a hunting trip or vacation into Mexico would be very reasonable. The total cost of our trip per person was $35.00 American money. We were away from home two weeks and traveled approximately 1,800 miles.

When entering Mexico one should have

all of their money exchanged at the border as when you are on the other side there is no more dollars, it is pesos, and consequently one should have Mexican money to pay for what he desires.

The State of Sonora is doing everything possible to facilitate the entry and stay into Mexico of all American tourists and hunters. Everybody is given very courteous treatment and are handled in a very businesslike manner. They want you to come and enjoy their hunting and visit their state in general.

We arrived at Nogales, Mexico, on December 1st, and immediately made plans to cross the border and proceed on our way. Leaving Nogales at about twelve o'clock, noon, we arrived at Magdalena at about 4 p. m. and had a good old fashioned Mexican meal and enjoyed the hospitality of the town in more ways than one. From Magdalena we proceeded to Santa Ana which is about 75 miles below the border thence turned west to Altar and Pitiquito. The country is a rolling, semi-desert from Santa Ana south to Hermisillo and west to the gulf. Traveling along the road one will see hundreds of jack rabbits and big fellows they are. They offer good targets for high power rifles.

FROM Pitiquito we turned south towards Pt. Libertad; our destination at that time was Datil, a ranch located about thirty-five miles from the gulf. We were informed that this country would afford us at least some hunting of the kind we desired. We were anxious to obtain mountain lion, wild hog (javalin), deer, and any small game that happened to be present. We arrived at Datil and there located a Papago Indian, Antonio Lopez, and engaged him to show us the best hunting grounds close to that location. He took us about fifteen miles west of Datil to a spring known as Picou. At this place he claimed there was plenty of lion, deer, wild hog, quail, wild burro, and thousands of fox and coyotes.

The country surrounding here is a semi-desert with low rolling hills. The hunting at this point is very easy as there is very little brush to contend with and one can ride a horse over 98 per cent of all of the territory. The deer here are quite plentiful, and any party could easily obtain all of the venison he desires.

About twenty miles north of this spot there is a range of mountains approximately five miles long which are very rugged. Our Papago Indian informed us that there were literally hundreds of big horn sheep in this range of mountains and if we so desired we could easily obtain big horn sheep from this camp in less than one day's ride on our horses.

We arrived at Picou early in the morning, made camp and rested easily that day glancing over the country in general, laying plans for the following days hunt.

walked several miles without striking any tracks at all when about 11 o'clock Ada gave tongue on a cold trail that was at least three days old and we made her leave it as we did not want to work on any old trails. We saw plenty of lion tracks but could not strike a trail that was made the night before. We gave it up about 4 o'clock and went back to camp. When we arrived there the other boys were already in and had several deer hanging up.

ABOUT 5 o'clock that night several Mexican riders came into camp and remained with us for several days. They certainly are jovial fellows, anxious to talk and seemed to appreciate the American tourists' company. Everywhere we stopped the ranchers wanted us to stay and hunt. Everything is "Manana" meaning tomorrow.

The next day we hunted for lion, saw about five or six different lion trails but did not strike a fresh track. Arriving in camp found the boys had brought in more deer and wild hog. We now had more deer than we could eat and so gave several away to the Mexicans. Then we all agreed that we should kill no more deer until our meat supply was exhausted as we did not want to kill and waste the meat.

That night one of the Mexican riders

we would be able to strike him there early next morning. The next morning found us up and away at daylight. We proceeded to the kill. Ada stepped to the right of our course when we were nearing the kill as she could smell lion in the air. She gave tongue about 300 yards up the canyon. I could tell by her voice that she was on a track that had been made that night. I immediately went to her and brought her to the kill. All of the other dogs had it in their nose by that time and things began to pop. Hoover hit the trail where the lion had been lying down, and took it on the run. Boy, oh, boy! Things began to warm up fast. Ada, Razz, Smokey, Hoover, and Smith all were on a red-hot jumped trail and the way they did cry was something terrible. The Mexican fellows had never heard an American foxhound in full cry so consequently they thought hell was turned loose at an instant. Mr. Lion went straight up a rocky mountain to a bluff that was impossible to climb down for either man or beast. At the bluff he turned to the right along the edge of the cliff, following along the cliff for a distance of about half a mile he turned and went down the mountain in a flat about two miles across. When the dogs hit the flat they simply flew on that trail. We all followed as fast as possible and when we reached the far side of the flat we could hear them all barking treed. We were all very excited and rushed to the tree where Mr. Lion was perched thinking he was well out of any further danger. It only took one shot from a 30-30 to bring him down. When he hit the ground of course the dogs then have their fun, mauling him around in great style We started back to camp and on our way we took some pictures of the buck deer that the lion had killed. He was a big male, and I suppose he never had heard a hound before.

When we arrived in camp some of the other boys who had started on the lion chase had been left behind and had run into a bunch of wild hogs and brought in a couple more of them.

The next day all was quiet in camp. Everybody either spent the whole day telling lies, or was asleep. The following day we moved camp to a new location, about ten miles south, and there hunted in the dry creek bottom. There was plenty of lion in that location but we did not strike a hot trail.

I would like to make it plain that this country is very hard to run dogs in due to the fact that it is so dry and hot. There is very little water to be had and a dog must have water if he is to work hard very long when it is hot.

WE spent the next day loafing and went to Hermisillo after that, going straight through the country, via Datil, San Francisco and Los Negres. This road is terrible. Most impassible in many places. All along the road, about ten miles apart, are ranch houses, and every one of the ranchers are glad to have you stay and

(Continued on page 45)

Kenneth Thompson and B. A. Sweet—and deer that the lion killed. It was at this tree that the lion dragged his kill. B. A. Sweet is holding Ada, a wonderful lion dog—over 200 lions to her credit.

We were up the next morning early and started to go up the canyon in the hope of hitting a red hot lion track. Some of the boys went deer hunting and some wild hog hunting. Our dogs were: Ada, a real lion hound with over 200 lions to her credit; and Hoover, Smith, Razz, and Smokey. The rest of the dogs are all well trained hounds but have not had the experience on lion that Ada has had. We

came into camp and reported a lion had killed a buck deer about three miles from camp the night before. He reported that the deer was covered up by brush which meant the lion would be back there that night. We all decided we would go over and tree that very lion the next morning after he had eaten his fill from his kill. We knew he would stay very close to the kill to keep coyotes away that night, and

The Value of Scents

Among trappers the secrets of scent making and their use seems a closely guarded mystery but here the author gives some recipes that make worthwhile "off-season" reading.

By FLOYD McBETH

ARE scents of any value? This question has been asked thousands of times and the question is still open for discussion. But no two trappers seem to agree alike regarding its value. Numbers of writers have given their views, although some, no doubt, never set a trap with or without scent.

The value of scents in trapping is something that everyone will have to prove for himself, and I hope it will be understood that what I have to say is written as my personal experience and opinion rather than as an attempt to decide the question.

Scents, it has been my experience, are all-important in the trapping game. Some say that scents do more harm than good by arousing the animals' suspicion. Some trappers use scent only to attract the animals, and make good catches; others use bait alone and condemn anything in the line of scent. Some use neither scent nor bait, but depend entirely on "blind sets." Some trappers have no faith at all in scents while others regard almost as necessary as traps.

In the first place, a scent, to be successful, must do one thing: it must attract the animals to the neighborhood of a trap and keep them tramping and pawing until caught. The value of scents for trapping depends on the kind that is used and the method employed, the time of the year and the sex of the animal. If one will stop to consider just what scent is, and the object in using it, he must readily perceive its value, if the right kind is used, at the right time of the year. Scents are of various kinds and are expected to appeal to the animals in different ways. Therefore, before the trapper begins to make his scents he should have definitely in mind not only the animals he will use them for, but what instincts he expects to use in his appeal.

Scents, those prepared with the idea of appealing to the sex instincts, which is sometimes stronger than the instinct for protection, no doubt has its greatest value to trappers in connection with sets when used from January to March or thereabouts. At the mating season, if it contains the proper ingredients, there seems to be but little doubt but that it does possess great attracting qualities. Many different kinds of scents have been used. Some have been used successfully, but in using scents one should use good sound judgment, or he will make the animal suspicious, and harder to trap.

Most all beginners think with a good scent or lure that he can just cover a trap over at almost any point, place a little scent near, and skin the animals the

A collection of beautiful silver and cross fox pelts taken in Canada. The pelt in the center is a silver fox of extraordinary color and beauty.

following morning. Such is never the case, but rather, the trapper must first search about to ascertain if the animals he is seeking are located in or visiting the vicinity, then the runs are next. Almost every animal will constantly visit the same places when passing through. Then a spot must be selected where the animal is quite apt to stop. When the set is completed, a little scent may be placed on a bit of moss or grass nearby, in such position that if the animal is smelling about to locate, he steps directly upon the trap pan. It is true that almost all animals depend more on their sense of smell than the combined sense of sight and hearing, therefore any odor that is attractive to them may call them from a considerable distance.

THERE is one odor that is attractive to all animals, and that is the odor of their natural food. Most all wild animals are always hungry, and the odor of the food it prefers, even when wafted from a long distance by a gentle breeze, will quickly turn it in that direction. At other times than the mating season, animals live for the one purpose of eating.

The odor of fish-oil is probably more appealing to a greater number of animals than any other odor. All animals that will eat fish are attracted by it, and this lists a large percentage.

The best fish-oil is made by chopping up oily fish and placing in glass jars or bottles with covers tight enough to keep flies out, but not sealing, and allowing them to remain in a warm place for a month or more until the fish decomposes, leaving the oil on top. Animals that are attracted by fish-oil either alone or in connection with other scents, are coyote, fox, raccoon, mink, opossum and 'cats.

However, a base is usually necessary for any scent, and fish-oil is the commonest and usually the best thing. Some kind of scent ingredients will not mix satisfactorily with fish-oil, or spoil soon after mixing, and alcohol should be used at these times. Alcohol detracts from the value of some scents, and should be used only as suggested.

A good scent for the flesh-eating animals is as follows: Take three ounces of fish-oil, and add half an ounce of muskrat musk or beaver castor, and mix well. (Beaver castor is the best.)

Beaver castor is for sale by some raw fur dealers, as well as beaver trappers, but if unable to secure, muskrat musk is nearly as good. Muskrat glands are pear-like in shape and lie on each side of the vent, between the rear legs. The commonest method of collecting is to squeeze the musk into a wide-mouthed bottle, and for keeping over the summer, alcohol is used.

The musk from the muskrat glands is
(Continued on page 49)

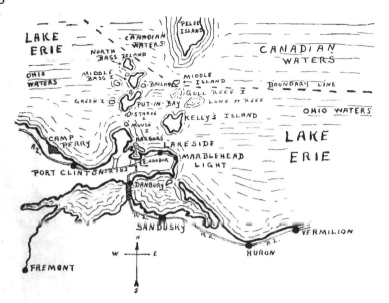

Put-In-Bay and the Islands, the Harbors and Marblehead Peninsula---A Vacation Land Where Game Fish Are Plentiful---Fly Casting, Bait Casting, or Still Fishing With a Bucket of "Minnies" It's All There For The Camper and Angler.

By

JAMES W. STUBER

Lake Erie Bass

The scrappers are of a size to make any angler proud.

THE sun just peeping over the horizon. A warm sou'westerly wind. Blue water with fleecy lace-like wave crests, tinged with gold from the rays of the rising sun. Gulls sailing lazily on outstretched wings. An eagle soaring high against the pale blue sky. Downy white clouds high overhead. Morning shadows gradually receding. Fishing boats in the distance, making their way to favorite spots. A sail boat careening in the breeze with a row boat in tow. The opening day of the bass season in Ohio Lake Erie.

We dropped anchor in the lea of a beautiful wooded island within sight of Put-In-Bay. It looked bassy along the shore. Rock cliffs jutting forty feet up from the water. A sand bar and a reef. That formation caught my eye. I made a cast. Wham! and the battle was on. A big small-mouth with the first cast. "Saw it comin' and was right there to meet it," I said to Fred Markinson, a Cleveland fisherman, who had accepted my invitation to open the season. He had previously remarked that he'd never been able to do any good at Lake Erie, in spite of all he had heard from fishermen who touted Lake Erie bass and bass fishing. Fred's eyes were a-gleam as he watched my bass race around the end of the boat, when I gave him line and let him go. He went for deep water. Fred was good with the oars and quickly worked the boat away from the shore. With a resounding splash the bass broke water and then I turned him and brought him towards the boat, jerking savagely and fighting every inch of the way. He made another rush and as he raced passed Fred who now had the landing net poised for action, my fishing companion dropped his pipe overboard and shouted: "My Lord. What a bass!"

I worked the fighting bronze-back towards the boat and finally tired him out. He was too big to lift. Fred slipped the net under him as he turned on his side and scooped him aboard. Four pounds of small-mouth. A pretty good start.

Now Fred wanted to try a cast. I took the oars. His first casts were fruitless but shortly I maneuvered the boat so he could put his pork rind lure right in where the reef came almost to the surface. He got a strike and lost it. Failed to set the hook. He made another cast and a two-pounder struck and came right out of water with the bait in his mouth. The hook held. The bass raced here and there, breaking water again and again. He brought the bass close to the boat on a short line and as he played the fish we saw four smaller bass racing back and forth with the hooked bass, evidently trying to take the lure from his mouth. The bass was soon boated. Markinson stood right up in the boat and

whooped with joy. A fisherman who had complained of punk luck had found himself and had been won over to Lake Erie fishing.

We fished around the end of the island and each lost a bass. I tried a spinner. A cast close to a large rock got a strike and I brought a two-pounder to the landing net. We circled the island again. We came back to where I had taken the first bass. There seemed to be a pocket there under the rocks. I made a cast and saw a bass rise and miss. Waiting a few minutes, I tried it again. I worked the lure slowly over the top of the reef and let it sink to deeper water and then brought it along with a jerky movement. Blam! I had another one. Out of water it came and as it hit the surface and jumped again the lure flew ten feet high in the air, and the bass was gone.

"Aw, that's a shame. These are the

fightingest bass I ever saw," Fred exclaimed.

Another cast right in the same spot without results. We rested and returned in ten minutes. Another cast. No results. I knew there were more bass there. The third or fourth cast brought a smashing strike. I hooked and boated another fighting bronzie of two and a half pounds.

We then got into a school of the largest rock bass I ever saw. It was a hit and run proposition and between us we landed nine, all of good size. At noon Fred had his limit of small mouth,—eight, and I had six. We had struck the right weather, the right day, and the right place. I had made a convert,—yea, an addict for Lake Erie Island bass fishing.

Put-In-Bay and the adjacent islands abound in small mouth bass, pickerel, and rock bass. I well remember some years ago, when I camped at Rattle-snake island with Senator J. F. Atwood, and Fred Heer, genial publisher of HUNTER-TRADER-TRAPPER. We all caught all the bass we wanted and had a delightful day at the island. On other occasions I have had good bass fishing at Kelly's Island. Gull Reef is good. And when the wind is right fishing is good at Starve island. Green island west of Put-In-Bay is a splendid place to go. There are bass all around these islands. The advantage of fishing at the islands is, that one can always find a lea shore. No matter where the wind is from, there is always some island or a side of some island where one can fish, even if the wind or sea is too heavy for open water. Wind and weather largely govern fishing conditions anyhow as every experienced bass fisherman knows.

ONE day last summer I fished the reefs with William Brown of Lakeside. With me were George Lawrence, well-known Cleveland and Florida sportsman and "Junior" Roy Elliott, a ten-year-old Columbus boy.

We dashed out to the pickerel grounds in one of Brown's comfortable speed boats. In twenty-five minutes we were on location. The boat was slowed down and we trolled with a small spinner, heavily weighted to take it down. One could recline and smoke, cruise easily about, enjoy the scenery and the day and catch fish. "Junior" got the first strike. A sharp tug, a "z-i-n-g" from the reel and then the recovery. The lad under instructions and much back seat coaching brought a two-pound pickerel to the boat. About the time the fish was boated, Lawrence caught one and then I got a strike and brought one aboard. Brown had a fish hooked and then "Junior" and Lawrence both began battling a fish at the same time. Fish were coming aboard too fast to string them. We caught about twenty-five in four hours of fishing. Both bass and pickerel can be taken on the reefs. We found excellent pickerel and bass grounds near Starve Island and again at Gull Island.

On another day we sped to the Island territory from Mack's in a speed boat out of Lakeside. Mack's like Brown's is a well known starting point. We located good territory for small-mouth, pickerel

and rock bass and found white bass plentiful near Mouse Island. White bass are located by watching the bass gulls. When they dart towards the water circling over the schools, the boat should be headed right for the school marked by hundreds of rippling circles and dainty splashes. The white bass are there. A small spinner is best. A piece of white oil-cloth or a bit of white rag or white rubber attached to a hook will suffice. A fly rod can be used to best advantage in casting the light lure. When white bass are biting they can be caught as fast as one can cast and place the lure where they are.

STILL fishing with a bucket of "minnies" is good sport in the territory. This is the nicest and easiest fishing one can imagine. The boat is anchored or perhaps permitted to drift slowly. When someone gets a strike, the anchor is let down and then you stop and fish until time to move on when they refuse to bite or when they quit. Sometimes it is necessary to move only a few boat lengths, when they will start again. Plenty of rock bass can be caught this way. Now and then an old lunker of a sheep head is hooked, especially if using crawfish. Now here's a little secret for summer fishing at Put-In-Bay, and the islands or points out from the Marblehead Peninsula: Use crawfish, hard ones, not over an inch or an inch and one-half in length,—the kind that you ordinarily throw away and never use. Bass and sheephead in these waters don't want larger crawfish. They also prefer the smaller minnows,—not over two and one-half inches in length. Small gold fish are

almost "sure fire" for these waters, and being carp and hard mouthed, a few gold fish will last a long time. I have taken as many as five bass on one gold fish bait. The color seems to attract them, especially if the water is cloudy. You don't use a cork. Six feet of gut leader should be used, on the end of the line, weighted with small split shot, eight or ten in number or more if necessary, to carry the line quickly straight to the bottom. You use snelled hooks not larger than No. 4. Larger hooks will catch in the honey-combed rocks and are hard to loosen. Big Cincinnati bass hooks are right for river fishing for small-mouth and for inland lakes, where one fishes for large-mouth, but the small dark snelled hook is just right for Lake Erie waters and will hold a five pounder if you play him carefully. The spring of the rod keeps the hook taut. With the small hook if the point catches on a rock, a little jiggling of the pole on a tight line will release it. The gut leader and dark hook is necessary as bass shy away from a line attached to a hook or from a shiny hook in these waters. I've seen them do it many times. Harry Crossley, chief of the Lake Erie district, of the Ohio Conservation Division "than whom there is no whomer" when it comes to bass fishing and knowledge of where and how to get them, showed me the secret of this gut leader, small hook fishing rig years ago.

One day I went over to East Harbor, a large bay-like inlet from Lake Erie, on the Marblehead Peninsula. Scouting about I found an ideal location at George Bohlings just east of the junction of Bay

(Continued on page 24)

Inspecting a nice string of fighting bass taken from the waters of the Lake Erie district.

Nagagomi Moose

By

J. M. KOVAL

The first note of the birch bark horn had brought the moose to the clearing.

"**H**URRY UP, we're losing time. This train can't stand here," commanded the conductor. "Yes, hurry," urged Howie, our head guide, "grab this duffle-bag, while I pull out the canoes." Immediately grub boxes, tarpaulins, tents, packsacks, sleeping-bags and guns toppled out of the express car while up and down the long line of train cars passengers strained their necks looking out the windows and wondering why the crack Transcontinental should stop in this wilderness. As this was not a regular nor flag stop, we had special permission to stop the fast Canadian National at this point. Before the heavy sliding doors of the express car were closed, our guides were busy counting the packs and bags strewn along the track. "Eight, nine, ten," counted Ernie, our second guide. "That's right and I'm glad they're down, for this is a real he-man's country we're going into and we need everything we've got."

Instantly the hustle and bustle was over, and the train (the last sign of civilization) was in the distance as we sat among the duffle to have a smoke. This was the beginning of our long planned moose hunt.

Almost every hunter sometime or other wants to bag a moose; to go to Canada on a regular moose hunt—the kind you read about. And to prepare months ahead, gathering information pertaining to maps, routes, guides and outfits. To go on an "honest to gosh" moose trip away up North, where the woods are virgin, where distance is measured by "so many hours by the paddle," where rivers flow North to the land of spruce, cedar, balsam, tamarack and pine, and the home of giant trout, pike and moose. The kind of trip the average American-citizen-hunter has

impregnated in his system waiting for a chance to burst. Moose! The word, itself, makes one think of something big and soon his thoughts run to all the stories he has read, describing the far North, telling of trackless forests where only Indian trappers have penetrated, where trees and waters are still the way God left them, where the air is pure, where there are rapids, falls, chutes, fast white water and portages where one must carry everything on his back to bring home the bacon.

Well, back here in the Conservation State (Pennsylvania), we have some mighty fine hunting; not virgin, but good. "Lefty", my partner, like myself, had hunted in every corner of our state for grouse, English pheasants, rabbits and deer. We each had bagged our bucks for the past three seasons, and like every other dyed-in-the-wool hunter, we wanted bigger game—to add a moose to the row of heads at our hunting lodge. So we decided to go for moose the following season.

Our local hunting was old stuff to us now and the desire to go to new stamping grounds was on us. For the past dozen years or so we had been devouring all the articles in all the outdoor magazines, where the word Canada or moose stuck out until we got tired of this and wanted to experience some of the thrills ourselves. Looks like we were forsaking our old camping and hunting grounds. Here we knew every creek and run and could tell by the different shaped mountain peaks where we were and how to get back to camp. Our week-end trips to our favorite hollows and ravines held no charm now. We wanted to go "where our rifles were the only ones to break the stillness." This deer hunting where one

had to share a runway with others, was too crowding. Hunting and fishing where one could hop into his car, drive over a concrete road and within an hour or two be wading a trout stream, or pushing through grouse cover, seemed too manmade. We wanted to go where we could leave civilization, where there were no beaten paths, nor roads.

The idea hatched in December. Soon we had maps and information from the Canadian government, the Canadian National Railway and Hunter-Trader-Trapper.

April found us with our heads still together and by July, the date was set. Hunting in New Brunswick and Nova Scotia did not appeal to us. The lake regions of Northern Quebec, where moose are called to one's canoe, looked too tame and Alberta and British Columbia were too distant, so we chose Northern Ontario, where the rivers are fast and flow north. There, to worship at the "Shrine of the Red Gods." Soon, letters were coming thick and fast from our guides. Actual letters from real moose guides in far Northern Ontario, who lived nearer to Hudson's Bay than to Lake Superor: up where we were dreaming of going. The contents of the letters we devoured to make sure we missed nothing. "Yes, moose are plentiful this fall," "A sport from Cleveland who was fishing and kodak shooting caught a six (6) pound 'Brookie' and counted 47 moose in 20 days on the river," "We supply everything but your gun." Passages like these were constantly in our minds.

THE middle of October found us in the big station at Toronto, boarding a northbound train. After passing through the cattle, sheep and farm country north of Toronto, we came to the original home of the small-mouth bass, the Georgian Bay district. Our window sightseeing continued as we crossed the famous French river, then to the Sudbury Mining district, the gateway to the new North. We were never here, but our past contact with outdoor periodicals certainly kept us posted with the hunting and fishing country we were passing through. From Sudbury, north, the Canadian National passes through never ending walls of coniferous growths on both sides, cobwebbed with thousands of clear lakes. Occasionally, a lumber camp was passed, or a tank stop where breeds and Indians lounged on the platforms of the clean little villages of log huts.

A Story of a Moose Hunt in Northern Ontario which satisfied the desires of twelve years accumulation in the hearts of these Pennsylvania hunters.

Casting for game fish on the shore at Lake Nagagomi provides a little diversion.

At Oba, the intersection of the Algoma-Hudson Bay Railway and the Canadian National, we were to meet our guides, canoes, camping equipment, etc. As the conductor passed us for the steenth time we asked him how far Oba was, when we would get there and was he sure the train would stop. "Oba, O-B-A. Change for the Soo." Standing on the platform among a pile of packs and bags, stood a big husky 6 foot 2 individual, whose face was screwed into an uncertain squint as he eyed the car windows. Did our hearts beat fast? Were we happy? What if we had missed our guides? No one need tell us who he was. "Lefty" already was shaking hands and introducing himself.

The engine took water, the station master hurriedly exchanged reports with the conductor, the baggageman loaded barrels, etc., for "The Pas," "Fort Churchill," "British Columbia," and points Northwest, while we helped the guides load our own precious cargo of tents and strapped bags which contained our bed and board for the next two weeks. Were we in new country? Were we nearing "The Happy Hunting Grounds"? Ask Lefty. Soon the monotonous grind of the car wheels told us Oba with its population of thirty-seven (37), was left behind and for the next three hours we sat back and plied our guides with questions of "bush life".

The train now ran along the "Height of Land". The source of many rivers flowing north into Hudson's Bay, filled with trout, pickerel and great Northern pike, along whose shores the moose makes his home.

Our map told us we had crossed the Missinaibi, Fire, Kabinakagami and Shekak rivers. Farther on where we were going, where the map looked whiter, were the Pitopika, Otasawian, Pagwachuan, Kenogami and the Negagomi. Rivers of beautiful Indian names. Only a native could do justice to their pronunciation.

Nearing our jumping-off stop, we spied an airplane heading north. Now there is nothing more appreciated to a lost, sick and hungry party in an impenetrable wilderness than a searching airplane soaring overhead, dropping parachuted bundles of food and medicine. Manna from the heavens. Even the toughest sourdoughs who

disdain the comforts of civilization, accept the airplane as the greatest invention the mechanical genius has given to the people in the uncharted, unexplored lands of the north. But, this same carrier, if not restricted, is going to be responsible for the depletion of fish and game in the inaccessible parts of Northern Canada, Yukon Territory and Alaska, where the "going in" and "coming out" constitute the biggest and best part of the trip. And this hunting country will be marked "shot out" to our son's sons. Airplanes are a great asset to the geologist, miner and surveyor in the far north, but should be discouraged as far as the hunter and fisherman are concerned.

"HERE'S where you fellows get off— Hurry up we're losing time," shouted the conductor. And this was the beginning of our long planned moose hunt. Here we were where the Canadian National crosses the Nagagomi river at its source. Just forty (40) hours since we left our homes in Pennsylvania—every minute of which we spent in traveling. The result of well timed plans. Our trip was to take us down the Nagagomi river ninety miles to the northern branch of the Canadian National Railway.

"Howie", my guide, arranged our packs, while "Ernie" and "Lefty" looked after theirs. City life at an end, "Howie", "Lefty" and I hit the "tump line" for a mile portage, while "Ernie" "lined" the canoes. Whenever possible, instead of portaging, canoes are "lined"—snaked down over the riffs and between the boulders by means of a long rope. The person lining, jumping from boulder to boulder or wading along shore. Pleasant work in October. While "Ernie" was freezing we were sweating.

Canoes loaded, "Lefty" and I took our positions in the bows with rifles ready and eyes glued ahead, watching for moose at every bend in the river. Five (5) miles of paddling brought us to "Over the Hill" portage, where camp was made in the dark. After a warm supper and stories from our guides, we hit the balsams. The roar of the falls that make "Over the Hill" portage, soon lulled us to sleep.

Daybreak and breakfast over, our belongings were portaged to the pool below, and our journey down stream continued. At "Rapids" portage, "Lefty" and I got out to snap our guides shooting the rapids. Can those fellows handle canoes? Wow! Pushing windfalls aside, shooting the small rapids and waiting for glimpses of moose, we had action aplenty.

Before noon of the third day we reached Lake Nagagomi. This is a very large, shallow body of water (about 5 miles across), whose shoreline is sandy and pebbly and balsam, spruce and tamarack clad. With a steady, determined west wind blowing, we pointed our canoes across the lake to a channel that would take us into Little Moose Lake. Half way across the white caps got so bad we began to take water. Every man sunk his paddle deep, pulled hard and we made the nearest shore just in time to crawl under the canoes and save ourselves from a cold rain and sleet that lasted three hours. Playing "Rummy" in the sand under an upturned canoe isn't bad pastime when there is nowhere else to go. With the wind, went the rain. Hustling, we paddled our way to Little Moose Lake and made camp where the Nagagomi river empties into it. This day we had seen flocks of ducks, two otter, caribou tracks, lots of moose signs, but no big game. With a bright fire in front of our tents we slipped into the eider-down bags cushioned with balsam boughs and dreamt of moose on the morrow.

In the morning, we skirted Little Moose Lake for moose, before continuing our journey down stream. "Lefty" and "Ernie" took one shoreline and "Howie" and I took the other. Foggy and bad light. The lake was cold and calm as we paddled our way along shore through the bull grass and wild rice that grew head high. Soon we came to open water. "See that black spot? See it move along shore? Lay down your paddle and get ready to shoot." These instructions came from "Howie" and I could tell by the quiver of his voice that he was making game. When I was discharged from the army, my eyes were O.K.'d as normal, yet I looked in vain. With a quiet twisting movement of his wrist, my guide pushed the canoe ahead without taking the paddle out of the water. We sat like two statues. Closer, closer. Sure enough the semi-visible dark object moved along shore unconscious of our presence. A bull with a rack big enough to take. The canoe now coasted quietly over the glassy surface, with only the ripple the bow made as it cut the water. We were almost in range and just as I was ready to squeeze, a flock of black ducks we overlooked flushed between the canoe and our quarry. The bull turned. "He sees us. Shoot, shoot." Bang-bang-bang—more ducks skimmed the water—the moose moved toward cover. Bang-bang-bang. As I pumped three more Mr. Alecs Americana jumped from side to side like a dog at play and trotted into the timber.

I HAD prepared six months to come over six hundred (600) miles, to lose a nice spread with 6 clean misses. More ducks rose as we paddled to where the bull was last seen. "Howie" soon had the case diagnosed. No blood—no moose. Presently we heard shooting from across the lake, in the direction "Lefty" had taken. Sounded like a shot-gun. Sure enough, "Lefty", a shot-gun enthusiast, thinking that I had filled my license, and at the same time scared all the moose from Little Moose Lake, enjoyed himself pulling ducks out of the air with a 20 gauge. Ducks for supper.

As we sat around the fire, after the day's hunt, great northern pike splashed in the fast shallow water where it spills out of Little Moose Lake and makes Nagagomi river proper.

From here down (North), our voyage was to be a never ending series of rapids, falls and portages, and let me state here, that he who elects to hunt on a river that is Hudson Bay bound, better be ready for hard work, sleet, snow and hours of sweating on muddy uphill portages. Three inches of snow that covered everything, greeted us in the morning. After breakfast, we launched the canoes in a snow squall. Rifles ready, we took our positions in the bows.

At "Koochigan Falls" portage, still snowing, the carry over was made with little ceremony. Nearing "Gull Rock Rapids" portage the snow turned to rain. Here we would have made camp, but our time was limited, so we went down northward toward the tracks to "Dirty Bush" portage. Camp was made here at 3 p. m. The rain had stopped and while "Ernie" gathered wood and made things ready for the night, "Howie", "Lefty" and I paddled back up the river where we had seen some very fresh signs. "Lefty" and I were posted on ridges (of which there are very few in this low, flat, swampy country), while "Howie" climbed a high balsam and began to call. "Moo-oo-oo-ugh", coaxed "Howie". Immediately we heard a grunt in a direction away from the river. "Ugh, ugh" and Mr. Moose headed our way. But the cracking of

windfalls and the grunts soon ceased, as Mrs. Moose bawled out a love call and soon we could hear the bull returning to his mate. Away from us. Seven times, "Howie" induced the bull to come our way only to have the whole show busted up by a plaintive bawl from Mrs. Moose, who always called him back. These certainly were tense moments; pantomime sighting, loosening clothing, freezing the trigger finger and feeling for extra cart-ridges. The bull must have detected a false note in "Howie's" love-making, for he returned no more. A fox barked in the distance, a great blue heron squawked at my left, the whiskey jays jibbered in

After the taxidermist got done with him.

the pines and a great horned owl noiselessly swooped around my head. "Lefty" and "Howie" soon joined me and in the fast fading light we paddled to camp—hot supper and the eiderdown.

UP at daybreak and back to our positions on the ridges. We went through the same procedure as the evening before. Twice, the bull came our way, but the wily cow always called him back. "Howie" knew moose. He soon joined me and we made our way toward "Lefty". Here we held a consultation. "Do you fellows want that bull?" came from "Howie." "Sure," we chorused. "Well, let's go in and get him—they won't leave very soon," replied "Howie", relieving himself of some of his clothing. "Any danger?" "Can't tell. Every moose I killed acted differently. No set rule," cautiously answered our guide, who was already quietly making his way into the bush and blazing the trees enroute. About a quarter of a mile from the river we came to a clearing overgrown with hard hack blue berry bushes and waist high Xmas trees. A beautiful place for moose love-making. "Howie" cleared his throat and the serious expression on his face told us he meant business, as he raised the birch-bark to his lips. "Moo-oo-oo-ugh." The first note brought the bull out into the clearing. We heard his antlers, as he swished

through the pines. At about 100 yards he stepped into an open spot and the "Savage 300" broke the stillness. The 180 grain Westerns did their work well for when we reached him he was practically dead.

That afternoon, with canoes loaded to the danger line, we proceeded down river shooting the safer rapids and cutting portages whenever possible.

After 2 hours of flat water, as we were rounding the tail of an S bend, we heard splashing just ahead. Canoes abreast we paddled fast and as the river straightened out ahead of us, a nice bull who was feeding along shore, plunged into the river and headed for the opposite shore. Just like a moose—a foolish move. Running the gauntlet is always uncertain and as he raced through the shallow water (this was a cross-over), two body shots were scored. He made the opposite bank. Just as he was lifting himself out two more well directed shots ended his struggles.

Two moose in one day. We made camp on the spot. "Howie" and "Ernie" prepared camp while "Lefty" and I gathered balsam boughs for our beds. While thus busying ourselves we flushed a flock of grouse who made no effort to get away. They would fly onto the first limb of a tree and stretch their necks toward the finders of our cameras, as we took their pictures. That night as we sat around the fire, our guides told us that grouse were scarce, also, that some years ago, like the snow-shoe hares, they were very plentiful and one could supply the larder by knocking them off trees with a long stick. In the States these wary birds were diminishing rapidly and yet no one hunted them here and they were scarce. We were further informed that this condition existed in this North country before and that in time they would become as plentiful as before. Everyone was happy as we related the day's experiences and our dreams of the far North were a reality. We were camped on a virgin river that had never been lumbered—whose shores probably never will be profitable to lumber, for the big timber reaches only a few hundred yards from shore. The rest, being muskeg and bog and where there always will be moose. As the Northern lights danced through the sky, a wolf on the opposite shore serenaded the moon and an extra layer of balsam boughs assured us of a comfortable night.

FOR the next two days we were bucking "Jack Pine" portage and sweating at "Big Rock (Canyon)" portage on our way to the rails, the home of our guides and the end of our water journey. Here we left the Nagagomi river to flow into the Albany, that river made famous by the Revillon Freres Co.—"To Hudson Bay without a portage."

We were homeward bound. But the thoughts of the North still linger and even today we are planning another trip to God's country.

Canvasbacks

A day with the ducks on Chesapeake Bay.

By TALBOTT DENMEAD

THE canvasbacks and other ducks that winter at the head of the Chesapeake Bay, generally leave that part at the mouth of the Susquehanna River, which is widely known as The Susquehanna Flats when the weather gets very cold and the shallow waters freeze over, and take up at least a temporary residence further down the bay; this affords some good shooting immediately south as far as the mouth of the Patapsco River on the west shore, and on both sides of the bay. Of course this section has many ducks during the whole season but the number is augmented by birds from the Flats when the mercury gets pretty low. One of the best known sections for canvasback shooting under such conditions is on the Eastern Shore of Maryland, at the mouth of the Chester River, and is known as East Neck Island.

In this vicinity are located some of the most widely known hunting clubs of the upper Chesapeake, among which may be mentioned Cedar Point, Ringold's Point, Frying Pan Cove and Belt's Bar Clubs; and it is interesting to note in passing that the membership and guests of these shooting clubs on East Neck Island include among other prominent men some of our most famous physicians and surgeons.

Let us spend a day together at the Belt's Bar Club after the lordly canvasbacks, red head and other ducks that may be attracted by our decoys. Shooting is done from blinds on shore, for which reason points of land projecting some distance out into the water are the best locations for good shooting.

It was 4:30 a. m. on a cold, clear, crisp December morning that Captain Spence rattled the shovel in the coal scuttle, and called out, "Time to get up, boys." "Good morning, Captain, what are the prospects for some canvasbacks today?" asks the least sleepy, as all pile out of the warm covers and reach for some heavy clothing. Now, the Captain, besides being the best fisherman in those parts, is a natural born duck hunter, and has quite a reputation as a prophet on matters pertaining to duck hunting and fishing; so we were sorry to receive from him at this time a most discouraging reply to our query. "Not so good, too calm and mild, the canvasbacks have probably all gone back to the Flats".

It did not take long to dress and stow away a good breakfast, and get down to the blind on the point not far from the Club House where we planned to shoot, and we helped the Captain get out the decoys and everything ready before legal shooting time. It did not take long for

the Captain is also most methodical as well as a prophet and always keeps everything in good order, and arranged so that there will be a minimum of effort while at the same time maximum results will be obtained.

For example, no one gets any kick out of taking up the decoys, when the day's sport is over, and the hunter is cold and tired, and perhaps there is ice on the decoy heads; it is just hard work; but the Captain has a "system" for this job: exactly thirty-five yards straight out from the outer edge of the shooting blind, which incidentally will hold five hunters, and should be built to hold not over three, he has anchored a small cork buoy; it does not disturb the ducks, and can be easily located early in the morning before dawn when it is almost impossible to accurately estimate distances; the result is when daylight comes the decoys are found to be neither too far nor too near the blind; the little buoy also helps the hunter in calculating how far off the birds were that he killed, and also missed.

The Captain has five heavy lines something over fifty yards long to each of which is attached by short cords two feet long, ten wooden decoys, canvasbacks mostly, fifty in all; on one end of each line or rope a couple of yards away from the nearest decoy is an anchor which is carried out by boat and dropped overboard about even with the cork buoy; the other end is tied to the blind or shore, and there you have fifty decoys all set; when the day is over all that is necessary to take up the decoys is to stand on shore and haul in the ropes; to make the stool more life like, and break the monotony of the rather straight lines of decoys on the ropes, about 25 singles are placed around and in between the strings; and the scheme works.

WE were all set at legal shooting time, which is one-half hour before sunrise, but we had not seen any ducks up to then; our blind was on the river side of the island, and we could not see out in the Bay; a careful search of the waters with binoculars in the uncertain light failed to reveal a single bunch of good ducks, although there were scoters, whistlers, and mergansers scattered here and there, and also a small bunch of whistling swans; not a canvasback. "Well, perhaps they will come into the river to feed later," said Howard, but the Captain "allowed" the ice had left the Flats and the birds had returned to the head of the Bay, about forty miles north.

By ten o'clock we had not had a single

shot; the best part of the day, in the opinion of most duck hunters had passed, and it looked like the Captain had guessed right. There were a lot of single whistlers (goldeneyes) cruising around and some white winged scoters, locally called tar pots, but they would not decoy. I had a twenty guage "Sportsman" three-shot automatic in the blind and decided I would like to try it out on one of the scoters that would occasionally fly by just outside our decoys, but with no intention of decoying, if one would only come in close enough.

"Say, you fellows—the next tar pot that comes by that is in fairly close I am going to try this little twenty on," I said. Howard laughed, "Why, that pop gun won't kill one of those tough babies, you are wasting your time and ammunition." But I persisted, and in a few minutes along came a scoter.

"Keep off this bird, you fellows, he is mine is he comes in close enough." He kept on coming in a straight line parallel with the shore, closer than any previous one; remember, the Captain's cork float was a measured 35 yards from the muzzle of the gun; the bird was not over two feet above the water and would pass outside of the decoys; at the proper time I arose in the blind, led the old boy about three or four feet and pulled the trigger; down he came approximately eight yards outside of the buoy; not bad for a twenty on a tough old bird like a scoter for they

(Continued on page 25)

Two generations of phrynosoma cornutus, the horned lizard, commonly called toad. They are discussing the remains of a tarantula which the larger of the two has just dispatched. The horned toad will not eat the spider.

The King *of* Spiders

Everyone has heard stories regarding the deadliness and ferocity of the tarantula. Now read this authentic story into which has been crowded as much romance and interest as in a most fascinating novel.

By RAYMOND W. THORP

WHAT would you do, my friend, if, while you were soundly sleeping the sleep of the just, something happened to bring you suddenly awake, and upon awakening you discovered that a giant tarantula nestled snugly upon your naked chest, or arm, or mayhap your face? Would you be frightened? Would you cry out? Would you leap frenziedly to your feet, screaming and brushing at the unlovely creature?

The chances are that you would do one of these things, or all of them, or something equally foolish. The fact is, too, that a large percentage of persons placed in such a position would do the same as yourself. Indeed, I will go so far as to say that right now you are thinking: "Well, my smart friend, what would *you* do?" I shall tell you. I would reach up, take hold of the creature, remove him from his resting place, and place him elsewhere, so that he would not be crawling about where he didn't belong. If, which is very improbable, the spider struck me while I was putting this plan into operation, I would adopt the same procedure, augmenting it perhaps by rubbing the stricken portion of my anatomy vigorously for a minute or so, then roll over and go to sleep. I most certainly would not kill him.

Most people, outdoorsmen as well as others, have the fear of snakes and tarantulas ground deeply into them. Well, I will admit that, in case the intruder be a rattlesnake, I have no remedy or plan to offer. There is a vast dissimilarity in rattlesnakes and tarantulas. A rattlesnake is dangerous. To graphically illustrate the fear and regard that most people hold for the great spider, even in a region where it abounds in numbers of millions, I will recite an incident which happened recently, coming under my observation.

A nature photographer is walking along the rim of a great wash or dry canyon that winds snakelike through the city of Los Angeles and into the outlying districts; winds, indeed into the uplands and onto the bleak gray walls of the Sierras. Below this man, great groups of men are working with pick and shovel in the rock-strewn depths of the *Arroyo Seco*.

Suddenly he stops short in his tracks, leans forward a trifle, and stares at a little group of men in the canyon. Even as he gazes the men draw back; the knot grows wider. Exclamations ring out upon the air. The observer notes that the workmen are all staring downward, toward the center of a human circle which they have made. He is unable to see however, the object under discussion. One man, evidently bolder than the rest steps forward, long-handled shovel in hand. Reaching out the full five-foot length of this implement, he seems to be carefully gauging his distance.

THEN he strikes. Again exclamations. One among the crowd shouts, "You've got him, Joe." They close in, gingerly, about the point where the shovel descended. White men talk loudly, authoritatively, evidently propounding their weighty views on what has taken place. Mexicans talk in their quick Spanish-lingo, gesticulating at the same time, toward the spot.

The observer leans forward, brows knotted, eyes trying to focus upon the object indicated. The distance is too great. He is about to give it up, and has about decided that a rattlesnake or Gila monster has met its doom when, cutting through the dry atmosphere, a phrase is caught:

"Tarantaula! *Si senor;* a bad *hombre!*"

So. Much ado about nothing. A tarantula has been killed. Another "big, bad wolf" of spiders has been sacrificed to ignorance. Another fuzzy, ferocious-appearing, five-inch specimen of the family *arachnida,* harmless to man or babe, but stamped with the brand of Cain. A tarantula dies, to lie in the pitiless rays of the burning sun, an element to which he has always been unaccustomed, until his body has been devoured by the red desert ants. Our nature photographer shrugs his shoulders, mutters something under his breath, and meanders into the hills adjoining the canyon.

Too bad, Mother Tarantula, you should not have left that safe burrow, high up in the plot of adobe. You should not have left your little white cunning babes, waiting for you to return with food to the cool recesses of your subterranean home. Waiting for that nice plump cricket or cicada, which, according to your very minuteness, you could have feasted upon for days and days. Nay, even a roach would have sufficed; but you must have been very hungry, indeed, to allow your great fuzzy brown *mater to* exert herself in the killing sunshine. Nature intended for her to hunt only at night.

Ah, well; such is life. Mayhap the Government will make an appropriation to feed you, so that you may grow up to be hideous and ferocious-appearing; to be killed by stick, stone or shovel. You had no right to be born looking so formidable, you sheep in wolves' clothing!

Where, babes, is big black Papa? Well, you don't have to tell me, for I know better than you. He will never leave his burrow by day. That is why I know it was your mother who was killed in the canyon. You must shift for yourselves, now that she is gone, for Papa lives in a separate home where he will not invite you to stay. He may come over to see you some day, but it will not be to bring food for your microscopic but capacious maws. He will, if he comes, eat you. But if he doesn't act quick, your nearest neighbor, perhaps your aunt, will beat him to it, for your species are devout cannibals. It seems that the man with the shovel has destroyed a whole family. If not, however, you will grow big and strong, to be killed, mayhap, by *phrynosoma cornutum* or *pepsis formosa*. If the carnivores overlook you, the vegetarians are yet killers, you know; and then there are the ignorant men with shovels. They are hard to convince that you are harmless and amiable.

But *are* you harmless? I grant that you cannot hurt human-kind, but big black Papa, and Mamma, when she was alive, were destruction itself among the insect world. With their great, curved fangs, dripping venom when about to strike, they were death, even to small birds. Yes, Papa and his kinsmen, *Avicularia* and *Eurypelma*, are the kings of the spiders.

SWIFT of foot, quick to jump far, either forward, backward, or sidewise, of a mien and countenance ferocious enough to belong to a bad dream, the tarantula is a killer. Not for nothing was he equipped with formidable fangs, shaped like boat-hooks; perfect counterparts of cat's claws. Yet, in spite of all this, I take him up gently, let him lie upon my hand, my arm, my neck; even my face. He is afraid of me.

But even were he not afraid, what would it matter? Let us see. I take a parlor match, place the spider in an erect position upon my forearm, and tickle his sheathed fangs. No appreciable result that way. Next I try another tack; I strike quick jabs directly at the fangs. Ha! A sudden interest; a stiffening, a shifting, ever so slightly, of his position.

Again I strike. Now the *arachnid* rears the fore part of his body somewhat; the gleaming tips of the shining black fangs emerge part way. It won't be long now. I strike again; and, as sudden as the lightning's flash comes the return. The tormenting match gone, the fangs descend upon the flesh, and are buried deeply and firmly. So firmly, in fact, that it is with some trouble that I disengage them. The twin punctures are plainly visible, in fact, more so than if a rattlesnake had delivered his fatal stroke. While the arm swells, I repeat the performance, or rather, induce the spider to do so until at last, fatigued and with his supply of venom exhausted, he ignores my insults and sulks. I put him down, rub my arm vigorously, and wonder at the folk-lore which has established this creature as a man-killer.

A Mexican, who has approached and is standing at what he considers a safe distance, murmurs: "*El Senor* is crazy!"

But *El senor* is not crazy. It is true that the tarantula is a carniverous *arachnid*, maintaining his existence only through his power to kill. He has a potent poison, but potent only against the creatures upon which nature intended him to feed. A man or child who has been struck by a tarantula generally swells at the stricken portion of his body, but after a few days the soreness is gone, and no ill after effects are forthcoming. Remember, too, that the *arachnid* seldom will strike at a human being. In all cases where I have been bitten, this was caused by my teasing the spider with some object at which he struck. This was removed as he was in the act, and naturally the open fangs, descending with power, sank into whatever they encountered; in this case, my arm.

There is tremendous power in the legs of the giant spider. To find this out, one has only to place his hand upon one and press down. It is almost impossible to hold the beast in one spot without exerting enough pressure to smash him.

After one has handled tarantulas for a time, the utter absurdity of newspaper stories concerning the spiders and their fierce animosity toward man comes home to him. The stories become then, not absurdities, but malicious lies upon one of nature's most interesting, amiable creatures.

BEFORE humankind the tarantula is timid. Moreover, he is a master of strategic retreat. Yet he will, say, the columnists, spring suddenly from a bunch of bananas upon a stevedore, receiving clerk or merchant, and deliver a mortal wound. The "bunch of bananas" story is the one most frequently quoted, because the writers of same have a faulty theory that tarantulas can only be imported from

tropical countries. They do not know that there are as many of the creatures in our own Southwest, as in any other portion of the globe of the same dimensions.

What bewilderment, what fear, must have been the portion of the foraging mother as, coming out from behind a stone into the brilliant sunshine, she faced a crew none of whom knew her true nature, and one of whom, in the next instant, dispatched her?

Well, we cannot lay the blame for such acts of blatant ignorance upon the shoulders of our own race, even though we, as a rule, embrace the popular but false belief. The idea that the trantaula is dangerous actually originated and is yet fostered in the folk-lore of the Spanish-speaking peoples of Old Mexico, and the Southwestern Indians. This fact seems the more remarkable when we realize that both peoples named have lived in close proximity to the giant *arachnida* for centuries. Mexicans live in positive dread of the hideous sheep in wolves' clothing.

The truth is, children may play with tarantulas in perfect safety. It is a common sight in districts where the great spiders abound to behold tiny tots of four and five years handling them fearlessly. They even allow the creatures to crawl about over their persons. English-speaking children use them in a game. It is a comical sight to witness a white child, armed with a huge *arachnid*, chasing after a terrified, screaming Mexican tot.

The tarantula has his dread enemies in the realm of nature. *Phrynosoma cornutum*, the horned toad, is a destroyer of the *arachnida*. However, these two seldom meet, unless placed together by human hands, for the former goes to bed at night, like a gentleman, and the latter retires in the daytime, as does his prototype, the lion. The tarantula has, however, an hereditary enemy; one whose only aim in life is the killing of *arachnida*.

This is Eurypelma, a tarantula of Honduras. Photo courtesy of the Bureau of Etnology, U. S. Dep't. of Agriculture.

This is the killer wasp, termed by some the "tarantula killer," and known scientifically in Europe as *pompilus forfosus*, and in North America as *pepsis formosa*.

A close look at this formidable monster shows us that its head, thorax, abdomen and long, spiny legs are black in color. The wings are a light reddish-brown, with black spots at the tips. When the trantula observes the familiar, hated cockade of this fast pursuit plane hovering nearby he, figuratively at first, and actually at last, gives up the ghost. Death is near when those powerful wings, bearing a two-inch body, settle toward the earth. For *pepsis* is a burrowing wasp, and he wants his burrow ready-made. In other words, he kills the owner of a tarantula burrow and takes possession. And this, the home of arachnida is well worth the taking by any creature whom nature has decreed must live in the earth. Unlike others among the multitudinous spiders, of which there are more than 25,000 known species, the tarantula craves a solid instead of a gossamer home. Each tarantula has its own particular abode which it builds, inhabits for a season, and deserts.

THIS is a perpendicular tunnel with a circular entrance. The tunnel is about 12 inches in depth; and about halfway down there is another, but horizontal, tube which leads back into the earth for several inches. This is Mr. Tarantula's living room. Here he sits, and with his periscope eyes watches the open door above him. One may glance down into such an abode at almost any time of day and discern those gleaming headlights, pinpricks in the blackness. It is when a shadow, passing above, clouds those lamps, that the *arachnid* prepares for death. So, as the terrible tryst generally takes place in late afternoon or early evening, and as the day is drawing somewhat to a close, let us take a look-in at such a duel.

It is a day in the season for parenthood of *pepsis formosa*. Mr. Tarantula knows this, and knows his danger. He has twice in the afternoon, witnessed the blotting off of the light from above. He is hungry, but he is careful. So, with hunger gnawing at his vitals, he stays at his lookout post, waiting for night. A half-hour, an hour, passes by slowly. The shadows deepen; it is well past 5 o'clock. Crickets and cicadas begin their trilling, clicking songs in the grasses above. Enough! The hunting season is drawing nigh, and the giant *arachnid*, feeling the need of early sustenance, casts his fears aside, and, with a quick springing crawl, emerges from his hiding place.

Too soon. Ere he has traveled twelve inches from his tunnel entrance he realizes his mistake. It is not as late as he thought: the sun is not yet behind the mountains. He turns to beat a retreat.

Too late! There is a droning from above. Full-motored, with wings blurred as an airplane propeller, *Pepsis*, swooping down from the heights of a nearby pepper tree, prepares to strike. There is no time for retreat, no chance for escape,

nor is there a chance for a long-range duel. It must be close. It must be bayonet work. The *arachnid* turns, faces his enemy. He has two bayonets; *Pepsis* but one. He is the most powerful of the two, and by far the most deadly. He could easily kill a wasp, if he would but fight the latter. But remember this; *no arachnid has ever killed such an opponent*. Why? Well, you will soon know.

Here and now the giant spider does a peculiar thing. Cat-like, he throws him-

Close-up view of the underside of a half-grown tarantula. Note the great fangs, partly unsheathed. No other creature in all nature possesses like apparatus of such prodigious size. Were the fangs of a six-foot rattlesnake built in like proportion to size of body, they would be almost one-eighth the length of its body.

self upon his back. Yet, unlike the cat, he does not unsheath his fangs. Instead, he simulates death. How futile! *Pepsis* knows this peculiarity of the *arachnid* as well as we humans know the same trait in the opossum.

Everything is now in readiness for the tarantula to commit suicide. The killer, swooping in, observing closely, notes that the fangs, of which he stands in awful dread, are closed. He settles for a moment, then drops, throwing his stinger directly between the fangs and into the mouth of the *arachnid*.

THE great fangs quiver, then droop, inert and futile. *Arachnida*, by attempting a simpleton's trick on a Napoleon of warfare, is now completely disarmed. The dreadful poison throwers will never operate again. The wasp now withdraws his stinger and, throwing it into high gear once more, delivers the second and final blow of the conflict; a thrust into the thorax of his silent foe. The first stroke has rendered resistance impossible; the second has paralyzed all body movement.

Tarantula is *hors decombat*. Tarantula is dead.

Well, now, what will the victor do? Is he a carniverous creature? Will he feed? No; he is a vegetarian. Whereaway, then, will he set his course? Will he rise, this great wasp, terror of the *arachnida*, and go hence, to his family, mayhap, singing his droning song of triumph? Is he like a bomber who, once his object has been accomplished, has his business finished, and forthwith attempts a getaway? No. None of these things are true. Let us see.

EVENING is here. The sun is now behind the brown hills. Soon darkness will have arrived, and *arachnida*, in droves and multitudes, will come forth. Our valiant victor, our living war plane, which combines the duties of observation, pursuit and bomber all in one, must be about his business. What needs be done must be done now.

Twelve inches away from his erstwhile tunnel home lies the great tarantula. The conqueror now seizes him by one long, furry leg; next, he sets his own motors to running. There is a low, musical drone, —a continuous blur of wings, the load begins to move, slowly at first, then, with the power of *Pepsis* full on, is gradually dragged toward the entrance to the spider's den. At last, after five minutes of hard work, the feat is accomplished. The two disappear, the victor and vanquished, the dead and the living, into the earth. One who chose to investigate would now find out the secret of the whole proceeding. *Pepsis formosa*, using the body of his dead enemy as an incubator, lays his eggs therein; eggs that are to bring forth more such killers as he.

Now, as night's shades are being pulled across the barren hills, our amateur, homecoming along the trail that leads down along the rim of the Arroyo Seco, passes close to the spot where the tragedy has taken place. Of it, however, he of course knows nothing. But he is well-versed in the meaning of the night noises underfoot. There is a rustling of grasses, a sharp clicking, sounds of cicadas' song being cut short. Then, there are also dull, rasping sounds.

The great tarantulas have emerged from their dens, and are hunting. The rustling sounds are made by the carnivores. The clickings are the last dying struggles of myriads of insects which have been attacked by the monsters. The raspings are caused by the spiders' using their legs to sweep the day's accumulation of den-dust from their posteriors. There is wholesale death and feasting going on underfoot, and our amateur curses softly because he is minus his camera lamps. So, while gullets are straining and larders are being stocked, he walks on out of the picture. After a while the cicada become silent, the toads stop their gutturals, and the crickets their clicking.

The great tarantula, king of the spiders and also of the night, stalks abroad with his fangs unsheathed.

That interlude of silence that comes between the first break of day and the rising of the sun.

Michigan's Highest Lake

An interesting story of fishing and camping on Lake Guthrie.

By G. C. JAMES

A ROBIN awakened us this morning. He evidently intended to rouse us in time to see the sunrise, for it was just after daybreak when we heard him calling. We had put in no request for such an early call. However, we are grateful for him. Jess Smith and I have always loved that interlude of silence that comes between the first break of day and rising of the sun. It is to us as though the world waits in breathless expectancy. Outside the bedroom window the screened porch overlooks the lake. The air is fragrant with the wild roses that seem to grow everywhere in this section. A warm, southern breeze from down the lake wafts their fragrance to us.

We are staying two weeks at Lake Guthrie, the highest body of water in the lower peninsula of Michigan. The lake reposes like some rare gem in a setting of high hills nearly 1500 feet above sea level. South of the Straits of Mackinac the land rises to a high plateau which continues to a point near the headwaters of the Rifle River near West Branch. In Otsego county it reaches its highest pinnacle just a short distance north of Guthrie. The water from Lake Guthrie flows in opposite directions draining into widely separate regions. The water is clear as crystal, with gently sloping beaches of clean white sand, and all about the lofty pines, many so large one cannot reach around them. As Jess and I emerge to watch the sunrise behind the pines on the east shore we are struck by the wonder of it all. Everything there is held in a lovely stillness—the slender birches whitely streaked against green woods beyond, the tattered sprays of russet maple leaves, the broad scribbling of mauve shadows along the dim and curving lines of the shore. Everything is quiet and tranquil, with the quietness and tranquility that belong to early dawn and early dusk when things are scarcely awake and barely asleep. Far down on the east shore a tiny fawn, just out of the spotted coat, plays and gambols

along the sandy beach while a more cautious mother deer emerges slowly from the thick undergrowth near the point jutting out into the lake near the channel into Section One Lake. Both pause to drink then turn and enter the thick cover. Now Jess is a hunter of deer and he loves to see them at any season.

A red-wing blackbird "konk-a-ree'd" from the top of a dead cedar overhanging the lake. A muskrat ran from the lake into the little spring creek at our back. The whistling wings of a black duck breezed our heads as he sped south down the center of the lake to join others of his kind on lower Section One Lake. A black bass leaped full length out of water not twenty-five feet from where we stood, then swam into a school of minnows nearly at our feet. That was enough for Jess. He walked into the cabin and soon came back with his casting rod and a red head Bassoreno swinging from the end of the line. The first cast he made was fruitless. He cast again and his line snarled into a beautiful backlash. One of those tight ones that make the most patient fisherman fume. The lure lay motionless on the surface of the water. Jess fingered the line in an endeavor to untangle it.

WE heard a splash. The lure had disappeared. The line tightened, the tip of the rod jerked and Jess was fast to a fish with a beautiful backlash in his line. He struck the hooks home and prepared for action. He was standing on shore and there was no boat to follow the fish about to relieve the tension. The bass came up and emerged from the water standing on his tail as he shook his great head. The lure rattled and shone in the early morning sunlight, the ripples widened and startled minnows sought shelter in the shallows. There Jess was fast to a fish weighing about three pounds and full of morning vigor. The bass sounded and raced up and down the beach while Jess backed up the better to ease up when the time came

Once again the fish leaped and then appeared to weaken. We did not rush the fish and gradually he slowed up to the point where I could slip the net beneath him. And ten minutes later the sweet fragrance of frying black bass—fried in good farmer's butter—was wafted out to the beach to mingle with the fragrance of wild roses. Jess is a cook of the woods. He can fry potatoes in the grease left from frying black bass, browning them just right and seasoning them to taste. Black bass, potatoes, fresh bread and good butter and a hot cup of Java and we are ready for the day's fishing.

Our boat, with outboard motor attached, rested in the water beneath the little Norway Pines in front of our log cabin. We load our tackle into it and chug away. First we round the eastern corner of the lake and fish the waters of Black Bay. An island shelters a mammoth black bass, but he is not eating this morning. Probably gorged on minnows and frogs and is as surfeited with food as we are. A faint breeze ruffles the water as we head her south to try for pike off the point. The pike do not take the casting lures so we settle down to still fishing. We use chubs for bait and shortly after our anchor is out and we are discussing the beauty of this wilderness lake so far away and alone from all travel, we note my line is tightening. I give the fish a bit of slack. If it is a pike he will bite the minnow from the rear, no doubt to kill it, and then turn it around to take it head-first so the fins will not scratch the mighty throat as it slips down the gullet. That first twitch may be the killing stroke and would I strike, it would pull the minnow from the fish's mouth. I wait and give out about fifteen feet of line which is rapidly taken in some mysterious manner beneath the surface. There is a pause, then a steady pull. Time enough has elapsed to enable the fish to enclose the entire chub in its mouth, so I strike swiftly and strongly.

(Continued on page 30)

18

Valley of the Arickaree, where Forsyth's Scouts and Roman Nose's Cheyennes fought Sept. 17, 1868. Photo by Brininstool, 1917.

The Hero *of the* Arickaree

Personal experience of John Hurst of Forsyth's Scouts at the Battle of Beecher Island.

By E. A. BRININSTOOL

Author: "Capt. Benteen in the Custer Fight," A Trooper with Custer," "Capture and Death of Chief Crazy Horse," etc.

AUTHOR'S NOTE: During the summer of 1917 I became acquainted with John Hurst, a member of Forsyth's Scouts, who was then living at the Soldiers' Home, Los Angeles, at which time he related to me the following account of his personal experience in Forsyth's fight on the Arickaree Fork of the Republican River, in Eastern Colorado, in September, 1868. This nine-days' siege on Beecher Island (as it was later named) is without a parallel in American Indian warfare, 51 frontiersmen standing off some 700 Northern Cheyenne Indians, with no food but their dead horses about them.—E. A. Brininstool.

"I was born in Lisbon, St. Lawrence county, N. Y., Feb. 19, 1941, where my childhood days were spent on a farm. In 1859 I went to California and worked at the lumber business until the outbreak of the Civil War, in 1861, when I enlisted in the First California Volunteer Infantry, and was sent to Arizona with others to relieve the regulars who were guarding the Overland mail route. I was stationed at various army posts in Arizona and New Mexico during my three years' service, being mustered out at Los Pinos, New Mexico, August 31, 1864.

"I then started across the plains for Kansas by way of the Santa Fe trail, arriving in Leavenworth in November. Shortly after Price's Raid I went to work for the United States government at Fort Leavenworth, driving mules, hauling sup-

plies. etc., until 1867, when I was transferred to Fort Harker, Kansas, August 20, 1868. I there joined Forsyth's Scouts the latter part of the same month.

"Love of adventure, which is inherent in all American frontiersmen, and becomes a sort of second nature, prompted me to join the Scouts. I was young, hardy and strong, and eager for anything in the way

Inscription on one side of Beecher Island Monument. Photo by E. A. Brininstool.

of excitement—plenty of which I got during the ensuing six weeks!

"If I remember correctly, we went to Fort Wallace, Kansas, with eight days' rations and four pack mules loaded with doctors' supplies, axes, shovels and picks. We made a circuitous route, as far as Beaver Creek, following up that stream for some distance, and then bore south to Fort Wallace, where we rested a few days.

"From here we were hurried away because of an attack made on a Mexican wagon train near Sheridan, Kansas. It was encamped between Fort Wallace and Sheridan. Two men were killed and some of the stock run off by the Indians. Sheridan

at that time was the western terminus of the Kansas-Pacific Railroad, and all freight going west was hauled there by wagon.

"As soon as the news of the killing reached Fort Wallace, we started in pursuit, with six days' rations. We found the Indian trail, and followed it for some distance; but finally it petered out, and we lost it, the Indians having scattered and broken up into small bands to elude pursuit.

"HOWEVER, we continued traveling northward. that being the general direction of the trail. We further expected we might run across another trail, or perhaps the Indians themselves; but we saw nothing until we reached the Republican river.

"After scouting around until the morning of the fourth day, we picked up a small trail running up the river, which we followed until evening, when we went into camp. The trail continued to grow warmer as we advanced, other trails leading into it.

"Next morning we continued the pursuit, and it soon became evident that we were not very far behind a large body of savages. Soon we discovered the marks of the lodge-poles dragging on the ground. Indians, when traveling, strap these lodge-poles on each side of a pony, making what they call a 'travois.' On these the savages carried their belongings.

"On the fifth day, as the trail kept enlarging and becoming more and more distinct, some of us became greatly concerned as to the wisdom of following such a large body of Indians with such a small force of scouts, as it was evident they had their families with them, and could not travel as fast as a war party. We realized that we would soon overtake them.

"Making known our anxiety to Colonel Forsyth, he halted the command and called us about him, asking us if we 'didn't enlist to fight Indians with him.' That ended the discussion, but, all the same, it did not convince us of the wisdom of the course we were taking.

"However, we followed in silence until the evening of that day, when we came through a narrow defile in the hills, which opened into a beautiful valley. We thought we were on the South Fork of the Republican, but it later proved to be the Arickaree branch of that stream.

"It was a lovely spot, with plenty of grass for our jaded horses, and we halted that afternoon about 4 o'clock and made camp. I am sure that providence must have had a hand in directing our operations that afternoon, for had we progressed half a mile more, we would have ridden directly into an ambush which had been skilfully prepared, and the command would doubtless have been slaughtered to a man.

"BUT aside from the trail we were following, we saw nothing whatever that would indicate there was an Indian in the country. I was on guard that night, and Thomas Murphy was my partner. We cooked some beans during our watch, for the men who were to relieve us, and had a square meal ourselves—our last, by the way, for nine long, dreary, exhausting days.

"After we had stood our watch out, we were relieved, and lay down with our saddles for pillows, and our guns at our sides, and were soon asleep. We had not heard a sound while on guard, that would indicate there was any danger near. Little did we dream of the awful peril that was right at our door!

"The next thing I recollected was the sound of shooting, and the guards shouting 'Indians! Indians!' We all were on our feet in an instant, grabbing our rifles and preparing for action. In the dim morning light, we could see three or four Indians driving off several of our animals which had pulled their picket-pins.

"Colonel Forsyth gave orders to saddle up at once, and we were soon standing by our horses awaiting further orders. Just then a few of the men got permission to drive off a bunch of Indians who were hiding behind some rocks on the hillside to the north of our position. When these men got on high ground, they shouted to us to 'look up the creek'—and such a sight! Indians by the hundred were everywhere in view! They seemed to spring from the very earth; out of the tall weeds and bushes along the creek; from the depressions in the ground, and began swarming out over the hills! It was the most thrilling and awesome sight I ever saw, and I have often thought what a marvelous moving picture it would have presented on the screen.

"But to know it as it really was, and to realize that those savages were after our scalps, gave us no time to think of anything but our own safety. The spectacle was appalling! Hundreds upon hundreds of Indians were pouring down upon us, all mounted on their war ponies, in full regalia, with feathers and plumes flying, and the sunlight glittering on spear, gun and lance! Was it any wonder that some of our men were fairly overcome at the thrilling panorama?

"Quickly we took in the situation. We knew instantly that we would be no match for that army of redmen in the open, 'for they outnumbered us, seemingly, twenty to one. We were encamped directly opposite a small island in the Arickaree, which

John Hurst in 1917. He has since passed away. Photo by E. A. Brininstool.

was covered with tall grass and small, scrubby trees.

"At the suggestion of Jack Stillwell, a beardless boy of but 19, but a veteran in frontiersmanship and plainscraft, and one of the brainiest, bravest and coolest of all the Scouts, Colonel Forsyth gave orders to 'make for the island.' I do not know how the order affected the other men, but to me it was the most welcome and timely one I ever received in all my army experience.

"In other historical accounts of this fight which I have read, it has been stated that we moved across to this little island in a solid body, with our horses in the center and the men in a circle about them. This is most decidedly erroneous. There was no regular order preserved at all, but we all made a grand rush for cover like a flock of scared quail.

"IMMEDIATELY we were pretty well scattered over the island, which was, I should judge, about one hundred and fifty yards long and perhaps seventy-five yards wide, making plenty of room in which to hide from an enemy. Our horses, of course, we had to simply tie to the

bushes, and they were all killed in a very short time.

"It appeared to be a great surprise to the Indians how quickly we got out of sight, and we could tell from their yells of rage and disappointment that they were greatly exasperated in not having first taken possession of the island themselves. Had they done so, the fight would not have lasted fifteen minutes, and not a man would have been left to tell the tale, for out there in the open we would have been immediately surrounded and cut down. It was this getting out of sight so quickly, and keeping under cover, that saved the lives of every one of the survivors.

"Hardly were we located on the island before the Indians were charging through us—not in solid bodies, but either singly or in groups of a few warriors. Scouts Armstrong and Barney Day were by my side at the right and left, each by a small tree, and Jack Donovan and others were at the west end, while others were in the center, all pretty well hidden, and shooting whenever the Indians came within close range.

"Our bullets, coming among them from all directions, thus seemed to daze the savages. We were all armed with Spencer seven-shot carbines, and that was another thing which puzzled the Indians. They could not understand how we were able to load our guns and fire so rapidly.

"There were three men in our command who played the coward. Much as I hate to say this, it was a fact. They utterly refused to fire a shot, but kept themselves hidden. I shall not mention their names. One of them, who happened to reach the island at the same time as myself, and who tied his horse to some bushes near mine, was shaking like a man with the palsy, and seemed utterly unnerved at the awful predicament we were in.

"I tried to encourage this fellow by saying, 'Now, Frenchy, we are in for a devil of a fight, and so let us fight like men!' However, it was all to no avail. He made a run for the bushes and took no part in the fighting.

"I recollect that as the last of our horses was shot down, I heard a voice from the Indians exclaim, in good English, 'There goes their last damned horse, anyway!'

"Soon after the fight began, our surgeon, Dr. Mooers, was struck in the forehead by a bullet, and although he lived three days in an unconscious state, he never spoke a rational word. Lieutenant Beecher was also shot in the side, and after lingering in agony until nightfall, he, too, passed away.

"It was unfortunate that some of our horses were located within the zone of fire near where many of the men were fighting. This brought the latter in range of bullets that were intended for the horses. Colonel Forsyth stood up giving orders and encouraging the men, until shot down twice. The last order I remember hearing him give was, 'Men, dig holes in the sand and make banks for protection!'

"While looking through the tall grass, I saw an Indian run his pony into an old buffalo wallow that was partially filled with water, and it seemed to tax the strength of the pony to extricate itself. This gave me a good chance to take a pot shot at the Indian, but I did not see him fall. Another warrior, coming from the north, almost charged over me on horseback, and certainly would have done so had not his pony shied to one side, which made it so hard for the Indian to keep his seat that he had no chance to shoot at me. I was glad his pony carried him along, for had he fallen, it would have meant death for one of us. I took a shot at him as his pony raced by, but did not see him tumble.

"My near neighbors, Armstrong and Barney Day, were both wounded in the early part of the engagement, and ran to other comrades to have their wounds attended to. That made me feel mighty lonely. I was afraid the Indians would get between me and the other men.

"There was much shooting at the east end of the island, and I thought it was the Indians, as I did not know at the time that Stillwell and some of the others were there.

"I KEPT close watch, and soon saw an Indian creeping through the grass toward our horses, and then I felt sure that all this firing was from the Indian ranks, and that they were closing in around us. This idea proved erroneous, but I am merely giving you my impressions as things appeared at the time. I thought we were all going to be killed and scalped, or captured and held for torture. I think this belief was quite general among all the men.

"I recall hearing Colonel Forsyth call out and ask if anyone could pray. He said, 'We are beyond all human aid, and if God does not help us, there is no chance for us.' I have since thought, in the light of subsequent events, what an awe-inspiring thing it would have been to the Indians if a man of God had broken out in a loud appeal to the Great Spirit for aid. However, nobody volunteered to offer prayer.

"When I saw that Indian creeping toward our horses, I fired at him, and then, without waiting to see the effect of the shot, I jumped to my feet and rushed to where some of my comrades were located. I think it was a healthier location than the one I was in. I found that some of the men had dug holes and made banks of sand around them, while others were using the dead horses for breastworks. So I dropped down behind a dead animal and went to digging myself, thrusting my hands feverishly into the loose sand in my haste to create a shelter from the bullets which were whistling all around me. Digging was easy after I had worked down through the grass roots, and I soon had a place deep enough for protection.

"While I was at work, Sergeant McCall and Scout Culver came in, and getting down behind another dead horse, they started digging. They had been at it but a very short time, when some of the men on the inside of the circle shouted, 'If you fellows on the outside don't get up and shoot, the Indians will be charging right over us!' At this criticism, both McCall and Culver arose to look for Indians. Their heads were fully exposed to the enemy. Suddenly 'Bang'! went a rifle. The bullet grazed McCall's neck and struck Culver in the head, killing him instantly. That was the last exposure of heads during the fighting!

"Shortly after this, Scout Harrington came staggering in, covered with blood from head to foot. He had been shot in the head with an arrow, and the barb was yet sticking in his skull. Some of the men tried to pull it out, but the barb was imbedded so deeply that it could not be extricated.

"Scout Burke then came in where we were and began to dig a hole near us. He kept at it until he had dug down to water. As we were very close to the stream, water was located very close to the surface. The hole soon filled, and he took his canteen

and filled it and passed it around several times until all within reach had been supplied. It was a boon to us, particularly to the wounded, who were becoming feverish and very thirsty.

"Burke then related to us a somewhat laughable experience. It seemed that he did not get across to the island with the rest of us when we made the first grand rush for safety. During the fighting he saw an Indian some distance away—too far, he figured, for a successful shot, so he commenced to crawl to a hummock of sand which lay between him and the Indian, and from which vantage he thought he could nail the red devil. Burke hitched carefully along until he reached the sand hummock, and then slowly straightened up. Suddenly, to his surprise and horror there arose from the other side of this identical hummock that same warrior! Burke said he was so surprised that he forgot all about shooting. He stated that he merely punched his gun at the Indian, shouting 'BOOH'! and then ran for the island, expecting every second to feel a bullet in his back. No shot was fired, however, and he glanced back over his shoulder, to see the Indian running in the opposite direction as fast as he could leg it.

"THE next excitement was when a white flag was displayed by the Indians for a parley. We had quite a controversy over the advisability of recognizing it, finally concluding it would not do to trust them, as they might take advantage of an armistice to rush our lines. I have since thought that as there were a couple of dead Indians lying at that end of the island whose bodies they had not been able to rescue, they may have attempted this ruse to obtain possession of them.

"These two Indians had been shot by Lewis Farley, the best rifle shot in the whole command. Farley had been lying in the tall grass on the north bank of the stream, with a broken leg. Both these warriors were in plain view of him as they crept along a ridge of sand. Farley shot them both through the head, and when I saw the bodies, both Indians carried rifles as well as bows and quivers full of arrows.

"The killing of these two warriors had an intimidating effect on the others, and stopped that mode of warfare. Farley was brought into our rifle pits about dark that night. When the relief command reached us, his leg was in such an awful condition that amputation was immediately necessary, but he died that same night. No braver frontiersman ever lived than Lewis Farley.

"After the white flag incident, the fight was resumed with sharpshooting, but there was no more charging across the island. The songs of their squaws, which, in the early part of the fight, had been joyful and exultant, with the expectation of an easy victory, were now turned into sorrow and doleful lamentation over the loss of their own braves.

"Night came at length, as a welcome shadow to hide us more securely from our dread enemies, and enable us to care more

Battle monument of Beecher Island where Colonel Forsyth with 50 scouts fought a large body of Indians and was besieged for eight days until relief arrived and the Indians retired. Photo June 2nd, 1931, by Emil Kopac.

(Continued on page 31)

How Do They Get That Way

What happens when a red headed woman embarks on the sea of matrimony with a dyed-in-the-wool fisherman.

By BESS L. MORRISON

Bess Loring Morrison and her "Slime shyster".

"**G**OTTA present for you," announced H. C. (my recently acquired better half) as he bounded up our front porch steps one September evening, and pressed a small cardboard box into my hand. It's bracelet, I thought as I eagerly unwrapped it. Then I tried to force a smile, as I gingerly withdrew a painted contraption, bristling with hooks.

"It's nice," I stammer, "but what on earth is it?"

"That," boasted H. C., "is a bass getter, and guaranteed to catch more bass than 'Insull' caught suckers; and look at that action," he added, snatching the thing from my fingers and manipulating it crazily through the air.

When I had married, three blissful months before, I knew I was teaming up with a dyed-in-the-wool fisherman, but this was the first I had discovered, that he was "balmy" about it.

"Only two weeks fore," he babbled, "and I am going to show you the best bass lake in the state of Minnesota. Charlie Turner tipped me off to it," he confided.

For two weeks thereafter, each evening, friend husband brought *me* a present; each having some special merit. He would bore me almost to tears, explaining that they were underwaters, surface lures, or whatnot; which was all Greek to me, for all I knew about fish, was, that's what we ate on Fridays.

It was the $1.25 tag on one of those gadgets that "burned me up." And H. C. had been talking economy! Why I could have bought a brassiere, for what one of those fool things cost, and still have had enough money left to go to the movies. But it seems that when men have a hobby, they lose all sense of relative values. And yours truly, had been trudging eight blocks to save two cents on a pound of butter.

"It's going to be a cold day when I do that again," I vowed. But I relented somewhat, when two days later, found us skirting the shore of a lovely Minnesota lake, shimmering in the green forest, like a sapphire, set in an emerald matrix. To me, who had known, only the prairies of Kansas and Nebraska, it appeared that the trees almost reached the sky. I breathed deeply of the spicy air, redolent with the fragrance of pine and balsam.

We drew up shortly, before a great log building, and in answer to our honk, were greeted by a lank Scandinavian. "We are the Morrisons," announced my husband, extending his hand.

"Oh, yah!" replied our host, as he pumped H. C.'s arm vigorously. "Ve save special cabin for you, but it's too bad you didn't come last veek. They ain't bitin' so good now," he added apologetically, as he twisted the end of his blonde handle-bar mustache. H. C. scowled in lieu of a reply. "I go get your key now," proposed our host.

"You would drive 700 miles to a lake where the fish are not biting," I gibed, "but it serves you right, when we could have gone to the World's Fair, just as well, and you could see all kinds of fish."

"See 'em!" snorted H. C., the color rising in his face, "now who the—"

I WAS truly glad, when our host emerged from the lodge with our key.

"Yust follow this road and you can't miss it," he explained, pointing along a winding, bumpy, trail, that paralleled the lake shore. Down that cow path H. C. herded the protesting car at break-neck speed, with me bouncing around, like a dice in a cup.

"Where's the fire!" I demanded, plopping down with a thud, after I had just bumped my head against the top of the car. "Huh?" grunted H. C. giving me a sidelong glance. "Hey! Look at that fish jump up out yonder," he yelled, pointing to a ring of widening circles in the water; then tore madly at the wheel, to keep from hitting a tree.

"By George, that was a bass!" insisted H. C. I had looked quickly, but I could see no fish, and I wondered if he were subject to hallucinations.

"Whew!" I was sweating bullets by the time we had sighted our cabin of peeled spruce logs, nesting in the evergreens. But I was petulant from having the breath shaken out of me by that awful jouncing, and was in no mood to appreciate it. "Well, here we are," announced the better half, jumping out of the car and piling out duffle and fishing gear. "Here! Grab some of this luggage," commanded my lord and master, as he picked up tackle box and outboard motor. Obediently, but reluctantly, I followed, lugging a heavy box of groceries. "Three months ago, I was his sweetheart, but today, he regards me as his squaw," I reflected bitterly.

"Some swell dump," enthused H. C. when he opened the door. I put down the groceries and looked around, while I got my breath. That climb up the hill had winded me. A large room with rustic furniture greeted me. A stone fireplace at one end of it too. I had to admit it looked cozy, but I was still disgruntled; even though I could see a pressure stove and spotless cooking utensils.

"We're certainly lucky to get this cabin," raved H. C., "Charlie Turner told me, 'it was built and furnished as a wedding gift for the resort keeper's daughter, but her sweetie ran out on her.'"

"Lucky girl," I reflected, then asked dubiously, "Where do we sleep?"

H. C. opened a door and bowed foolishly, "Here we are," he said, with a silly grin.

My stars and garters, couldn't that husband of mine say anything else, than, "Here we are."

I sat on the bed and sank down, and down, but I didn't spring back. Suspiciously, I turned down the sheets, and found two feather ticks, piled on top of a freshly filled straw tick. The pillows were filled with fragrant balsam needles. Everything was so sweet and so different, that I found I was galling in love with the place, in spite of myself.

H. C. gulped his meal, then jumped up from the table and started stringing up a rod, leaving me sitting there with lunch only begun. I couldn't understand "what had gotten into him."

"WHEN you finish eating get into your old duds, and I'll show you how to fish," he proposed.

"That's going to be simple," I thought. He would just tie one of those red and white spoon things fast to my line and I could sit in the shade of a tree, drowsing lazily, with a fish pole in one hand, and a book in my lap. I would look at the bobber occasionally, when I turned the pages of my book. But what a rude awakening I had.

Once my clothes were changed, friend husband grabbed me by the hand, and galloped down the hill to the water's edge, dragging me after him, as if I were a cat he was going to drown.

"Now we'll get the boat," he explained.

"What boat?" I could see no boat.

"This one right here" he went on, pointing toward the end of the pier.

There I saw a rope tied to an iron ring. My eyes followed it to the end, where it was sort of holding up the end of a boat, that was otherwise submerged. "You can't kid me," I boasted, "I know a shipwreck when I see one."

"That boat's O. K. She was put in there so the seems would swell shut. Give me a hand and I'll show you." Together we dragged the boat to the shore and dumped the water out of it. To my astonishment, it floated. "Now I'll hold it while you get in," insisted friend husband, steadying the craft by the gunwhale. The inside was dripping wet.

"Where's something for me to sit on?"

"Sit on what God gave you, and grab this rod." And suddenly, I found a pole thrust into my hands. I sat—and it dawned upon me why the word "obey", was put into the marriage ceremony.

Once the boat was untied, we started to drift out into the lake. "See how easy it is," said H. C., as he tossed a plug out about a hundred feet from the boat, with a little flip of the pole. "Now you try it," he suggested, handing me the pole.

I gave it a mighty swing. H. C. ducked, and the plug landed about ten feet from the boat.

"Didn't thumb your reel. Once we get the snarls out of this line, we'll try again." By this time, H. C. had the lure wound up within six inches of the tip of the rod. "Now get this," he continued, poising the rod in his right hand. "The swing, is a quick forearm snap, like throwing an apple with a sapling. Take your thumb from the reel a split second, here (and he stopped the forward motion of his pole, so I would 'get' the idea) then follow the lure with the tip of your rod, bearing down with your thumb very lightly upon the spool, increasing the pressure a mite, should your line start to belly up between the reel and the first guide; then clamp down *hard* just before the plug hits the water."

I didn't know at the time, but now I understand, that I, a novice, was being initiated, into that Great Fraternity that worships at the altar of the Red Gods. Again I tried; this time with better success. After a couple dozen casts, I seemed to "get the hang of it."

"Think I'll row back along the shore, and let you try your luck," suggested H. C., picking up the oars. As we neared a bed of lily pads he whispered, "try a cast here."

"Why all the shushing, is this against the law?"

"Stop being facetious. And for heaven's sake shut up!" snapped H. C.

For an instant my cheeks burned, then my wrath gave way to fear. Something had *happened* to H. C. He never acted this way before. His unreasonable anger at that honest man who told us the fish weren't biting. His crazy driving, up to the cabin, that almost wrecked the car. Bolting his food, like a famished person. And that fish he claimed he saw. There must be a reason. No symptoms appeared until we reached the lake. My stars, he had water madness! I had heard of it. A psychiatrist would call it a water complex. Well, I would take him to one if we ever got home. "I'll try here just to humor him," I reflected, as I sent my minnow and spinner sailing through the air. I started to retrieve my bait, when wham! my pole was almost jerked from my hands. I held on for dear life! I was not going to lose this fish, not Little Bright Eyes! I pulled, and the fish pulled; all the while H. C. shouting unheeded advice.

"If this fish is going to make this a tug of war," I announced, "I'm going to let it know that my hair isn't red for nothing;" so I pulled harder.

"Oh, Lord!" moaned H. C.

THEN it happened . . . Snap! . . . and the tip of the pole was dangling. I had broken H. C.'s pet rod. I wanted to cry.

"You told me to keep a tight line," I quavered. H. C. didn't answer, but his lips tightened into a thin line, and he cold, like I was the snow scene, from the "Two Orphans." I silently prayed, that he wouldn't hit me over the head with an oar.

Again the line tightened. "Play him easy and you'll land him yet," encouraged H. C., "to hell with the rod!"

Gradually I pulled the fish to the top of the water. One swipe with the landing net, and hubby had it in the boat.

"Well, I'll be damned!" he muttered as he released the hook. Then he walloped that poor fish over the head with the handle of the landing net, and flung it violently into the lake. "Don't you swear at me!" I shrieked, "just because I caught the first fish, you needn't get 'sore' and throw it in the lake. It was such a nice fish too, with a pretty fringe, from its head to tail," I pouted.

"Aw, forget it!" snapped H. C. unfastening my bait, "that was nothing but a stinkin' dog fish." Then he began rowing in stony silence . . . I wasn't exactly a singing lark, myself.

"Well, tomorrow's another day," he commented glumly, as he tied the boat at the dock.

And so it was. One of those nasty, drizzly days; when it looks as if it is always going to stop raining, then doesn't. "I've heard they bite better, when it rains," said H. C. sheepishly, as he screwed a new spark plug into the "outboard", "whatta you think?"

"Oh, sure," I replied blithely. If I were going to be a martyr, I might as well go all the way.

"ALL RIGHT, fix up some eats, and bring the wash-pan along," ordered my fisherman, as he pulled on his slicker, "I'm going on down with the motor, and get her 'perking.'"

I had heard of men that didn't know enough to come in out of the rain, but this prime of mines didn't have enough sense to *stay* out of it.

The little motor was stuttering when I reached the dock. The raw wind was kicking up some sizable waves, I noticed. "She may ship a little water, but you can keep it bailed out with the basin," instructed H. C., as he tinkered with the motor.

"Aye, aye, skipper," I replied, fear gripping my heart.

Our little boat bobbed about like a cork in the ocean. Water came in over the bow, every time it cut a wave. For every basin of water I bailed out, it seemed that two came in over the gunwhales. It kept gaining on me in spite of all I could do. Then of all times the engine stopped. We were drifting helplessly. This was the end! I *knew* it. I wondered if our bodies would ever be recovered. I looked at my husband, as I recalled those fateful words, "Till death do you part."

"Can't you do something," I implored. "Don't you see, that in a few moments this boat will be swamped!"

"It might at that," replied H. C. casually twisting a wire around a spark plug, unless you stop waving your hands, and start bailing again."

To think, that he could be indifferent at a time like this. He never did love me in the first place. Of course I was sure, else he would not bring me out on this lake to drown. Merciful Heavens! I wondered if I had married a Blue-beard. My bitter throughts were interrupted by the staccato popping of the motor. And the spray that whipped my face, mingled with salty tears. Finally we reached the lea of an island where it was calmer.

"SOON as we get the water out of this scow, we're going to troll for walleyes," proclaimed the better half, as he shut off the motor. We trolled, we cast, we still fished, all with negative results. We ate a soggy lunch. We were soaked to the skin. H. C. seemed to be enjoying it; while I had the good sense to keep my mouth shut. So engrossed was he with his fishing, that he had forgotten my very existence.

My feet were wet. My dress was wet, and our vacation was all wet; of that I was sure. I was cold and tired, and hungry. But he kept right on fishing, while I sat and silently "sizzled", as I thought up new terms of contumely for fishermen.

"Too windy, they're not biting," declared the "ball and chain", as he laid his rod aside, and started hauling up the anchor.

"You're telling *me?*"

"Better reel in your bait before I start the engine," ordered the man I had trustingly, married; ignoring my sarcasm.

As I started reeling in my foolish bait, I was glad I remembered that cruelty was legal grounds for divorce; if I didn't first get pneumonia and die. As the outboard started sputtering ,I felt a tug at my line. "Stop! I've got a fish!" I called. I was almost sorry, for if I were doing a job of martyring, I wanted to do it right. From my previous day's experience, I had learned, not to pull on my rod, as if I were trying to stop a run-a-way horse, and after some minutes of struggle, my so-called "better half" lifted my fish, a long, slim one, into the boat.

"First blood," he chuckled. "Now we can have fish for breakfast."

"Not that fish," I protested.

"Why not?'

"Because I'm going to have its picture, and we can't take it that early."

"Not a picture of that 'slime shyster.'"

"Well, whatever it is, I am going to have a snapshot. It is the first fish I ever caught, and I don't believe it is a shyster," I challenged.

"IT'S a Northern Pike, and you take all the pictures of it you want to," beamed the better half. "Slime shyster is a pet name the natives up here have for them."

I sat and held that fish, while we putt-putted, towards our cabin. Funny thing what that fish did to me. It made me forget the city, forget I was civilized. It even made me forget I was cold. It tore five thousand years from the book of time. Again, I was a primitive female. Should I have had hair on my back, they would have bristled. The wailing of the wind no longer frightened me. The darkness was no longer something to be feared, but only a peaceful mantle, that brought tired creatures, sleep.

My renaissance was abruptly interrupted when the boat scraped the gravel beach in front of our cabin. Looking up I noticed a flickering light in our window. "Whom do you suppose it can be?" I asked.

"I don't know, 'Old-Timer', but we'll soon find out," H. C. replied, as he placed the minnow bucket in the water, and weighted it down with a stone.

As we slithered up the path together, carrying the fish between us, I felt it was worth its weight in gold; for I knew it bound me and my mate with stronger bonds, than were ever forged at any earthly altar.

Upon opening the door we saw "Oscar", our friend with the yellow handle-bar mustache, kneeling before the fireplace fanning a small blaze with his hat. Silently we watched. Soon the larger fagots kindled into a roaring fire.

"By golly, I didn't heard you come," he explained. "Dis evening I saw you on lake, and thought you be cold. "That wind was raw," admitted H. C., rubbing his hands before the cheerful blaze.

"Here, take a swig. I brung you yug

(jug) of cider," grinned Oscar who stepped through the kitchen door and handed H. C. a two gallon jug. "That was very thoughtful," thanked H. C. as he raised it to his lips, and took a "long pull."

"Give the Missus some, I bet you it varm her up too," suggested Oscar, as he kicked a glowing ember back onto the hearth. As I had not drank from a jug before, I spilled some of the contents, before I acquired the knack. Heaven knows how much I drank, I had to drink fast to keep it from spilling.

"Turn around quick! you're scorching," said H. C., grasping me by the arm. When one side of me started to steam, he turned the other to the fire, as if I were a fowl roasting upon a spit.

NEXT MONTH

ROCKY MOUNTAIN MULE DEER
By K. C. DeWitt
A narrow escape from a wounded deer is the basis of this interesting story.

* * *

COUGAR STEAK
By Floyd Thornton
You never heard of such a thing? Well, you will have after you read this story about these big cats.

* * *

FISHING ON TOP OF THE WORLD
By Dunc Storms
Trout—plenty of them and "nothing under three pounds" in this wonder spot on "top of the world".

* * *

PREPAREDNESS
By Walter Arnold
Don't miss half your season's catch by not being ready. Here's how and when to do the necessary things.

* * *

And many other stories and articles written by H-T-T readers themselves. The kind you like to read and enjoy.

All in August Issue

"Now, that's what I call hospitality," chuckled H. C. who is slightly Scotch, "Oscar wouldn't take a cent."

"Then I'll give him a picture of my fish," I volunteered. I was feeling more generous every minute.

"Boy, oh boy! but this fire feels good," enthused H. C. as he rolled a new backlog into the flames.

"I'll say," I answered warmly. "I feel like a million dollars, I'll tell the cockeyed world."

H. C. gave me a sharp look.

SOON the aroma of country cured, smoked ham frying, mingled with the fragrance of the blazing pine logs.

"Never ate anything so good in all my born days," approved H. C. smacking his lips, after his third helping. "Give me another cup of coffee."

But when I got up, the funniest thing happened; the floor started rocking the same way the boat did when it was anchored, and I missed the cup partly, when I poured. "Harris, there is something wrong with me!" I cried, thoroughly alarmed.

My husband eyed me soberly. "It's nothing that you won't get over" he answered quizically.

"But I feel so queer. What is it?"

"It's that applejack. It has plenty of authority."

"Great heavens! you don't mean I'm—"

"You are — going to bed this very minute," insisted H. C. picking me up. The last thing I remembered, was someone unlacing my shoes, and then I was dead to the world. Even the porcupines gnawing didn't disturb me.

A tug at my arm aroused me; then a familiar voice, "breakfast is ready—get into your duds." It seemed I had not slept an hour.

"Snoring so loud I couldn't sleep, and would get up and get breakfast."

The meal was excellent. Strange, how some men who disclaim all knowledge of culinary skill at home, suddenly acquire it, when on an outing.

Soon we were headed for the lily pads. It was clear, and crisp and calm.

H. C. scanned the shore line carefully. "Over thert's an old stump," he observed. "See if you can hit it." I took careful aim, and just missed it.

"I'm snagged on something," I exclaimed, as my line tightened. Then the water fairly boiled, and a gleaming mass of fighting strength and fury, leaped high into the air.

"SNAGGED! I'll say you are. To the granddaddy of all the bass in this lake . . . give him line you darn fool," yelled H. C. as the bass hit the water.

"Who is catching this fish?" I asked, trying to keep my rod from trembling.

Whee-e-e-e-e! went the reel, the line scorching my thumb. "See I don't have to give him line, it takes it all by itself," I boasted. "You don't need to tell me—"

"Stop him, stop him! you idiot, or you'll lose him sure," broke in H. C. as he rowed after him. Again the bass leaped into the air, shaking his head, till the hooks on the plug rattled. I was praying the line would hold. Finally after what seemed an eternity, to my aching arms, the fish started to swim in circles around the boat.

"Now keep him coming and I'll land him," shouted H. C. ready with the net.

"Not by a jug full," I declared. "I caught this fish, and I'm going to land it or know the reason—"

"You haven't caught him yet," interrupted H. C. "Moreover, you should speak more respectfully of jugs."

Just then the bass started a great commotion in the water. H. C. made a quick sweep with the net, but the fish was quicker, and jumped not only over the net, but over the side of the boat, landing plop in my lap.

I dropped my rod, and grabbed it by the gills, and clung on for dear life, as my captive flopped about, knocking my skirts galley west.

"Help! I've got him!" I shrieked.

"Just like the fellow that was holding the bear," laughed H. C.

"Look out for those hooks, till I release that plug."

"See, I *told* you I would land it myself,"

I boasted, as I dropped my gallant warrior into the live net.

H. C. gasped, and mumbled something about the Providence that watches over fools and children. Then he thumped me so hard, between my shoulders, that he knocked the marcelle out of my hair.

"You're a brick," he grinned. "I wouldn't have had you lose that fish for a farm."

Before the morning was over, I landed four more; each strike sending a wave of panic through me jittery, until I started to play them; and then I settled down to the business of thoroughly enjoying myself.

"Just one more and we'll have the limit. I'll row slowly and you can troll," suggested H. C.

We had not moved a hundred yards, when I got another hit on the spoon bait. I set the hook, and played my fish carefully. I was learning. But just as I slipped the net under that old bronze back, he gave one more leap, and threw the hook.

"Well what do you know about that?" I groaned. "That fish would have weighed five pounds if it weighed an ounce."

"Maybe," replied H. C. with a twinkle in his eye, "and again maybe not."

All too soon our vacation was ended. My love for out of doors had only begun.

Back home once more, I was showing some of my fishing pictures to the 'girls' of the Thursday Bridge and Scandal Club. But they didn't 'click' despite my enthusiasm.

Finally Dolly Williams admitted "they were nice."

"What do you think!" I confided to her "H. C. is going to give me a 'Shakespeare' for my birthday."

"That will be sweet," she cooed, placing her cup in her saucer, "but don't you think that something besides a book would be more practical!"

Now can you "tie that?" How a girl thirty years old (though she only claims twenty-six of them) didn't realize I wasn't speaking of books. So I "up and told her," that "a Shakespeare with a handle could furnish more thrills than Romeo and Juliet ever dreamed of."

My only reply was a slight elevation of her plucked eyebrows. But as I went into the kitchen after the ice cream and cake, I heard her murmur to Sally Crosgrove, "My dear, how do you suppose she gets that way."

Evening scene at the Harbors. East, West and Middle Harbors are the homes of large-mouth bass, rockbass, bluegills, perch and catfish. "Greatest breeding grounds for game fish in the world".—Dr. Raymond Osborn, head of the Department of Zoology Ohio State University.

Lake Erie Bass

(Continued from page 9.)

Bridge Road and Route 163 towards Lakeside. Cozy cottages, good boats, a general store. Beautiful scenery. Right at the home of the large-mouth bass, catfish and bluegills. Mr. and Mrs. Bohling, gracious hosts. And just beyond is Guy Tibbels, on East Harbor, another good place right at the fishing grounds.

I tried East Harbor for bass. A weed bed caught my eye. Acres of lily pads looked like a good large-mouth habitat. Pushing the boat easily towards a bed of lilies I began casting with a pork-rind wobbler. It lit on a pad and as it slid into the water a big bass lunged and had it. The bass sawed away through the pads but I worked him out to the open and brought him to the boat,—a three pound large-mouth. A few minutes later I caught a grass pike. Then I tried the open water where beds of moss and marsh grass waved beneath the surface. I could see bass scurrying away ahead of the boat. I rowed easily, letting the boat drift now and then. I made an open water cast, and a bass splashed and took the lure. It was a two pounder. I used plugs and porkrinds and bass struck at both. Evening and night fishing are good at the Harbors. You get a real thrill when an old lunker of a bass lunges and grabs your bait in the dark or on a moonlight night. Bluegills can be caught by the peck almost any day.

There's a good camping ground at Jim's Place between West Harbor and Middle Harbor about ten minutes drive from Bohlings or Tibbels' and not far from Lakeside. The fisherman who has a camping outfit or a trailer camp-wagon, will be in luck if he stops at Jim's Place. Good water, shade, and cooling summer breezes.

I found good bass fishing at West and Middle Harbors too.

Fishing for bluegills at the Harbors was good sport. I tried a little worm fishing for bluegills. I used a small black cork and a snelled hook. Pop! would go the cork as it ducked out of sight, and then a big bluegill would come cupping out of the water cutting whrilly-gigs and putting up a fight that had a thrill all its own, especially when using a fly rod. I tried flies with small spinners and had luck, in late afternoon. The "blues" would smack the fly as soon as it hit the surface. I found a combination of Silver Doctor and Grizzly King to be good. A Black Gnat or a Cowdung also brought many strikes. I think a dark fly was the best.

In Sandusky Bay off shore from Zeller's Point,—Black Bill's place, there is good fishing for channel catfish and bull heads, plenty of bass are taken in this territory also. There is good fishing near Johnson's Island and near Marblehead Light, and also off shore near Danbury and Bay Bridge.

In a week's trip on the Peninsula and at Put-In-Bay and the Islands one can find such a variety of fishing and scenery, that he will keep busy every day. Fishing trips can be adjusted to fit the weather. When the big water is rough the Harbors can be fished. It's all right there, easy to reach without wasting time in traveling long distances to the various fishing grounds. It's far enough away from the hustle and bustle of business life and traffic, and yet close enough to keep in touch with the outside world. It's a delightful playground, that has largely been overlooked not only by sportsmen in other states but by Ohio folks as well. It's a great place for the women and kiddies. There's fishing for them too.

A tent at the Harbors. A moonlight night after a gorgeous sunset. Perry's Monument in the distance across the water at Put-in-Bay, gleaming faintly in the moonlight. A trip to Marblehead Light, old weird, historic and beautiful, especially on a moonlight night. Quietude and restfulness. A quiet pipe under the trees. A snooze in front of the campfire. The twitter of night birds. A plop of a feeding bass. Bullfrogs and crickets to sing you to sleep. The wind sighing softly through the trees. The music of the waves as they kiss the sandy shore. Burning embers burning ever lower. Aroma of smoke from a campfire. A refreshing night breeze. Stars above. The moan of a passing freighter far out in the big lake as it signals to another craft approaching in the dark. You crawl beneath the covers in your camp or cottage at bed time, rested, care-free, content. Another good fishing day on the morrow. You know the bass are there. Pickerel await you. Pan fish will rise to your flies or catfish to jerk the pole out of your hands. An inspiring sunrise, awaits you after your night of dreamless sleep—you sleep so soundly. Or if it rains and the weather man kicks up a fuss, you see Lake Erie in a stormy mood, but you know that the fish are still there and when Lake Erie smiles again there will be game-fish on your stringer.

CANVASBACKS

(Continued from page 13)

are very hard to kill at any distance with any gun. Incidentally this bird was mounted and now adorns the office of a Washington sportsman.

Twelve o'clock came and we still had not seen a canvasback; the Captain wanted to take up our decoys and put out a string of four or five scattered ones along shore and shoot a few whistlers which would not decoy to our stool but which had been flying around, singly, all day. "Nothing doing," said I, "We came after canvasbacks and no 'bull heads' interest me", you fellows can go up shore and try it if you want but leave those decoys alone"; and I had my way. At 12:30 the others decided there was nothing doing and went in to get dinner, leaving me in the blind alone to guard the outfit; and right then was where the fun began. They had hardly gotten inside the club house, which was less than one-quarter mile away, when the canvasbacks began to come around the corner in small bunches. Evidently they had fed the night before to their hearts (or stomachs) content and had been bedded out in the bay resting and preening their feathers where we could not see them; but the wind had been getting stronger and the bay rougher and the birds probably decided to come in to lunch.

THE first five decoyed, and I got just one; the quitters in the club house heard the shots but reached the unanimous decision that "Tal's shooting another scoter". But they were wrong; I got two out of the next bunch, and then a single which required both barrels of the twelve guage to stop him. Captain Spence by this time had some doubts about that scoter business, and he came out to investigate just in time to see the next bunch coming up the river towards the blind; in no time they were all back in the blind, but they scared off a good bunch while on the way; by the time they were settled the wind was blowing harder than ever and the canvasbacks were pouring into the river, but not all coming to our set up.

The first bunch that came in after we were all settled was a flock of about forty canvasbacks; they came straight in but a little high and fast, and the bunch split; I was shooting from the right corner of the blind, Captain Spence in the middle and Howard in the left corner; just two birds, both drakes, came my way, the rest veering to my left; they did not give the Captain much chance but the two on my side offered a perfect shot; Spence fired first and got one; Howard let go with the automatic and he got one. They turned to me and one of them said, "How many did you get?" and I had to reply "Not a blooming feather". It is easier to hit them when in a blind by yourself.

We all settled down after this, however, and the canvas kept coming; we kidded the Captain for prophesying that the birds had returned to the Flats and that we would have poor shooting; every time a nice bunch would round the bend

one of us would casually remark "Captain, I believe all those canvasbacks have gone back on the Susquehanna Flats".

The shooting continued until sundown; when we stopped we certainly appreciated Captain Spence's device for taking in the decoys, as we were tired and cold, and I was more than hungry; it took the three of us less than ten minutes to bring them all in and store them ready for the next time. I stood on the shore on our way back to the club house and looked back and the ducks were still coming in from the bay; it is always a wonderful and exciting sight. On arrival at the club house we counted our kill—37 ducks, of which 33 were canvasbacks; this was but a small percentage of the vast numbers which we had seen, and had left feeding in the river.

After a supper of beef steak and onions, and a dish of Captain Spence's favorite delicacy, fried eels, we drove to Baltimore, a distance of 90 miles. On the way up Howard while driving the auto dozed off—probably dreaming of canvasbacks—and we went off the road; fortunately there were no telegraph poles or ditches at that point. May the Canvas of East Neck Island supply sport and recreation for many of our mentally weary citizens for years and years to come!

Walleyes of Sisse-Bak-Wet

By JAMES CLYDE GILBERT

"**I** PROMISED to take the girls out tonight, but if you're only going to be here a short time I'll take you out where the wall-eyes run big," said Leo Manke, as he bustled about the kitchen of Otis Lodge.

"You be down at the landing in ten minutes and I'll be there with bait and everything," he added.

The blue water of Sisse-Bak-Wet Lake rippled pleasantly beyond the white birches and oaks of the sloping lawn. It is no small lake. It is a good day's row around the shore line, but one need not row an hour to find more fish than one needs. Above the blue waters, encircling the shore, are green trees. Across the lake, in the far distance, are purple, wooded hills. Your eyes roam upward to the fleecy, white clouds with a background of lovely blue, ranging from a light to a deeper hue. A poet or an artist could make an exquisite impressionist poem or a picture from Sisse-Bak-Wet.

When we started from our southern Michigan home I promised my good wife I would show her wild deer, perhaps a bear and would see that she caught big fish. I made good on the deer and bear when I took her down the Tahqueamenon River in Joe Beach's boat. I took her through the Superior National Forest of northern Minnesota and we saw wild deer in the quiet waters of the lakes at eventide feeding on the lily pads with the sun shining on their red coats. Now it was up to me to make good on the fishing. Leo Manke, the guide, would have to help me do that, for one is likely to be critical of a woman's first efforts to catch game fish. With a guide in the boat I would have to be polite and patient. Leo came and we pushed off, Madame, Donald, my ten-year-old son, and I. I gave my good wife my best Heddon casting rod fitted with line and snelled snap. Leo looked over my tacklebox.

"Everything but the right thing," he commented, and then proceeded to dig in his pocket. Up came a little tin box about three inches square. From the box

he took a special spoon lure which he attached to the line.

"Now cast over the bar as I row up," he said. (Never a word to me as to what I should use—he was going to see that the lady got fish.)

I fitted up another rod with what I thought would please the wall-eyes of

Mrs. Gilbert caught all the fish that trip.

Sisse-Bak-Wet and cast out in my best professional manner. As I cast I heard a little screech from Madame:

"Oh! Something's on the line! What will I do? Oh! Oh! He's pulling the line out!"

"Snub him hard," yelled Manke as he bent to the oars.

She "snubbed," and then the fun began. She had hooked into a big wall-eye and he wanted to go places. Down he went into the blue water. This like is over 200 feet deep in some places by actual

measurement and this fish apparently had found one of those places. Straight down he went, under the boat while Leo spun the oars and brought the craft about, the while he shouted encouragement and advice. Slowly she reeled in the fish, then out he raced, barking her fingers on the spinning reel handle. I feared for my pet Heddon and while Leo shouted encouragement and gave her points on handling the fish I yelled out to her to hang on to that rod, as it was my best one and had no other like it. Finally the fish tired of Leo's steady rowing and her pull and came in slowly and majestically like a big ship docking. Alongside the boat he came and the guide lifted him into the boat by the bronze leader. The fish was full of life and vigor and dashed about, requiring a little time to subdue. I was for having the lady fisher take the catch off the hook, but big-hearted Leo would have none of that. He disengaged the barb and threw it out where it trailed behind the boat. He picked up his oars and at the second stroke I heard the warning squeal, and sure enough the line in the rear was taut and the rod bending. We went through the same experience and in came an even larger fish than before. I changed lures, spit on the lure, prayed under my breath and did everything a man could do to bring luck, but nothing hit. Leo would advise me to use this, that and the other, though he had a peculiar glint in his eye. He was out to show me up. I knew it and could do nothing about it. I was glad to see the Mrs. getting fish for she is not an ardent fisherwoman, and I thought if she could be taught to fish she would be my constant companion. Always when we go into Alaska, British Columbia or the Yukon she stays in the hotels while I and the boys go into the hinterland. But now she was showing me up in a fearful manner. Donald was beginning to razz me. He was not fishing but was an interested spectator.

We rounded the point north of the cottages and began our back trek. The sun was sinking and the fish were feeding—

but not on my lures. Leo had put a spell on my tackle. The good wife insisted that I take her outfit and catch a fish, but I disdained it. I who had caught the Arctic Grayling in the Yukon, and who had crawled behind overhanging glaciers on the upper Skeena to fish monster rainbows and cut-throat would never consent to that.

The sun went below the western hills and we came in with six nice wall-eyes. I say "we." The lady caught all six. As we beached the boat Leo pulled out another of those spoon dinguses and said:

"Be out here early in the morning before sun up and follow over the same route we took and you'll get fish with this."

There was still light enough for a good picture of Madame and her fish and I snapped it. She who had never caught a fish in her life had bested me, and I had all the tackle a fisherman could ask for. But the cunning guide knew every fish by name in that lake and just when and what he would strike. So, fishermen with wives who would fish "if the fish were biting" go to Grand Rapids, Minnesota, drive out to Otis Lodge and ask Arthur or Mrs. Otis for Leo Manke. Arrive in time to take in the evening fishing and if you explain that your wife never caught a fish and is desirous of catching some of the famous wall-eyes (which you have often caught) you will be shown up as an amateur sure as you are alive, for I'm telling you there is something uncanny about Leo and his influence over those fish.

The next morning I was up at five and out on the grounds. I used all kinds of lures and caught many wall-eyes, throwing back the smaller ones and keeping only the large ones for icing. I found one of the best killers was a large feather fluted spoon of a weedless variety. I had such a Marathon spoon and also a Marathon hook casting spoon, black and white pattern. These brought the big fellows out of the deep.

I still think Manke cast a spell on the

Even little Donald Caught his share.

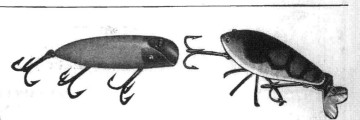

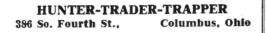

fish that first evening. I do know this. He has some supernatural power over those larger wall-eyes. He heard there was a World's Fair on at Chicago. He went out one evening alone and brought in the largest wall-eye of the season. He caught it in Sisse-Bak-Wet lake and if you were at the Century of Progress you may recall seeing it above the desk of the official in charge of the Minnesota State exhibit with name and date of catching engraved on the board on which it was mounted.

When Leo does not cast his curse on the fish it is easy to catch your limit. Donald, good fisherman in his own right, went out with me and came in loaded. We did not waste our fish. Otis Lodge caters to hundreds of vacationists and they all like fresh fish. The lodge is ten miles southwest of Grand Rapids, Minnesota. The main lodge is about a hundred feet from the shores of Sisse-Bak-Wet lake in a grove of hardwood trees. It has rooms and bath and is equipped with piano, radio and library for use of guests. We occupied one of the cottages off by ourselves. These are spread along twelve hundred feet of shore line, all of which is clear of underbrush and mowed by lawn mower. You need not be a fisherman to enjoy this place. The grounds are electrically lighted as well as the lodge and cottages. In the lake are wall-eyes and Great Northern pike, many of which we caught in our short stay. The lake is spring fed and has been stocked with from forty to eighty ten-gallon cans of pike fry each season for the last nine years. In little Sisse-Bak-Wet lake (connecting) are black bass, sunfish and bluegills. In seven nearby lakes, from three to eight miles distant, are black bass, sunfish, crappies and wall-eyes. Our cottage was serviced by maids and we had only to enjoy ourselves, fish, swim, play tennis and loaf. Itasca county, in which this lake is located, boasts more than 1200 lakes, the waters of which run into the Mississippi River and the Arctic Ocean. Thus no matter how much they are fished those waters connecting with the larger systems are naturally replenished each spring when the fish run in to spawn and remain to be caught.

Here is a beautiful spot where the seasons paint their pictures as on a vast canvas, for daily admiration from the windows of our cabin; a ruddy dawn burns through the distant treetops and the glow of sunset seems to pause, mellow and golden, on the bank.

Everything there was held in a lovely stillness — the slender birches whitely streaked against green woods beyond, the tattered sprays of maple leaves, the broad scribbling of mauve shadows along the dim and curving lines of the shore. Everything was quiet and tranquil, with the quietness and tranquillity that belong to early dawn and early dusk when things are scarcely awake and barely asleep.

There is much rugged beauty throughout northern Minnesota. We traveled from the Superior National Forest down through to Itasca county camping out, staying in tourist's camps, abandoned mine buildings and fashionable lodges as the mood struck us. In the open, when the

Shoreline of Sisse-Bak-Wet Lake, Minnesota

weather was good, we threw our Maupin sleeping bags down under the trees and slept. When we had access to a gas station with air we blew up our rubber mattresses and placed these under the sleeping bags. No matter how rocky or rugged the ground the combination meant a night of comfort. We would awaken to the leap of trout in the stream at our feet or the mighty splash of a feeding black bass or Great Northern pike. A white mist followed the streams, and the moon rose full over the highlands.

We fished many streams and lakes throughout the north, saw wild game of all kinds and took our leisurely course here and there where fancy beckoned. Perhaps we would look at the map of Minnesota and see a chain of lakes miles away in what looked like wild territory—an absence of towns would indicate that. We would start out and in a few hours would be winding up some old road, almost impassable with brush and overgrown shrubs. How delightful it is to accept the hospitality of a roadside wood, when rain sweeps across hillside and plain, as it did one day in Itasca county. The sturdy tree branches were tossed by the wind that roared down the valleys from the hills. Rain may pour and wind may rush across the treetops, but once under the hardwood's kindly shelter, only stray spatters penetrate and the wind seems but a murmur. And when spinning along hot, dusty roads, brief glimpses into wayside woods, where shafts of sunlight pierce the gloom, or checkered shade and sunshine adorn their smoke-brown carpets, always impart a sense of refreshment and rest to a tired fisherman.

It is a joy to vacation in a care-free manner amid such pleasures.

SPLENDID SALMON FISHING

THE attention of salmon fishermen is called again this year to Anticosti Island, in the Gulf of St. Lawrence. A. O. Seymour, general tourist agent of the Canadian Pacific Railway, states that the island, which is accessible from Quebec city via the steamer Fleurus during the season, has fifteen rivers ranging from two rod to eight rod capacity, and that outings of 7, 14, 21 days or longer can be arranged. Sea trout, brook trout and lake trout are also found in most waters, and provide excellent sport. The Fleurus

leaves Quebec every Thursday at 8:30 a. m. from June 21 to Aug. 2, and intermittently thereafter. The sum of $237.00 covers round trip steamer fare from Quebec, meals and berth included, approximately 7 days fishing with all necessary services except tackle, and special non-resident fishing license.

Fishing rights on Anticosti Island are owned by the Consolidated Paper Corporation, which in 1933 inaugurated the system of leasing their property to sportsmen. The island is also noted for its fine hunting. Shooting privileges were extended for the first time last year, and will again be available in 1934. Formerly a sanctuary for wild life, the island now abounds in ducks, geese, snipe, deer and other game.

A LADY ANGLER

I READ the fishing stories from your subscribers and once in a while there is one from your lady friends so I am taking a chance with this and want to show that all the fishermen, or I should say fishers, are not of the sturdier sex. I had just rather go a-fishing than anything I know of, and when anything prevents my going with the he-man of the family I just don't get over it very soon. Now for the big one that *did not* get away.

I had been catching medium sized fish all summer and my man would beat me on size and I had remarked that if I could just get the largest one on some trip I would be happy to stop and let him get the larger number. I had fished down stream on this particular trip and he had chosen up-stream (I believe he thought up-stream would be the most producctive). I had a pretty fair catch and was about to turn and fish back toward the car, when I saw a dreadfully hard place to get at, willows and brush very closely interwoven and a nice deep pool just back of it. Now I could do nothing but poke my pole through this tangle and use but a couple feet of line, which I did, with a great big night crawler all wound around the hook. I kept well back out of sight and had no more than set the hook into the pool just where I thought it would do the most good when I thought an alligator had started for Florida with it.

Of course I could not raise it up straight out of the water for the pole went into the pool through a six-inch hole in the willows, so that was the way I had to get

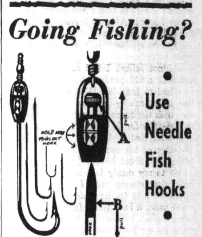

it out, and when I got that fellow up to where I could see him I just almost jumped in to keep him from leaving the hook. Gosh, but I was afraid of losing my prize, and who wouldn't be, after trying for years to get one like him. I knew my man would not believe I had ever hooked him unless I could produce the evidence so I just had to keep him. Well I maneuvered that baby inch by inch until I could grab him with the corner of my jacket, and just in time too for if he had made one good flop with that little hook just caught in the edge of his upper lip I would not be telling you about him. I just hugged that whale to my manly bosom and backed off from that stream until I just knew that no matter how far he could jump he would never make it back to his family under that overhanging willow. Well, I finally got down on my knees and eased him out onto the ground and would you believe it, I was so nervous and incredulous that I could have had such luck that I really wondered if I had a trout or was it just a carp. I finally decided it was a much coveted trout, and wound up my line (I ouldn't have fished another minute for I was so shaken up) and putting the big fellow under all the others I went back to the car. My husband had already come in and was laying his fish out in a nice row, to impress me, I suppose. He said, "What do you think of that for a mess of fish?" I said, "Gee, you sure do have all the luck," and started laying mine out, the smallest one first and so on up to next to my big boy. Then I counted them and said, "Why, that's funny, I thought I had another one, guess it is so small I can't find it in this bag. Oh, here it is," and I laid that big brown eyed baby out beside his little row, and he looked and gasped and said, "Where in — did you get that?" Well, I was so happy I could have cried for I had beat him once, and if I never do again I can always tell about that one. Now maybe you have gotten the idea from this fuss I have been making that that fish weighed at least ten pounds and was a yard long. I'm going to be truthful and tell you that he was 14½ inches long and weighed something like two and a half pounds, but that is "some fish" for our small streams. Of course our lakes give up the really big ones, but I am content, and as our season opens May 15th I am all set and ready to go. You ladies who have never taken up fishing, do so before another season draws to a close. Don't let the men have all the fun.

EDITH NOWLIN,
Salt Lake Co., Utah.

———o———

STURGEON SPEARING

Have read with interest several stories by Mr. C. Roy Teller about fish house spearing in winter. Well would like to say he sure knows what he is talking about when he says there is a lot of fun and sport in it. Well I fish that way every winter on Old Lake Winnebago which by the way is the largest fresh water lake in the U. S. A. within the bounding of one state. This lake is about thirty miles long and twelve miles wide, but it

is very shallow, averaging about sixteen feet deep. As we have an open season for Sturgeon spearing this year will try and tell you about it.

THE fish shanties used here are about six feet square in size, some larger and some smaller, with a hole in the floor about two by six on the average. This is about the size hole you make in the ice, then after putting your shack over this hole you cut the ice out so that it slopes out under the ice so you can see out under the ice farther. Then bank your shack all around with snow to keep out the wind and cold. Now after you have started a fire in your stove you are all ready to fish. For a decoy we use a white enameled minnow about six or eight inches long, although some are a longer and some smaller. This is made of wood and weighted with lead to make it sink. Then you cut some fins out of tin and put them on and you have a nice minnow that swims quite natural. You drop this in the water and move it about a few times and then let it rest for a few minutes.

One I speared last February. It is 5 ft. 3 in. long, weight 60 lbs.

Although the sturgeon is a bottom feeder he sometimes comes up to look at your minnow. After you have moved your minnow about for some time and it has come to rest you see a dark shape coming slowly up from the bottom. As the sun strikes it, it becomes a deep brown and stops for a second at your minnow or it may move right along through the water. You take your spear and slowly lower it in the water until you get one hand on the end, then you aim for a spot as close to the head as you can and throw it hard. These spears are made of eight feet of one-half-inch pipe filled with lead for about three feet on the lower end. A hole is drilled in the pipe about two feet from the end and a strong rope about three feet long is tied in there and onto your spear. There is a flat spring welded onto your pipe just above where this rope is

fastened. This is to hold your short rope and keep your spear in the handle.

As the spear strikes the big fish he starts going places unless you are lucky enough to break his spine. As the sturgeon struggles the spear comes out of the handle and he is fast to the short line or tumbling line as we call it. Your spear is fastened with about thirty feet of strong line on the top of the handle. You may have quite a fight on your hands if he is a big one as some of them weigh up to two hundred pounds although the average is about forty-five. The first thing the sturgeon likes to do after you hit him with the spear is to roll and twist. If your spear did not come out of the handle he would soon tear loose, so after he swims around for awhile you draw him up and get the gaff hook in and out he comes, and you think it's some prize if he happens to weigh seventy-five or a hundred pounds.

There is a lot of luck in catching them as you may fish all winter and not see one, or you may get several in one day. Although you see lots of other fish you are only allowed to spear sturgeon and rough fish. The limit on sturgeon is five a season. The season is from January 5th to March 15th.

It is only about once in five years that this lake clears up so that you can see bottom, and that's about as often as you can get sturgeon.

BERNARD BERGEN,
Fon du Lac County, Wis.

———o———

THE May issue of the Du Pont magazine contains an article referring to the fact that cellophane is used as a fish lure. A sportsman wrote in saying that he discovered this use by accident when he lost his bait box and decided to try the shiny wrapper from his cigar.

———o———

MICHIGAN'S HIGHEST LAKE

(Continued from page 17)

a log, for there is no turmoil. But just for an instant. Then there is no fooling on the part of the fish. He tears from the near surface to the bottom of the lake and directly under the boat. The line saws along the slippery, watersoaked wood of the boat bottom and I stand up frantically trying to bring the fish around. Jess heads the boat into the wind and the line releases. Still the fish bores down into the water and my reel screams as it whirs. Fortunately there are no weeds or logs to obstruct the line and the fish has the freedom of the entire lake. Out the line goes to within twenty feet of the end. It is time to stop fooling and get down to business. I tighten down on the reel with my thumb and the pressure stops the fish. Slowly it widens out in a great circle seeking to throw the line by jerking. It does not come to the surface. It is a pike, I am sure. Gradually I pull in the line with the tugging fish still unseen. Then there is slack as the fish runs under the boat. I absorb much line in the reel and wait his next move. It is not long in coming.

Straight away he swims slowly but doggedly and with alarming strength. In vain do I thumb the reel. He goes out relentlessly. The sun is beating down hot and strong on my neck and perspiration is running into my eyes. There is no breeze. Jess keeps the boat headed just right. He has pulled in his tackle long ago and is now helping me bring the monster to net. The line slackens and I reel in frantically while I can safely do so. Soon deep, down under the boat we see a long, white twisting belly. It is a Great Northern pike and he rolls and shakes his great body, opening and shutting his shovel nose jaws like some prehistoric creature of another world. Up, up he comes. Too big for the net. Where's the gaff? As usual, in the tackle box unjointed and no time to put it together. The big fish comes alongside the boat, Jess reaches over and grasps it firmly behind the gills and pulls it into the boat a splashing, threshing thing that quickly tangles all lines and lures together as he fights for the freedom he will never again enjoy. Enough fish here for three days, hungry as we are. We slip the noose through his lip and tow him gently behind to the live box before our cabin. Here we release him. More threshing then sulking in a dark corner while two smaller black bass weighing three pounds seek the safe seclusion of the opposite corner.

WE hastily eat a lunch of cold bass and bread washed down with hot tea made from spring water. We find we have time to fish the north branch of the Au Sable before fly fishing for bass in the evening. We jump into the car and twenty minutes later we are wading the north branch while brook trout leap to the flies we offer. The run is all to fish about seven or eight inches long, though Jess hooks one that gives him a good battle before breaking loose. This is a game preserve and deer cross our river again and again ahead and behind us while partridge feed on the wintergreen berries in the open, sunny patches beneath the white birches. At the big rock a mile below the ford Jess tangles with a big brook trout which he finally lands in the shallows. We each have a half dozen nice trout, enough for any fisherman. As the sun casts long shadows across the sparkling waters of the old North Branch we turn our way homeward. It is hot in the closed car that has been standing all the afternoon in the sun high on the west bank of the river. But with a good speed we soon have a refreshing breeze blowing in. A big buck deer, with antlers well out of the velvet, stands not sixty feet from the road and wheels and leaps away as we near, his white flag aloft, head back and heels flying. He makes for the swamp at the head of the river near dam two. Far to the left on the jack pine plains we see other deer moving into the hills for the night's feeding.

Home again through the gathering dusk. Home to the old log cabin by the lake shore. This old cabin is made of logs we pulled from the lake—old boom sticks of pine that were used to encircle the saw logs of the late seventies and early eighties,

for once there was a mill at the north end of this lake. These old boomsticks which had lain in the water a half century, when dried out on land, made good timbers, sound as a dollar. It is a cozy old place, not elaborate, but fitting the surroundings of tall pines and murmuring waters. We are alone on this lake, as wild as it was ten centuries ago. We have two weeks' supply of food, bacon, flour and canned goods. A spring back of the cabin and a pump at the door furnish our water. We are too far back to have electric lights or power, but a Coleman Sportlite lantern in each room makes night as bright as day. We also have a Coleman cook stove which we use when the days are exceptionally hot and we do not want a fire in the big range.

IN these days of heartache, bank failures and depression, it seems to me more people in the crowded cities would seek the quiet peace and solitude of such places as this. North of Saginaw Bay, on the east side of the lower peninsula clear to the straits of Mackinac, may be found abandoned farmhouses and neglected farms, rich and ready for the workman to produce a living. Marshes furnish wild grass for stock until clover can get a start and logs are plentiful for fuel. This land is held by defunct banks now in receivership or by individuals who have too much of this type of property and are ready to sell it cheap on most any terms. Even improved farms of all sizes are for sale now. There are wild berries by the hundreds of thousands of bushels going to waste each year in this section that might be canned or dried for winter food. Deer could be killed and the meat jerked for winter as was the meat of our pioneer ancestors. When suckers run in spring they may be caught by thousands and salted in barrels for winter food. The land will produce if properly selected in hardwood areas. Even if the markets are a bit dull now at least the worker can raise enough for his of breadline and eviction. It will pay to own use. And the wild beauty of the country is such that that alone should compensate one for the change for here at least one has security free from the fear of breadline and eviction. It will pay to investigate this summer. Bring your fishing tackle and come along.

———o———

THE HERO OF THE ARICKAREE

(Continued from page 20)

properly for our own wounded. It was a dark, rainy night, and our first work was to get the wounded all in and dig a place for them where they would be protected from the rifle firt of the Indians, which we knew would be renewed with greater fury than ever on the morrow. The Indian loss already had been heavy, and we knew they would make a desperate attempt to end the matter with the light of another day.

"After digging a pit, in which the wounded all were placed, we got the saddle blankets off our dead animals, and made as comfortable beds for the men as

possible. We then secured all the ammunition in our saddle-bags, after which we cut the hams off the dead horses, into small strips, which we hung up in the trees to dry, as our food supply was all gone. Next, we dug trenches connecting all our rifle pits.

"Colonel Forsyth then called a council to determine what was to be done. Our guide was Sharp Grover, an experienced frontiersman and Indian fighter, and Forsyth asked him what the chances were of sending men through the Indian lines to Fort Wallace, for reinforcements. The distance was about 125 miles. Every mile of such a journey would be fraught with danger, even if men could slip through the Indian cordon about us.

"GROVER said it would be impossible for a man to get through the lines. He went on to explain what the Indians did in such a situation as we were in. He said that as soon as it became dark, the Indians would creep in closer and form a circle about us so small that it would not be possible for a man to get through without being detected.

"We all stood around listening to the dark picture he painted. After he had finished, young Jack Stillwell, the boy of 19, but who had all the nerve and courage of a Spartan, spoke up and said, 'Colonel, I'll go if I can get someone to go with me, providing anybody wants to take the chance.'

"An old scout named Pierre Trudeau—old enough to be Stillwell's father—replied, 'I'll go with you, Jack.'

"Thereupon, Colonel Forsyth wrote a message to Colonel Bankhead, the commanding officer at Fort Wallace, explaining the terrible plight we were in. He then inquired of Grover if wagons could be brought directly across country from the fort to us. The scout replied that the country was so rough that it would not be possible to do that. Stillwell was thereupon directed to return by the way of Custer's trail, made in 1867, which ran directly north from Fort Wallace to the Republican River, and then to follow the river to our position. This made a distance of about 130 miles, and accounts, in a measure for the long time occupied by Stillwell on the way, as well as the fact that he had to travel slow for the first day or so to get entirely clear of the Indians.

"It turned out, however, that Grover's description of the country was all wrong, for we returned to Fort Wallace straight across the country. Sharp Grover was the man who ought to have volunteered to carry the message, but my opinion is that he was afraid to take a chance.

"We expected to get relief—if at all—in about six days, providing the scouts got though all right. After Stillwell and Trudeau left, we just settled down to business, for we did not know what the Indians might do before morning, and so we kept diligent watch all that first night. There was no attack, however.

The next day was one of watching, for instead of any more attacks such as the Indians pressed on the first day, the fighting was all confined to desultory firing by the Indian sharpshooters.

"When night fell, Colonel Forsyth deemed it advisable to try and get two more scouts through, not knowing, of course, if Stillwell and Trudeau were successful. I do not remember the names of the two who volunteered on the second night, but anyhow, they were unable to get through the lines, as every avenue of escape was too closely guarded, and the scouts soon returned.

"The third day was a repetition of the second—very little firing, but close watching on the part of the Indians. Evidently they were going to try and starve us out. And it certainly looked like their plans would carry out.

"After dark on the third night, Colonel Forsyth again called for volunteers, and Jack Donovan and A. J. Pliley started out, with directions to come back straight across the country with soldiers and an ambulance and medical supplies, together with plenty of food. They had many thrilling escapes, but after many privations they met Colonel Carpenter of the Tenth Cavalry who was out on a scout, and guided him to our position.

"While the scouts were out trying to bring relief to us, we who were left on the island, were having a serious time. The Indians gave up the siege after the fifth day, and some of the men were prompted to advise saving the lives of those who were uninjured by striking out for the fort, and leaving the wounded to their fate, thinking none of the volunteers would be able to get through.

"WHEN this talk of abandoning the wounded reached Colonel Forsyth's ears, he called us together and made a nice talk. It was very touching and soldier-like —so much so that I did not hear anything further said about abandoning the wounded. Forsyth told us he expected us to remain with the command until the men he had sent out, had had time to reach Fort Wallace, and that it was our duty, from a humanitarian standpoint, to stick together at least until we felt sure the men had failed to reach the fort.

"'After that,' he concluded, 'I will have no further claims on you, and you can do the best you can to save your own lives.'

"We then all swore we would never leave the wounded, but would remain and die with them, if necessary.

"Our dried meat gave out in six days, and then we had nothing to eat but the dead horses, which were festering and decaying all about us, and when we cut into the meat, the stench was frightful, the meat having green streaks running through it. The only way it was made at all available for eating, was by sprinkling gunpowder over it while it was cooking, which partially took away the bad odor. We had no salt, and our systems were craving it.

"I recollect that one of the men found a small pork rind in his haversack. He chewed on it until he thought he had sucked all the goodness out of it; then he spat it out. Another man then found it, and he, too, chewed on it awhile, and then

threw it away. Later on, I discovered it kicking about in the sand, and tried my hand at it. It seemed to me that nothing ever tasted so delicious.

"ON the eighth day several of us made quite a march about the near country, looking for game. We located quite a prairie dog town, but none of them came out of their holes. I made up my mind that I would return in the morning, and try and kill one.

"Accordingly, the following forenoon, which was the ninth day of the siege, I went out to the prairie dog colony and watched for quite a bit, but none of the animals appeared, and I began to feel pretty discouraged. I had kept up fairly well to this point, as I was 28 years old and a pretty husky youngster; but I now began to think we would all starve.

"I was having the blues mighty hard as I started back for the island, empty-handed, and with a stomach that fairly seemed to touch my back, so empty it was. I had not gone far before I saw some of the men running toward me, and motioning for me to hurry. I thought the Indians were returning, and I started on a dead run for my comrades. I was too faint and exhausted, however, to run very far, and soon fell to the ground, completely all in, scarcely caring whether it was the Indians or not, so discouraged and disheartened was I.

"Happening to look up, I saw three horsemen riding toward me. They did not look like Indians, and I gazed long and earnestly at the advancing riders, soon discovering that they were white men. It proved to be Jack Donovan and the relief party. Never before or since have I been so glad to see the face of a friend, and the sudden transition from despair to safety was too much for my overtaxed nerves, and I broke down and wept like a child.

"There was great rejoicing that day, I can assure you. Donovan had to tell his experience over and over again. We moved the wounded back a half mile or so from the river, to escape the terrible stench of the dead horses. If I remember correctly, we remained there three days after Stillwell's relief party came in. He was one day behind Donovan, but of course had further to go considerably. After we had taken care of all the wounded and rested a few days, we started back for Fort Wallace.

"In due time we arrived at the post, where we were most hospitably received, and given the freedom of the fort. General Sheridan issued an order to give any of Forsyth's men any position they were qualified to fill in the Quartermaster's Department. In a few days I went to Fort Harker and secured a position as wagonmaster, hauling supplies to Camp Supply, in the Indian Territory, while Custer was operating further south.

"But in all my experience fighting redskins on the Plains, and the Apaches down in Arizona, I never went through anything that compared to the terrible fight on that little island in the Arickaree, where Death stood at our side for nine awful days."

WATERCRAFTING

Motor Boating on Swift Waters. Photo by C. S. Simonson, Vernon Co., Wis.

Timely Hints for Boat Fans

By W. A. KIMBALL

FOR those living on the coast and using either sail or motor boats—there are a few regulations which must be observed and for the first-timers owning craft on tide waters, the following hints might be timely as the boating season will soon be on in full swing.

Those people who wish to operate boats on tide water or ocean—bay, harbor or sound—or in a river which is not entirely an inland sheet of water—there is no examination, no operators license or no cost in owning and using a motor boat on such waters. There is, however, the federal tax on boats from 28 to 50 ft. in length of $10.00. Between 50 and 100 ft. there is a tax of $40.00, but for the owners of smaller craft under 28 ft. there is no tax.

A government license number is required on all power boats, but it is issued free and never has to be renewed. There is no examination demanded to get the boat number. All of the above details, of course, apply to boats used solely for pleasure purposes and not used for carrying passengers, or used for hire.

Some states require taxes on boats used within the borders of the state and if in doubt as to your state taxes on boats, write your State Board of Navigation, usually located at the State Capitol Building.

If you own a cabin cruiser, you have probably kicked about lack of head room, after bumping your head, but remember if you had plenty of head room on the boat the lines of the boat would be so

queer that they would attract smiles from other boatmen. You are naturally proud of your boat and good lines are important in the looks of your craft. For visitors it is often wise to caution them right at the start as to head room of the cabin and tell them to "duck" when they go into it. After such warnings, any bumps they may get is entirely up to them and it won't be long before they will automatically "duck" their heads.

Too high a cabin makes for drift sidewise in heavy winds and much time and distance is lost in a day's run due to drift.

Many boat fans like both sail and power boats that they combine their sail boat with motor and to me this is the ideal boat. In a good breeze there is a big kick to sailing and when the wind leaves you adrift, far from the port, the old motor is a blessing. You can usually get home on time with the powered sail boat. One does not necessarily need a high powered engine, just enough power to get the boat through the heaviest tides around the waters you sail in. Speed is not so essential as a lower powered engine and a reliable one in all weather. The marine motors with make and break ignition are particularly good for boats where the engine is exposed to weather as spray and water will not interfere with the ignition. This type of engine is very popular with sea coast fishermen who depend on their boats for a living and as a means of getting back to port in all kinds of weather.

Bass water in Little Miami River near Clifton, Ohio.

NEIL MacDOUGALL, dean of Lakehead sportsmen, was chosen honorary president of the recently organized Thunder Bay Fly and Bait Casting Club of Port Arthur, Canada. The purpose of the organization is to improve the skill of members in fine arts of angling.

Mr. MacDougall is known to a large number of the fishermen who visit the district, many of whom bring him their prize catches for mounting.

FISHERMAN'S LUCK

WANDERING back over years of varied experiences in fishing and hunting, many of the memories most happily recalled are not of my own minor triumphs but of the successes of others. This is one of the things which makes the sports of fields and waterways so thoroughly enjoyable—you can wholeheartedly rejoice in the good fortune of others, friends or strangers.

It was along Paint creek, not far from Chillicothe, Ohio, and I had a wonderful rod, magnificent reel, a very fine silk line and a beautiful lure. The outfit was purchased with loving care, each unit painstakingly selected. Don't mind confessing a deal of pride in the equipment which cost approximately $100.00.

As I stood on the bank casting without success, a small colored boy happened on the scene. His admiration for my tackle was spontaneous and outspoken.

"What's yuh aimin' to do, ketch out all the fish in Pa'nt creek? That sure am a swell-elmigant fishin' pole."

I put the rod into his hand, gave him some instructions, and told him to try his hand at casting. He was a happy youngster, so was I.

After a few minutes he "'lowed it warn't his way of fishin'," so I reeled off some line, also gave him a hook. He secured a sapling pole and went down the creek, remarking "there warn't no chanct" to get a fish within my casting range.

An hour went by without a strike when I saw the lad returning. On a string were three of the prettiest fish I ever saw. I would have felt elated to have landed them with my splendid equipment.

"Ketched out all the fish 'round here?" he asked.

I merely smiled—said nothing in my admiration of the trio of beauties in shimmering scales in which the lad showed no interest but seemingly ignored as not meriting recognition.

"Gettin' nigh suppah time—I'se goin' home."

He meandered out of view and shortly thereafter I put away my tackle and returned home—empty handed. But I had a pleasant afternoon, one that lives happily in memory just because a boy caught three fish and I could rejoice in his success.
W. H. SHEELY.

KENTUCKY PALISADES

FROM my earliest recollections, I have always wanted to view those towering cliffs along the Kentucky river, long known and referred to by writers as the "Kentucky Palisades." Many times in many places have I viewed them along their hundred mile stretch through the beautiful blue grass region of Kentucky, but it had never been my privilege to see them as one unbroken whole.

In the latter part of August, 1933, I found opportunity to gratify that longfelt desire. Leaving Pineville, Ky., one Sunday morning, my brother-in-law and I moped along in our old Chandler down to Irvine, on the Kentucky river, about one hundred and fifty miles from our starting place. We had all day to make the trip, but arrived about three in the afternoon. We spent the night with relatives, and in the morning went down to the river to launch our long-dreamed-of expedition.

Due to the very nature of the trip, our equipment was necessarily meagre. A twelve-foot Acme folding canvas boat, a one and one-half horse power outboard motor, a remodeled pup tent, Ford round ten gallon gasoline tank, waterproof floor cloth for the tent, camera, binoculars, very little bedding, go-light cooking outfit, water jug and a few groceries.

Our destination was to be Frankfort, the state capitol. The distance from Irvine to Frankfort, by river, is one hundred and fifty-nine miles. The river has been locked and dammed for all this distance, and much more, so we were assured nine feet of still water all the way down and back. It was eight o'clock before we "steamed" out from under the old railroad bridge at Irvine and ambled our way down the watery lane. The water was deep and as smooth as glass, so we got along fine. About noon, some fifteen miles down the river, we sighted a nice place for lunch, and crawled out on the bank to eat a well-prepared lunch fixed by the folks at home. After lunch I happened to feel for my pocketbook, and felt that dull, sickening thud when I missed it. I had left it in my other clothes where we spent the night. Since both of us put together didn't have more than seventy-five

cents, there was nothing to do but to go back and get it. So the long fifteen-mile trip back up the river. The pocketbook was recovered without mishap, but we lost five hours of valuable time. It was dark that night when we reached lock number eleven, and pulled in for camp. We made it a point to camp each night on government property, at one of the locks. The lock keepers were most kind and courteous, some of them donating tomatoes, cantaloupes and kindred edibles. After supper the locktenders, or "lock masters", as they are officially called, would "come out and see us" and we found them loaded with river lore and information that was indeed a welcome treat to us. Also we interested them some. Folding canvas boats were not thick in "them parts" and a carbide lamp was a source of wonder. A tremendously heavy dew (to us), made things good and wet next morning, so we were late in getting away. We soon found that on the river heavy dews were the rule rather than the exception. By noon we reached "Old Boonesboro", the site of the first important settlement in Kentucky, the scene of many Indian skirmishes, perhaps the beginning of the settlement of that "Great America" west of the Alleghenies, and above all, that spot in song and story so dear to the heart of every red-blooded American school boy. We spent about one hour there, but the place has lost its original charm. Swimming pools, bathing beach, hot dog stands, and beer gardens, would make old Dan'l Boone turn over in his grave if he could. What a pity these historic shrines can't be turned into state or national parks for the benefit of future generations. The high cliffs of limestone begin to set in about Boonesboro. We passed through the Boonesboro locks without incident, and were soon on our way. Just below Boonesboro a new state highway concrete bridge of rare beauty spans the river.

WE camped for the night at Lock No. Nine at Valley View, beneath a big elm tree, about four feet in diameter, and with a shade spread of more than one hundred feet. Almost over our heads was the abandoned bridge of a branch line of the L. and N. railroad company. Looks like it might have cost a cool half million dollars. All day long the trip was a mixture of scenic beauty and grandeur. Willows and alders with here and there a giant sycamore, made the river a silver broadway in a green field. Behind these rose the perpendicular white limestone cliffs, anywhere from two hundred and fifty to four hundred feet high, making an unforgettable spectacle. It has been my good fortune to travel over thirty-eight states and five foreign countries, and never has it been my privilege to witness such a continuous stream of unprecedented mixture of scenic awe, grandeur, and beauty. Occasionally a flock of white herons or "cranes" would appear, seemingly from nowhere, and sail down the river ahead of us for a mile or so. Now and then the shrill cry of a hawk would break the stillness, and a search with the binoculars would reveal a nest high on the crags, with a head or two sticking out of the twigs. Muskrats, squirrels, and little blue herons, or "shitepokes" were always in evidence. The watermelon and cantaloupe season was on, and the rich river valleys were full of them. We could buy five or six cantaloupes as big as footballs, for a quarter, with one or two smaller ones thrown in for good count. We lived high throughout the trip.

JUST above Camp Nelson we viewed for the first time in life a little natural wonder known as "Chimney Rock". Chimney Rock is a tower of stone, possibly seventy-five feet high, completely detached from adjacent cliff, looking not unlike a large smokestack of the cities. One marked peculiarity is that the bottom is smaller than the top. It is a silent witness to the fact that no earthquake of any marked severity has occurred in this region for perhaps one hundred thousand years. The light was all against us for a picture, so we decided to wait for the return trip. A few miles below Chimney Rock, at Camp Nelson, we stopped for gas and oil. We camped for the night at High Bridge. The camping place here was rocky, so we motored back up the river a mile or so, to a more agreeable spot. High Bridge and vicinity is one of the show spots of Kentucky. A steel railroad bridge, three hundred feet high,

we were prepared for plenty of water under us, we were not very well prepared for very much above us. We found a desirable camping place opposite the lockkeeper's home at lock number five, and soon had a fire going. We cut a lot of high weeds handy and set the tent over these, then a waterproof floor cloth, made a real bed. Supper of hot coffee and trimmings over, we turned in for the night and slept like two logs. The next morning the seventeen miles to Frankfort were soon negotiated, and after loafing for an hour or so, we were ready for the return trip. Camped that night at Lock Five, same place as the night before. The next night we camped at High Bridge again. We were off early next morning, arrived at Clay's Ferry on U. S. Highway No. 25 about ten a. m. Left my buddy in charge of the stuff, caught a bus for Irvine for the truck. At three p. m. we were all loaded and headed for Pineville, and rolled in there safe, sound, dirty, and tired at eight o'clock that night.

The total cost of the entire water trip, not including the things we took from home, was $4.80, most of which went for gas and cantaloupes. We were gone nine days.

For a pleasant, instructive, cheap, healthy, and above all else entertaining

It took "Old Man River" two hundred thousand years to carve these cliffs.

towering perpendicular cliffs, Boone's Cave, Government lock and dam, power plant, Dix Dam, thirty-five mile long Herrington Lake, Harrodsburg, (oldest town in Kentucky), Shakertown, and many other things, make it a tourists' paradise, for a time, at least.

A FEW miles below High Bridge is Brooklyn. Here a covered wooden highway bridge, built in 1838, spans the river. This bridge has been condemned, however, and a new steel concrete structure stands just below it. Just below Brooklyn is a "Double Chimney Rock". That is, two chimneys together. It is larger in size but probably not so tall as the one up the river.

That afternoon it began to rain. While

vacation, I know of nothing that will compare with a canoe or light outboard motor trip through the "Kentucky Palisades."
DR. J. H. HENDREN,
Pineville, Ky.

WRITE! WRITE!!

EVERY Trapper reading H-T-T write at once, telling all you actually know about biological survey POISON and how said POISONERS are destroying our fur and feathered wild life. Address your letters to Thomas H. Beck, Dept. of Agriculture, Washington, D. C., who is Chairman of President Roosevelt's Wild Life Restoration Committee.

Write now, boys, before it's everlastingly too late. DUNC STORMS.

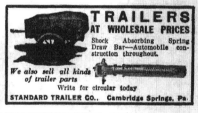

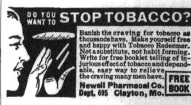

Picking Your Hunting Grounds

By C. S. LANDIS

Guns and Ammunition Editor

THERE is no time like this summer to take your rifle and pack and scout out the place you will hunt this fall, and trap in late fall, winter and next Spring.

This is even more important than your firearms—and we will discuss both of them together.

Never wait until the last minute to obtain up-to-date information on the game and fur supply in your favorite hunting ground. Knowing this, you will know in advance exactly which arms to take along — .22 rifle, .30-30, 12 gauge shotgun for ducks, 16 or 20 for bird shooting, and about how much of each type of ammunition you may require. These early summer hikes and varmint hunts are exactly the news service on such matters that you will need to supply.

There may be little feed in your game district by fall. Nuts may be scarce. Weed seeds dry and fallen—and scarce even before falling. Grouse may have had a touch of grouse sickness. Rabbits may be in one of their lean years. Squirrels may have migrated. Ducks and geese may find no food or water—and pass on. Try to get a line on things as the season advances. Look for fur sign, and look for game sign. Look for future prospects —and oil up the proper guns when the time comes.

The excessively hard winter just passed; too much or too little rain during spring and summer of 1934; a change in variety

and in location of the farm crops in your district, or severe woods or grass fires, especially in choppings which were your favorite rabbit, grouse, deer or trapping locations, all will have a bearing. A change in farming may have made a very material difference in the local stopping-over of ducks and geese if there is not much fall wheat or corn locally for them

to feed on. Or marsh plants, wild celery, and tubers. On the other hand, there may be a super-abundance of several of these, and certainly that will determine your location.

State Game Commission figures and propaganda may mean little or nothing locally. What you will need to know accurately is the probable conditions of feed, cover and water, and game supply within the 5, 10 or 20 miles area you will cover, and particularly within the 3 to 5 mile area you will expect to hunt or trap most extensively.

Fields that were planted in buckwheat, wheat or corn last year and were full of small game, and fur, may be as bare as a

barn floor this year. Maybe the farmers owning or controlling your favorite shooting and trapping grounds got together since last time you were out and agreed to sell the shooting and trapping rights, or either, and trespass notices that mean no hunting and trapping to you may be posted all over the neighborhood. This may mean that you will arrive with no place to hunt and trap and with an outfit that must be radically changed when you drive on into another district. The time to discover these very important matters is before you drive or ride the 200 or 500 miles, or maybe only the ten miles to your favorite location.

Then there is the matter of your hunting or trapping companion — or friends. If you like to shoot birds, and the other two fellows are confirmed rabbit hunters, that won't work. You will always want to follow every cover that looks "birdy" and every covey that rises. They will insist on trotting along after the beagles or the hounds—and beagles or hounds is simply another word for a nuisance to you.

You will get sore because the birds are flushed wild, and they will become angered because you walk in on the dogs.

Most marriages that go on the rocks do so because the two persons concerned find in time that they have not a single thought or recreation in common. They never want to do the same things the same way and never both want to do the same thing at the same time. It is that way in

Woodchucks are the standard "summer game" for thousands of riflemen. A pair killed by the Gun and Ammunition Editor.

the hunting field and in the trappers camp or cabin. A bird hunter, a duck hunter, a rabbit hunter and a deer hunter would make a quartet that no possible line of logic could solve. A muskrat trapper and a fox trapper would not be likely to get along, and a rifle nut and a shotgun fan would soon tire each other with constant ranting on different subjects of no particular interest to the other.

This matter of opinions on guns has split many a hunting camp and trappers setup. If one chap is a lever action fan and the other a bolt action enthusiast, and both are loud and talkative, each on his own favorite topic, look for heavy squalls long before the first blizzard is over. Each man will be ready to murder the other—simply to shut him up. Any old trapper will confirm this.

The auto or pump gun enthusiast may be gall and wormwood to the chap who insists on using nothing but a 20 gauge or .410 caliber double barrel, and who simply cannot see a speck of decency in his companion after three months of having pump gun and auto loading slaughter, efficiency and effectiveness crammed into his ears. He may go out in the open air and tear his hair and say to himself, "Why, oh why, didn't I pick a partner who wants to do what I want to do and who thinks as I think. Damn that windy nuisance in the tent!"

WHEN your crowd wants to hunt as you hunt, when they hunt like you do, and when they prefer to go where you prefer to go, camp where you select camp, and work and loaf as you work and loaf, keep clean and neat, or dirty and unattractive, as you keep yourself and your belongings —you should get along. Religion, politics, financial condition or age, notwithstanding.

A high strung, nervous, fast walking bird hunter will be ready to murder a slow, pattering, fat, good natured, lazy old squirrel hunter who just loves to loaf along and look at the tops of the hickories and now and then bring down a gray squirrel. A wiry, quiet moving, fast thinking, mountain-bred deer hunter will be bored to death with a slow, noisy, out-of-breath, middle aged, city-bred friend who simply cannot keep up with him and who insists upon "hallooing" so that he can be heard two miles off, every time his friend gets ahead of him and out of his sight in strange woodland. And especially in a chopping, and vice versa.

Opposites simply do not get along in the shooting game. They do not get along in camp. They do not get along on a deer drive simply because they find it impossible to understand or put up with each other's failings. They will find fault with each other and fight, in a rifle club. The man who finishes his score first will often greatly annoy the man who is still shooting and the man who has fired his 10 or 20 shots simply cannot understand why the other chap insists upon taking his time. Each—as you will notice, has adopted the style which suits his nervous and physical makeup, but such style does not suit his shooting companion.

Therefore, find the chap who likes to hunt those things and in the manner that you hunt. Find the man who walks with the same speed afield as you use, who is

as slow as you are, or as fidgety as you may be. If you both like to talk and can talk on congenial subjects—talk. If you are both quiet as two clams, sit and think and let him sit and think and don't bother each other.

Before a week is out each of you will agree that you have the best shooting or trapping partner the world ever produced and the wisest man on earth. Whatever he does he is right in doing, because that is the way you would do it.

There are seldom any serious arguments on such a team. He wants to hunt the hollows when you want to hunt the hollows. He strikes out across the high country when you think you ought to do so. He never runs off from you and does not lag behind until you lose him. If he cleans his gun, you clean your gun. If he doesn't, it never annoys you. The perfect man! He's your shooting pal and your trapping companion.

If he wants to trap the back pastures and old barns and outbuildings and rock piles for skunks, so do you. If he moves up to timber line or above, after marten, that's just where you will want to go—to trap marten. When you're right, you're both right. If you're wrong, you're both wrong. You climb the hill of adversity together and when you fall into a bit of coin, there is his share of the coin, which you didn't have to earn.

Finding and dating up such a man is four-fifths of any hunting or camping or trapping trip. Getting guns and ammunition for such a trip is easy—simply double what either of you may wish.

So you say, do you, you never saw such a man. Look in a mirror, brother, look in a mirror—there he is, and that is why hunting alone is so often so much more fun and so much more successful when you simply cannot find the perfect partner.

———o———

NEW GOODS

THE well known Winchester Model 60 single shot bolt action .22 rifle has been superseded by the Model 67—placed on the market quite recently.

This is a bid for the $5.00 trade—and a bid such as Winchester has not made in my memory. The new rifle has a 27" barrel—remember that, a 27" barrel, round, tapered, and fitted with German silver bead front sight and open rear sight with notched elevator. The rifle retails for $5.95 complete, tax included.

The rifle has an entirely new bolt action, a very short action by the way, it has a very good full pistol grip stock, with 13¼" length of pull, the pistol grip is only 3½" from trigger to end of grip, drops at comb and heel are sensibly designed, and the rifle has chromium plated bolt, bolt handle, and safety. The safety looks rather cheap as compared to the rest of the rifle and is merely a collar and fin which is raised from right to vertical position when the rifle is cocked by hand (it is not a self-cocker) and is snapped off easily to the right when the owner wishes to fire. However, the striker must be pulled clear back, an extra amount, to get the safety to engage fully and it is entirely possible for the inexperienced shot

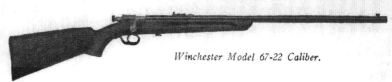

Winchester Model 67-22 Caliber.

to think he has the safety on with this
rifle and not have it on sufficiently far to
prevent firing the rifle.

Certainly this is a lot of rifle for $5.95
—but the safety should be redesigned so
that a person cannot mistake whether it
is on or only partly on—if the fin is truly
vertical or a bit past vertical to the left,
the safety is on, but there should be no
guesswork about it. The trigger pull on
the rifle of this model sent me, is exceptionally smooth and light and if others
sent out are half as good that will be a
point in favor of the Model 67.

This 27" barrel does not make this rifle
materially longer than its principal com-
petitor, for that rifle has a very long action and receiver with a 24" barrel, while
the Model 67 has a short action and a 3"
longer barrel. The over-all length of the
67 is about 42¼" which is just fine because
I never did cotton to these short barreled
.22 single shots for boys and trappers wishing a light rifle of not too great expense.

The 67 is better finished than some
rifles costing twice as much money, which
is a break for the buyer. You can do a
lot worse than the 67 for an inexpensive
rifle for the trap line, next fall.

New Stock for the 52 Winchester

THERE wasn't a great deal they could
do to improve the shooting qualities of
the Model 52 Winchester .22 long rifle caliber target rifle nor to improve the lock
time since the new Winchester speed lock
was produced so they have designed a new
stock which will be supplied on special
order.

I have one of the first of the new rifles.
It was claimed to be a heavy barrel rifle
but when it arrived it had the standard
weight barrel which is an inch at the
breech, approximately 11/16" at the muzzle and 28 inches long and neither Brother
Hutt nor Brother Pugsley can kid me into
thinking that is a heavy barrel 52.

As the new stock contains almost identical dimensions, from the trigger to butt,
to my own hand made 52 stock, naturally
I like the new one real well—but it took
years of argument to get them around to
those figures. The new stock has a length
of pull of 13¼" to 13⅜"—same as mine,
the length of trigger reach—trigger to grip
cap is the same, 3½", drop is possibly just
a trifle straighter, especially at the butt—
this new stock having only about ½"
drop at the butt, from the line of the bore.
The butt plate is large, being 1¾" wide in
the center, 5¼" long, heel to toe, same as
the plate on my rifle, and is curved just a
trifle in the middle. Why? No one knows
unless it is to fit the "figger" of the average Yankee who is long, slim and bony.
The rifle fits very close on the shoulder,
the drop is a trifle too straight for comfortable offhand shooting, especially with
iron sights, some will have a bit of dif-
ficulty to see through the sights clearly,
offhand, but this is a stock for prone shooting and prone, you need a very straight

stock and then some. It will suit the lanky
shooter fine and the stouter one quite
well, but he may demand hacking off the
toe of the butt just a trifle more.

The fore-end of the new stock is a good
beaver tail design—and the butt plate is
"beaver tail" so now we have a 52 which
is beaver-tail fore and aft. In fact the
first factory rifle with a beaver tail "fanny"
to come on the market.

You will recall that a few years ago
every rifle crank was demanding a rifle
with a minimum chamber. Then the next
craze was for boat-tail bullets. Next
came the beaver-tail fore-end and now we
have the rifle with the beaver tail fanny.

The general idea is that the heavy barrel 52's were becoming much more common and the stock made for the original
weight 52 was a trifle too light for a
rifle so heavy at the bow. So they designed this new stock specially to bed the
heavier barrel and to balance better at the
butt—made the new stock heavier all over
at the butt end—thicker through, heavier
wood, wider and longer butt and more
wood left in the musket butt. That tends
to make a heavy barrel rifle with at least
a trace of balance, which is a good idea
because a heavy barrel match rifle with a
puny stock on it has the balance of a
freight engine and is not much handsomer.

So, now if you see some chap going
down the line at a shoot with a 52 which
has a real elevation something like Aunt
Samantha you know it is the new model
with the beaver tail butt, speed lock, beaver
tail fore-end, probably heavy barrel and
special sights—and if the fellow carrying
it can't hit anything with it—it's his own
fault because manufacturing an alibi which
will hold water, when using one of the
latest 52's is a pretty tough job. Everyone knows they shoot.

It is beginning to soak through, also,
at New Haven, that the regular 52 rear
sight is not all it might be, so they are now
supplying on special order, standard barrel
rifles with five different iron sight combinations, including the Lyman No. 17A
and 48J which is listed as combination No.
5, and the heavy barrel rifle with two different sight combinations, including the
Lyman 17G and 48J which is the better.

If you need a 52, order one of the new
ones, and count yourself lucky that you
didn't order too soon.

———o———

FRITZ AND JOSEPHINE CALL

AT some time, or other, every rifle
shooter in the Eastern section of the
country who attends small bore tournaments has laughed at Charley Johnson's
"eel hound"—an English setter that
jumped into the inlet down at Sea Girt and
retrieved an eel pot containing three eels,
each 36" long. This dog was the pet of
the shoot and always had a great time.

Eventually good feeding and too much
petting spelled her finish and then Johnson,

who is internationally known as a match shooter, decided to raise a pair of pointers that would be very much "one man" dogs.

So, he taught them their commands in the Swedish language and the pups are unable to understand any English. Even Mrs. Johnson cannot make those dogs come in or go out of the house.

Very recently the two "Swedish eel Hounds" and Charley Johnson called in state on the Arms and Ammunition Editor of the HUNTER-TRADER-TRAPPER bearing a

whole arm full of silver plate they had just won at the Tri-State Yacht Club Bench Show in Maryland. Fritz took 3rd in the Dog Prizes and Josephine won the First Place for bitches.

You haven't heard the last of Fritz and Josephine. A pair of pointers as good as that and who cannot understand a word of anything but Swedish—will be heard from —especially in the shooting game. The prospect for amused comment is almost unlimited.

Guns and Ammunition Questions
By C. S. LANDIS

A .22 SEDGLEY- COLT REVOLVER
Editor Guns & Ammunition Dept.
Dear Sir:

For years I have desired to own a .22 caliber revolver weighing around 20 ounces, with medium barrel length and fixed sights. I would carry this while trapping and along on game hunting trips.

I have written various gunsmiths and the leading manufacturers giving them my ideas. The gunsmiths did not seem to care about tackling the job and the companies absolutely refused to deviate from their standards.

The Colt Woodsman was tried and although this is a fine arm in 4½" length, failed to suit me. The target revolvers in .32/.38 and Colt Police Positive, fitted with 6" barrel and target sights, are fine but not exactly what I wanted.

It seemed absolutely impossible to obtain the kind of gun I wished. The Bankers Special has a 2" barrel, rather large grips and is on a regular .38 frame. It is badly proportioned but O. K. as a companion to the .38 Bankers Special and .38 Special, using cheap ammunition.

In a recent trade I took in a light frame .32 Police Positive 4" with rubber grips and in perfect condition. For a while I reloaded and packed this gun about and it was not bad at all. However, I got an idea that this gun in .22 caliber was just what I wanted. But it must be a factory job. I had already written to the factory a long time before and was advised that no fixed sighted gun in .22 caliber was to be had and that their regular target model was superior. That of course is true if you can see the thing that way.

I wrote R. F. Sedgley, Inc., of 2311 N. 16th St., Philadelphia, Pa., and noted from their folder that they rebuilt New Service and Single Action Colt revolvers for .22 long rifle and .22 Hornet cartridges. I then wrote them about my problem of changing the .32 Police Positive 4" revolver into a .22 long rifle. Mr. Sedgley promptly advised me that they were in a position to do this work at a very reasonable cost. I sent the .32 in to them and after a time received the new .22 caliber Police Positive revolver. The last word in a small bore pocket arm.

A .22 long rifle cylinder was fitted and a .22 caliber Police Positive barrel was cut down to 4½", a fixed sight was incorporated, 1/16" wide, as on the P. P. fixed sighted models. The rear notch on the frame was made square to correspond with the front giving a fancy Patridge sighting effect. The barrel and cylinder are fitted to very close adjustment and all chambers align perfectly with the barrel. There is no play in the locking of the cylinder or forward. The firing pin hole in the frame was welded shut and a new one milled higher in the frame to take care of the rim fire ammunition. The firing pin was remodeled on hammer and was left movable and round on the end as in center fire arms. The trigger was checked very deep and sharp as was the back strap and trigger pull honed down to a very fine pull just below 3 pounds.

The entire gun was refinished and to say the least it equals any factory job I have ever seen. I tried this arm under practical conditions and can do as well as I can with any .22 caliber I have used up to date. It is much more handy to carry, is balanced as well as any, and shoots better than I can hold. I tried Peters .22 long rifle Filmkote, Western Super-X, U. S. Speedsters, the latter both dry bullets, Remington Kleanbore lubricated, Winchester Super-Speed Kopperklad and Remington HiSpeed lubricated. The Remington HiSpeed lubricated shoots by far the best in this arm. This gun does not have a recessed cylinder head but I have fired 500 rounds of various high speed ammunition (long rifle only) in it and there have been no ruptured cases or even indication of excessive pressure.

I was greatly surprised with the work of the arm and with the excellence of the workmanship. It is far better than I ever expected was possible. I have several other .22 caliber revolvers and pistols but you will find this one in the pocket holster most of the time afield.

Most shooters like target sights and 6" barrel, but for my purpose this gun is supreme. I expect to have additional work done by Sedgley and when I do, have no doubt as to their following my specifications.

Gordon C. Boser,
Springville, N. Y.

REPLY

A. The Guns & Ammunition Dept. Editor is well acquainted with R. F. Sedgley, and with the high quality of his workmanship— owning two of his rifles and having been in his shop numerous times. I have shot the .22 Hornet revolver Mr. Boser speaks of, and in two models, and except for the excessively sharp report indoors, it has features to commend it. Would prefer, however, other calibers in hand guns.

As to whether the average revolver user would prefer fixed or movable target sights, will depend on a number of things, one being whether the gun with fixed sights happens to shoot to center with the ammunition the gun owner prefers to use. A fixed sight arm is preferable for holster use, but not for target work or the use of various types and makes of ammunition.

Editor G. & A. Dept.

A DEER RIFLE FOR A 14-YEAR-OLD BOY
Editor, Guns & Ammunition Dept.
Dear Sir:

I have been hunting in Pennsylvania for fourteen years and this year I want to take my boy who will be fourteen next birthday. We will go for deer and bear. He is good with a gun of 22 caliber which is too small for such game.

I want to buy him a new rifle for this purpose and would want something light, yet heavy enough for deer and bear. Any advice you can offer will be of much value.

I've been using a .35 Remington, but I think this arm too heavy for him and I also would prefer a bolt action. Here are a few of the arms that I have in mind: How is the .25 high power and the 250-3,000, both in the bolt?

Andrew Pechio,
Youngstown, Ohio.

REPLY

A. A boy 14 years old (better be certain it will be legal for him to hunt in Penna. at that age) could not be expected to handle a heavy weight rifle in the hard-to-climb Pennsylvania mountain country. Especially is this so in those districts in which all the mountains run in parallel ranges and the bucks hang out mostly on the upper rock ledges and ridges. On the sugar-loaf hills and the mountain-top plateaus the climbing is not so strenuous. Also, remember that he would not be allowed by law to use an auto-loading or self-loading rifle of any caliber in that state.

As you know, his chance of getting a deer is fair, about 1 in 20, but his chance of a bear is probably not over one in 7,000, so that the bear part of it need not be considered heavily.

Assume that at 14 he will find the recoil of a .30-30 or .32 Special excessive, especially if a medium sized city boy. Therefore, I would suggest rifles like the slide action Remington Model 14A in .25 rimless caliber, or the .25-35 Winchester Model 64 lever action, the Model 94 .25-35 carbine or the .250-3,000 Savage lever action Model 99-R with 22" barrel. Outside of the carbine, these are all a trifle on the heavy side for such a lad, therefore he might actually

(Continued on page 49)

SKEET and TRAP SHOOTING

SHOOT ALL YOU CAN

LET every one attend as many skeet and traps shoots this summer as possible, and take as much part in them as your circumstances will allow. This fine sport will not only coordinate your mind and muscles, but it will lead your thoughts out and away from yourself and bring to you an ease of mind (if you have worries, and who hasn't?) that you had not believed possible.

With the whole world steeped in trouble as a direct or indirect result of the depression, thousands of persons are nearing the "cracking point" by allowing their thoughts to become too self-centered. But the pleasant associations of the skeet field and the trap field, unlocks the shackles that hold us in the prison of unrest, the fetters fall from our thoughts, and impressed by the disinterested earnestness of the competitors, the mind soars to new heights of freedom as it slips from its burden of troubles and cares.

Don't go to the skeet field or the trap field to find pessimists. They are somewhere offering one another little consolation by declaring that all the world is wrong, but they have no place with the crowd of happy optimists found at the traps.

Skeet and trap shooters are a cheerful lot. Their smiles are infectious; their ways are attractive; their manners are sincere. Associate with them a few hours and your blues, if you have any, will be forgotten. You will become so absorbed with the work at hand, that you will forget all about the good job you once had, the bills that cannot be paid, the things you want but cannot buy—for a time the world and all therein, is yours.

Take the family with you. The wife and children will enjoy getting away from the daily grind as much as you. No matter if Johnny does yell loudly because he cannot have all the ice cream he wants; and what if little Mary shrieks because a sweat bee stings her dimpled arm? You will feel a lot better as you ride or walk homeward, because the family was with you.

WILLIS O. C. ELLIS.

———o———

THE MT. WASHINGTON SKEET CLUB

WHEN you want to think of a really live and wide awake skeet club, it isn't necessary to let your mind wander to the East or West coast, and vision some of the fine clubs found at those places in action. All you have to do is to think of the Mt. Washington, Ohio, Skeet Club.

This club is located at Cherry Grove, Ohio, on Route 125, about fifteen miles from Cincinnati. It has a number of live, active members and it is one of the best skeet clubs to be found anywhere. Its targets are "in the air" every Sunday morning.

Mr. Martin A. Lang, 2719 Woodburn avenue, Cincinnati, Ohio, is the Executive Vice President, and the genial head of the association. He, himself, is an expert

Martin A. Lang, Vice President of The Mt. Washington Skeet Club.

skeet shooter. On April 8th he led the field with a score of 49 out of 50.

The 22nd of April this club sponsored one of the biggest and best merchandise shoots ever held in Ohio.

The merchants of Cincinnati donated three dozen prizes, ranging in value from a fine fishing reel to a can of automobile polish. Between these two extremes the prizes were many and various, and included meat, spark plugs, whiskey and gin.

This big event drew many shooters from the southern and southwestern counties of the state. Although the weather conditions were far from ideal, and the high, tricky wind blew many targets out of their true courses, some really fine shooting was done.

The high guns were S. Knab who broke 49 out of 50, and R. Bressler who smashed 48.

Below are the names and the scores of the winners in the 50 target event:

S. S. Knab	49
R. Bressler	48
Walter Muderback	45
B. Vollmer	44
E. V. D. Smith	44
Robt. Charge	43
Roy Linsey	43
J. Geiger	42
C. Meyers	42
Walter Green	41
John White	41
A. Leif	40
John Wallace	40
W. Wherry	39
Frank Height	39
Dr. R. R. Hill	35
Dr. J. W. Kirgan	33
Raymond Abbott	33
Ray Wallace	31
R. Burton	31
Wilbur Sauer	30
Ed Elston	29
Ray Davis	29
C. G. Wehr	28
H. Shaw	28
I. Tainer	22
Frank Ellis	28
Russel Scott	28

The tie scores were shot off the last Sunday in April, but we were not given the results.

This club has developed a new game called "grouse shooting." Better visit the club and try it. 'Tis said to be great sport.

———o———

SEA GIRT IN THE MOUNTAINS

LATE word is that the Sea Girt Small Bore Shoot—known officially as the Eastern Small Bore Tournament, will be held this year at the Maryland State Rifle Range at Cascade, Md. instead of at Sea Girt, N. J., as heretofore.

The Maryland N. G. Range is at an elevation of approximately 1450 feet, and is about one-half mile from Blue Ridge Summit, Pa., a station on the Western Maryland Railroad.

This range is about 40 miles southwest of Harrisburg, Pa., about 70 miles from Baltimore and about 90 miles or so, from Washington, D. C. It is easily and conveniently reached by direct motor trail from almost any point in Pennsylvania, New York, New England, New Jersey, Ohio, Indiana, and other nearby states, but it is not easily reached by railroad from the North or East as the Western Maryland cuts so little ice as a passenger railroad in Pennsylvania that most people don't even know where it is located.

It is claimed that the Maryland N. G. Camp Grounds contains a very good club house, ample huts to house all the competitiors, a bathing lake,—right at the club house, ample targets at 50, 100 and 200 yards, and that a fine shoot is practically assured. This for the information of those readers of Hunter-Trader-Trapper who may wish to attend.

The Gun Editor is one of those who very greatly regrets to see the passing of the Sea Girt shoots. There were sentiments connected with the Sea Girt tournaments not present at any other shoot in this country. However, for the present, they are gone and now small bore rifle and pistol shots of the East and Central West will have opportunity to see how they like a tournament held in mountain country. The dates are June 30 to July 4, inclusive.

——o——

WE STAND CORRECTED

WE are in receipt of a nice letter from the Reverend O. E. Braune, Newark, N. J., calling attention to an error that crept into our columns some time ago.

This minister is an ardent skeet shooter. He loves the sport. All the time he is trying to beat his own best records. One of his most difficult shots is the outgoes from Station 6. He followed the general advice of holding above and ahead, on this target. But he simply could not connect. He was so discouraged that he despaired of ever making a perfect score. Then right at the last, when he had all but given up, he interviewed such famous "skeeters" as Treager, Dr. Scranton, Garland and Thummel, who told him to hold "under and ahead" on the outgoer from Station 6. That did the trick.

Reverend Braune desires to pass this information along to others with the hope that it will help some boost their scores.

This minister also declares that since he has taken up skeet, his shooting on quail and jack-snipe had improved thirty per cent—just another well authenticated testimony that skeet shooting does boost one's field scores.

——o——

WINS GOVERNOR'S CUP

THE Governor's Cup which has been the object of annual competition for many years among trapshooters, was this year awarded for the first time for skeet.

This highly prized trophy was won by a Mr. Shepard of the Sleepy Hollow Gun Club, Scarborough, New York, with a score of 96 out of 100.

——o——

SOUTHERN CALIFORNIA SKEET ASSOCIATION

THE seventh match of the Association, April 29, found a grand camp meeting framed for the Waltonian Field including the regular shoot of the Hat-Whangers Club of Al Lucas.

Waltonian One shot its regular match with San Diego; and by special arrangement, San Diego also shot its match against Waltonian Two the same day. Santa Barbara, behind on its match against the San Diego from the 15th, came down to shoot up this back match, using the San Diego score against the Waltonian Champs against the scores made on the field by the Channel Town boys. Long Beach, also scheduled to shoot up a back-match with Santa Barbara and its regular

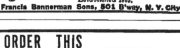

match with Waltonian Two, failed to appear and lost the two matches by default.

Los Angeles Skeet was unable to get a team, due to members being out of town, and postponed its shoot with Santa Ana until the 6th of May.

Over at Annandale on Saturday afternoon the Scottylites and the Golfers engaged in their scheduled fracas, LASM winning 347 to 345 and largely due to the hot shooting of Mr. Stockberger.

AT ANNANDALE VS. LOS ANGELES—SANTA MONICA

J. Maltman	24	25	24	73
Mrs. S. R. Small	24	23	25	72
R. Wilfong	21	25	25	71
R. Vosburg	21	23	23	66
A. J. Storer	20	20	23	63
				345
D. T. Stockberger	24	25	24	73
Don Morrison	23	22	25	70
K. T. Fay	25	23	21	69
A. L. Bloomfield	24	22	22	68
R. C. Scott	23	22	22	67
				347

SANTA BARBARA VS. SAN DIEGO

Santa Barbara	Events			Total
Higbee	22	24	20	66
Smith	24	21	24	69
Wilson	24	23	23	70
Brooks	23	22	23	68
Nelson	24	22	21	67
	117	112	111	340

San Diego				
Beckwith	24	24	20	68
Lutz	22	23	20	65
Miller	20	20	20	60
Perkins	22	23	19	64
Myrick	22	24	25	71
	110	114	104	328

WALTONIAN No. 1 VS. SAN DIEGO

Waltonian No. 1				
Lucas	23	25	25	73
Slater	24	24	24	72
Morgan	21	23	24	68
Bellende	24	20	22	66
Frew	24	24	25	73
	116	116	120	352

San Diego				
Beckwith	24	24	20	68
Lutz	22	23	20	65
Miller	20	20	20	60
Perkins	22	23	19	64
Myrick	22	24	25	71
	110	114	104	328

SAN DIEGO VS. WALTONIAN No. 2

San Diego				
Beckwith	23	21	21	65
Lutz	21	19	20	60
Perkins	23	24	23	70
Miller	20	24	22	68
Myrick	23	21	25	69
	110	109	111	330

Waltonian No. 2				
Delmar	22	24	24	70
Copley	20	19	21	60
Perk	20	23	22	65
Smock	24	20	22	66
Basso	23	22	19	64
	109	108	108	325

WALTONIAN No. 2 VS. LONG BEACH

Waltonian No. 2				
Delmar	25	24	23	72
Copley	21	23	24	68
Perk	21	22	23	66
Smock	20	22	23	65
Basso	23	22	24	69
	110	113	117	340

Long Beach lost by default.

REMINGTON BIDS YOU WELCOME

THE Remington Arms Company recently opened a display room in the Empire State Building at 34th street and Fifth Avenue, New York. It is very finely fitted up with easy chairs, lounge, tables

containing many of the better known magazines of the day, including the Hunter-Trader-Trapper.

Around the walls are show cases containing plain and fancy grades of all the Remington shotguns, and rifles, and boxes illustrating most of the different types of Remington Kleanbore metallic ammunition and Kleanbore shotgun shells.

A special invitation is extended by the Remington Arms Company to all readers of the Hunter-Trader-Trapper to visit the showrooms while in New York City. The editor of the Gun and Ammunition Department was one of the early visitors to this display and wishes to advise that it is well worth seeing.

—o—

IT was announced recently, that the Remington Arms Company, Inc., had also acquired the business and assets of Parker Bros., of Meriden, Conn., well known makers of the famous Parker double gun and the Parker single barrel trap gun.

Parker guns have been on the market since 1868 and have always been celebrated for fine finish and good shooting qualities.

These most recent additions make one of the most complete tieups in the arms and ammunition field—duPont, Remington, Chamberlin, Peters, Parker powder, repeating sporting rifles, repeating and self-loading and O. & U. double shotguns, clay targets and target traps, Peters and Remington ammunition, and Parker double guns. All quality merchandise and all sold through a nation-wide hook-up of salesmen, jobbers and retail dealers.

Readers of Hunter-Trader-Trapper will want to know of these latest developments in the manufacture and sale of arms and ammunition. They can look for them monthly and right up to date, through these columns.

—o—

IT will be of interest to many shooters to learn that the Peters Cartridge Company, Kings Mills, Ohio, whose fine shot shells and small arms ammunition are so well known everywhere, has been acquired by the Remington Arms Company, Bridgeport, Conn.

It is understood that the Peters Company will continue to manufacture high-grade ammunition as heretofore, the only change being that the company will be controlled by Remington.

May the new deal prove pleasing and profitable to all concerned!

—o—

REGISTERED SHOOTS TO BE HELD IN JULY

SKEET

BABYLON Skeet Club, Inc., Babylon, L. I., N. Y. July 4.

Waltham Gun Club, Waltham, Mass. July 4.

Connecticut State Individual Championship, Remington Gun Club, Lordship (Stratford), Conn. July 8.

Connecticut .410 Bore Championship,

Hartford Gun Club, Hartford, Conn. July 22.

Wichita Gun Club, Wichita, Kan. July 29.

TRAP

N. C. R. Gun Club, Dayton, Ohio. July 4.

Rockwell City Gun Club, Rockwell City, Iowa, July 8.

Izaak Walton League Gun Club, Omaha, Nebr. July 15.

Inland Empire Gun Club, Spokane, Wash. July 22.

Long Beach Gun Club, Long Beach, Cal. July 22.

Quaker City Gun Club, Philadelphia. July 28.

Meaco Gun Club, Chillicothe, Ohio. July 29.

TRAP STATE SHOOTS

Wyoming, at Laramie, July 7-9.

Indiana, at Winchester, July 17-19.

Michigan, at Mt. Clemens, July 20-21-22.

Iowa, at Cedar Falls, July 23-25.

—o—

PAUL NORTH DIES

IN the recent passing of Paul North, well-known Ohio sportsman, trapshooting lost one of the pioneers in the development of the sport.

In the '90s he brought out the first successful automatic target-throwing device, known as the "Magautrap". Later came his Leggett traps, then the "Ideal Leggett", followed by the "Miracle", "Wonder", "Blue Rock" and "Expert" traps for trapshooting and the "Wonder" and "Blue Rock" singlever skeet outfits.

Last year Mr. North disposed of his business, the Chamberlin Cartridge and Target Co., to Remington Arms Co., Inc. The firm is now known as the Chamberlin Trap and Target Works, with the plant at Findlay, Ohio.

—o—

OAKWOOD GUN CLUB

Of North Canton held an all day skeet and trap shoot Decoration Day, a registered trap shoot with 16 entrants was held in the afternoon. P. Radabaugh and Joe Seaborn won the prizes in the 50 handicap event, each breaking 44 targets.

100 REGISTERED TARGETS

50-16 Yd. Targets		50 Handicap Targets		
Guy C. Hiner	48	P. Radabaugh	18	44
Alvin Sims	48	J. Seaborn	21	44
A. F. Kraft	48	J. Sargent	22	43
Joe Seaborn	47	L. T. Bair	18	42
R. C. Brower	46	A. F. Kraft	24	41
J. A. Sargent	46	Wm. Morgan	17	40
W. R. Lentz	45	Guy Hiner	23	40
W. H. Patterson	43	Alvin Sims	24	39
L. W. Becher	43	L. W. Becher	22	38
F. C. Becker	42	R. F. Horn	18	38
P. Radabaugh	42	F. C. Becker	20	38
Wm. J. Morgan	41	W. R. Lentz	22	37
L. T. Bair	39	R. C. Brower	17	35
R. F. Horn	38	W. Patterson	20	35
Wm. Umstattd	33	Wm. Umstattd	16	31
Professional—		50 Skeet—Cont.		
O. L. Bassler	45	Geo. Wade		33
100 Skeet Targets		Mc. Farren		33
R. F. Horn	87	Weisong		28
Harold Noaker	72	Bob Brower		25
75 Skeet Targets		Carl Godsmith		19
W. R. Lentz	64	25 Skeet Targets		
Mr. Zettler	62	O. L. Bassler		25
Dr. Toot	49	R. C. Brower		23
Earl Walters	49	Joe Seaborn		18
50 Skeet Targets		Mr. Farmer		17
A. F. Kraft	47	Winkleman		15
Guy Hiner	44	F. C. Becker		13
Mr. Riley	37	Glen Rorabeck		12

Coon Hunting

SAVE THE DEN TREES

ON the 24th of April the Ohio Division of Conservation had a meeting for all sportsmen of this county and adjoining counties and gave a few talks and showed a few motion pictures.

As I see the situation they are not doing as much for the coon hunter as they are for the fisherman and the bird hunter. They said that some coon hunters are banding together and buying the dens from the farmers. Of course I know they are raising a lot of coon and turning them loose, but this is not the best way to help the coon hunter. Every year there are a lot of den trees cut down.

The proper way for the state to help the coon hunter is to buy or lease the dens from the farmer and after this is done and paid for, then raise the coon and let them go in the dens owned by the state. Most den trees are not good for much more than fire wood. I think this the best step the state could take in helping the coon hunter.

I think the expense would be far less than the money they are spending for the fishermen.

The state has a good game warden for this county and I have not heard a word against him. Every coon hunter ought to send a postcard in to the Ohio Division of Conservation and tell them what he thinks of the idea. The game warden of every county knows who the coon hunters are and, if the state wanted to know where the dens are, he could get the coon hunters to go with the state men to the farmer to buy the dens.

I also want to say that I am a reader of that good magazine, the H-T-T, and I think every sportsman should take it.

BILL CONNELLY,
Fulton County, Ohio.

---o---

A REAL COONER

I HAVE read with pleasure many coon hunting experiences, also the opinions of many as to the best strain of hounds for coon. After 55 years of experience, I am convinced there is individual merit in any strain.

In Williams County, Ohio, we have a scarcity of timber but numerous tile drains and the coon den in them more than in timbers so in order to tree you must have dogs that are fast on trail and to have any pleasure they must be open on trail, with good hound voices. Max, a redbone, is just that kind of a dog.

On November 15, 1931, midnight, my hunting partner and I started one of the best coon hunts I have ever had. We

Last Fall's Catch

were back at four-thirty with six coons, all caught singly, three on ground. They just can't run ahead of Max. Some dogs will in a loss return to a certain spot time and again while the trail grows colder. Max goes farther on.

The hunt last fall, I wish to describe, was the kind I like. The night was dark and misting and the first strike got to a big tile. The second ran 40 yards but had to tree on a red oak. After shooting him out, I said to Wilbur Hatfield, the present owner of Max, "I wish we could strike one that we could have a real chase." Just then Max opened, apparently where he struck the one we had shot off. This trail led in the opposite direction. This wise old Ringtail followed standing corn fields, wheat fields, then across 40 acres of fall plowing. Then had to climb a ten-inch blue ash on the edge of a thicket. The ground was very soft and the kind that sticks to your boots and I thought we never would get out of some of them, but I am there for the kill. The dog got out of hearing. We went on until we could hear him talking treed. He had run him two and three-quarter miles, the most of it muddy corn and wheat and fall plowing fields. I don't want two like that in one night, but got a real kick out of it.

I consider Max one of the best dogs in Ohio or any other state. He is one hundred percent coonhound.

JAMES SNOW,
Bryan, Ohio.

---o---

COON HUNTING IN ARKANSAS

BEING a constant reader of the good old H-T-T magazine and a confirmed coon hunter, I always turn to the coon hunting section first.

I lived in Arkansas for 16 years before I moved North and naturally did quite a

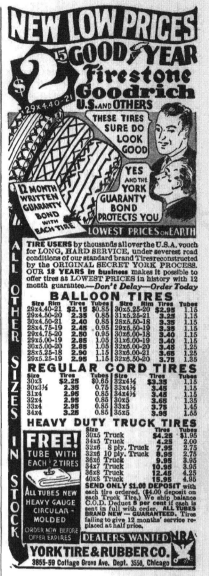
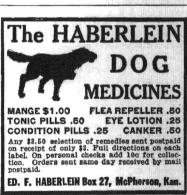

bit of coon hunting. So I will relate a rather exciting coon hunt in the White River bottoms.

On the 30th of November, my father, Jack Wingardt, a hunting partner of mine and I loaded up the old sedan with camping equipment, guns and dogs and started for a week's camp hunt on the river bottoms. We arrived at our destination about noon, and spent the rest of the day putting up our tent and making a couple of houses for the dogs. The next day was spent hunting ducks as we were camped right on the bank of the river with cypress lakes all around us.

We killed all the ducks we could use and found coon signs all around the lakes, which made us anxious for night to come. As this was the opening night we decided to get an early start. Now it was about the last day. Old Queen, a black and tan bitch about 9 years old belonging to Jack, and Trail, a 3-year old Walker Bluetick, both open trailers and good tree dogs.

DAD said he would stay in camp and see that the coons didn't carry away any of our provisions. So Jack and I decided to hunt an island on the other side of the river so we got the dogs in a boat and paddled across. We landed the boat by an old log and let the dogs out and were fixing up our carbide lights when old Trail opened up on a warm track. Then old Queen joined in and before we could get our light fixed we heard old Trail telling us to come and see what he had put up, so we hurried to where he was and found him standing on an old log about 10 feet off the ground barking up a tall pecan tree. I shone my light over the tree and saw Mr. Coon away up in the top. Now in the top of a white river pecan tree means up in the air, Brother. Having a 20 gauge loaded with No. Fives Jack said I would have to stretch the barrel but the second shot he tumbled out. After letting the dog shake him we started on. In the meantime Queen had been trailing off to our right down an old slough bed so we got Trail started with her and after about half a mile they jumped Mr. Coon at a small lake and believe me we had some swell music for a while but it didn't last long for Mr. Coon had to take a tree but he took a good one for when we got there we found they had treed up a big cypress with two or three holes in it. So we put them on a chain and led them for a couple of hundred yards and turned them loose again. This time they struck a hot track almost under our feet and ran straight for a small lake. Here Mr. Coon proceeded to give Trail a few lessons in swimming. Queen, the old dog, was almost given out so she stood on the bank and waited for the coon to come out. However, when Mr. Coon would get out of the water he would get out on the opposite bank run down it a ways then get back in the water again. Well finally Trail caught her in the lower end of the lake and we had quite a fight in the mud and water before I finally killed her with my hand ax. She was a large sow coon.

We headed back for camp and hadn't gone far when Trail opened up a run a short ways and barked treed. Arriving at the tree we found a small coon up a little tree

eating grapes. I kicked him out and let the dogs kill him. At this time we had three coons so we tossed to see who would carry the two coon and I lost of course, so I told Jack that the shortest way to camp was the sweetest, so again we started for the river when both dogs opened up on a red hot track. Jack said he hoped they treed in a den as it was his turn to carry the coon and we were both pretty well all in. The dogs were getting farther and farther away and going faster all the time. After running about a mile in a straight line and the dogs out of hearing I decided that if they were running a coon he must have had wings for those dogs were sure traveling. As they were running towards the boat we followed. On arriving at the boat both dogs were awaiting us. So we loaded them in the boat and rowed across to camp. Dad was up waiting for us and said he had heard the dogs running over on the island and that they had run to the river opposite camp and stopped when whatever it was they were running had

Three nights' catch of opossum, coon and skunk with old Trail.

taken the river. He said he had heard something come up the river bank below camp but didn't know what it was. As it was 3 o'clock we hit the hay and the next morning I went down and saw where a deer had come up the bank so that explained why our coon had run so straight and fast.

We stayed there and coon hunted for a week and had many a good coon chase and caught lots of coon. Hereby spending one of the most contended weeks in my life coon hunting at night and fishing and shooting ducks in the daytime.

PAUL W. BAKER.

———o———

TWO KINDS OF FEVERS

EVERY outdoor sportsman is subject to two kinds of fever. One comes about the first of April and the other first of November. He does not require the attention of a doctor. The symptoms of April are the longing for the old river and the looking over the fishing outfit. Then along the latter part of October when the leaves begin to fall and the night air is crispy, you get that longing for the woods and the brown fields and long hikes. Then you begin to look over the "dogs for sale" ads and start to finger your old trusty gun.

I have had this disease every year for 20 years. Last fall I found a friend,

George Churchard, afflicted the same way, so we decided to try our luck together. He had a wonderful coon dog, seven years old, as good as ever looked through a collar. I had to buy a dog. I have had them from Illinois, Kentucky, Tennessee, Missouri and Arkansas, so I thought I would buy one from Ohio this time. I watched the ads in H-T-T and decided to send to a firm in Williamstown. I told them what I wanted and got just what I ordered. He is a nice bluetick, weighs about 60 pounds and minds instantly either at the kennel or in the field; in fact, just as good as a bird dog. I think he is almost perfect. Naturally, after he arrived and I tried him out and he proved to be satisfactory I was all set for the season to come in.

The season did not start out very good, too dry and tight, so I thought I would take the dog (Steamer was his name) out for a run on rabbits and, believe me, he was some rabbit dog. I shot a couple, put on his chain and beat it back home. I was really ashamed to run a coon dog on rabbits. These dogs are absolutely rabbit proof at night.

Late that afternoon a warm rain set in and as the moon was very dim, I thought, tonight's the night. My partner must have had the same feeling, for about 5 p. m. he called me on the 'phone and said what time do we start? Six o'clock was the time.

WE had to drive about twelve miles south from where we lived to get to our hunting grounds. We arrived at the end of our drive and had to walk two miles to get to the hunting place.

It was still raining and we were getting very wet and discouraged. Of course we couldn't find a dry place to sit down, when all at once we heard a great commotion over in a corn lot. We ran to it and found Steamer had rounded a good sized coon. He does not tie into his game, he just holds them in the one place. Old Blue came a tearing in, he does not stop for anything, even though it should be a bear. We held the dogs and let the coon run again for five minutes. (Suppose some of you coon hunters will laugh at this, but we hunt for pleasure, not fur.) They soon had him treed in a small pine oak. We then bagged him and started away.

In about half an hour Steamer opened up about half a mile south. He was coming north when Blue chimed in, they surely were coming right over a ravine over tree tops 'n' everything. It certainly was good for the ears and I was not even wet or tired then. They treed in an oak stub in the middle of a small pond. The coon was clear to the bottom but with a little coaxing he decided to leave. He jumped out of the top and the dogs soon put on the finishing touches.

We then started for the car. On the way the dogs started to act foolish. They would run up and down the fence then rear up on several trees. Old Blue finally straightened the trail out and then they were gone. They treed in about ten minutes up a very large elm. A couple shots from George's rifle and we started for the car again, with three nice coon. Oh, boy, but that walk to the car was a heart-breaker. We arrived home at 6 a. m. tired but satisfied. We had fairly good luck this season.

SMITHY,
Elyria, Ohio.

—————o—————

OLD BOB

SOME folks prate of friendship true,
Tell of all they'd do for you;
But to always be right on the job,
Give me my coonhound, old longeared Bob.

I know many dogs are better hunters than he,
But he has the first time yet to lie to me.
How many people can I say that about?
No matter how much of friendship they shout?

Many a night, cloudy and black,
I have followed old Bob on ringtails track.
Of all earth's music, could I have my choice,
I would listen to his well known voice.

No water too cold, no current too strong,
He still keeps singing his joyous song.
And when at last at the end of the race,
I shall never forget the look on his face.

The coon's up there far out on a limb,
That he's asking to be brought down to him;
And when that coon is in our sack
Old Bob is looking for another track.

Although he's old and his eyes are dim,
I still wouldn't think of selling him;
For Bob is my pal, the truest of friends,
And will be true till life's trail ends.

You'll think me foolish, not very wise,
To have this moisture in my eyes,
But still I can say till my dying day
He is one true friend you can't take away.

OLD COONHUNTER.

—————o—————

HUNTING IN OLD MEXICO

(Continued from page 6)

hunt. In this same locality one can get mountain sheep. They are always in the roughest, rockiest mountains, but we passed many ranchers that assured us if we would like to take a couple of days hunt we could secure plenty of bighorn sheep. All of these ranchers are very anxious to rent horses for one peso per day for each horse. Any of the ranchers will show you where game can be found. The people in this part of Sonora are not well educated as there are no schools in the outlying districts. There are, however, schools in all of the small towns, consequently many of them never leave the ranch where they are born. They live and die there, yet they are happy and never heard of the word "depression." In this same locality antelope can be secured but they are not plentiful.

After arriving in Hermisillo our intention was to proceed to the Yaqui river

country, 150 miles south and east of Hermisillo, but our time was about up as we could be gone only two weeks. We stayed in Hermisillo two days taking in the sights and the town in general. At night one can hear people singing and playing on all sorts of musical instruments everywhere, in the streets, in the parks, in the stores, and in the homes. It seems everyone is so happy that they must let their emotions peal forth at dusk.

We had information that it was possible to go to the Yaqui river country by auto from Hermisillo and in this part of Sonora, which is about 150 miles south and east of Hermisillo, a great variety of game can be secured, such as lion, cats, bear, deer, wild hog, jaguar, and all small game. There also are literally hundreds of thousands of ducks and geese around the lagoon of Guaymas.

The Yaqui river country is much more mountainous than in the western part of the state. There is also much more water. This far south one is just on the edge of the tropics and it is here that the jaguars are numerous. We encountered one party who claimed that he had killed 26 jaguars on one cattle ranch in this part of the country.

We started from Hermisillo to Nogales on our way home over a very good automobile road, arriving at Nogales the next day and from there to Escondido, a well-satisfied party of hunters.

There is one fact that I would like to make clear—that is, we started into Mexico not knowing where we were going —just hunting—and we had a fine trip, and any party of American sportsmen can take a trip into Sonora and have a wonderfully successful trip without knowing the country.

There are hundreds of ranches all over the state with thousands of cattle and any rancher is glad to have you as his guest.

Before taking a trip into Mexico I often asked the question, "Is it safe?" I would like to make this statement very clear. I consider it much safer in Sonora, Mexico, than in the City of Los Angeles. Absolutely all the people are very courteous and congenial. They certainly love to have the tourists make long stays at their particular ranches. One is absolutely safe. Any party going into Sonora will not find a "No Hunting" sign in the whole state.

Our dogs are good coon dogs as well as lion hounds. These three coons were caught one night on the trip.

Oregon Bobcats

By JACK ROBERTS

IT seems the bob cat gets it on all sides. Some call them weak, others desperate killers, so putting two and two together there must be both good and bad ones. Myself I don't like cats of any kind. The larger the cats the less I like them. I have trapped and hunted cats in Yamhill County, Oregon, for a number of years and still have lots to learn about them. I have read many stories by V. E. Lynch, Yancy and others, and I believe I am safe in saying they do not know all there is to know about cats either. I wish we had some of those monster cats from Maine here in Oregon. I have never heard of a bob cat weighing over 3 pounds in this part of the country. The largest bob cat I ever caught was in a No. 2 Victor. This cat measured over 60 inches, and was very fat, but I am sure it would not weigh over 30 pounds. I did not have any scales to weigh it with, so it is just a guess. This cat's hide was graded as an extra large, so would someone speak up and tell me what class those 50 pound babies from Maine are in? I suppose they grade them as short tailed cougars.

My experience with traps show that a No. 2 will hold a cat, if it steps in the center of it. If not, Mr. Cat will soon go on his way. There is no reason why they shouldn't hold some. All wild animals do not fight as hard as others do. I caught a coyote in a No. 2, but that doesn't mean that you will get everyone that comes along and steps in a No. 2. I wouldn't use anything but No. 4 traps any more where they are not set in water. I believe anyone that traps in the mountains will double their catch if they use large traps, but I don't believe anyone should get the idea in their head that there isn't anyone that can catch such game as cats in a No. 2. A good trapper can do wonders with a little trap where a dub will get nothing with a large one, so who knows. Mr. G. C. Brewer of Hoodriver County, Oregon, may be able to hang hides all around Mr. Lynch of Maine. I don't say a bob cat will not fight. They

will, and plenty. I don't believe I ever saw a cat give up till they were dead.

I used a 44-40 Colt revolver one winter while hunting with my dogs, and shot several cats with it. I killed but one cat with it with a single shot. Now, don't say, "You should have shot them in the head." That is exactly what I intended

The writer and his dogs with bobcat and cougar.

every time, but who can take a revolver and hit a cat in the head every time, when the cat is sitting in the top of a good sized tree. Maybe our friend, Lynch, can, but I doubt it, as in all the pictures I have seen of him and his cats he carries a shotgun. One cat I shot with this gun, I was after for several days. There was a little thicket near a goat pasture, and about every two or three days he would lay and hide there and wait for a goat. I had other places to go, so couldn't get there every day. About three weeks went by before my dogs picked up his trail. One morning I heard the music start and knew that he had killed his last deer or goat. They trailed him about two miles, and started to bark treed. After looking things

over, I finally spotted him about ten feet from the top of a large second growth fir. Now try and shoot a cat's eyes out with a pistol on a good cold day, that high up. Well, at the crack of the gun a cat, a limb and about a ton of snow came down. I had made a beautiful shot. I hit the limb he was sitting on dead center. I knew what had happened. The dogs had him up another tree, so I went over to shoot him in the head again. There he was—a nice large boy, unhurt, standing on a limb. A good big head, why anyone ought to shoot his head off. I sent a second piece of lead after him. Well, down he came and I saw he was hit, but when he hit the ground he was on his way and one dog was biting at his heels, but he would not stop and put up a fight. I could see one front leg swinging, broken in the shoulder, but if you think a cat can't run on three legs, get a dog after one and see. Well, I watched the race for about one hundred feet and I believe the pup would have caught him in a few more leaps, when in a hole goes Mr. Cat. This was a rocky den. There was no way to get in so the only thing to do was to go home, and see if he came out that night or died in the hole.

Well, next day finds luck in my favor. A light snow started to fall. Soon after leaving and upon arriving at the den I find Mr. Cat had just left not over ten minutes before. Well, I took time enough to dig out a rock and roll over the hole then away go the dogs. About fifty yards from the den they jumped him out off some thick brush. Down for the den he comes. Now, maybe you think a cat can't think quickly. Well, they sure can. When he saw the rock in front of his retreat, there was hardly a moment lost in figuring things out. I thought he would stop and fight, but not this cat. Up another tree he goes. Well, I started shooting at his body this time. I thought I might hit him in the head this way. After four shots, down he came, down but not out. He hit the ground and dove under a log and was

Last Season's bag of coon treed by the two dogs, Lead and Lightfoot, which were bought through an advertisement in Hunter-Trader-Trapper by E. F. Corliss, Cumberland County, Maine.

ready for fight at last. Old dogs could have finished him, if they were good ones. The two I had were only seven months old and were a little slow to take a hold, so the cat was getting the best of the deal. When I got up close, he came at me, but the dogs stopped him. I shot him twice in the head before he lay down for good, seven bullets from a 44-40—shot through and through before he went down to stay. Does that look like a weakling. This cat weighed about 25 pounds and was a Tom. I have shot several with this same gun some three and four times before they came down. You hear some people say, "Why, I heard of a fellow killing a cougar with a 22 caliber gun". Sure, that is true. I did the same thing once, but if I ever meet another when I have a 22, I hope it is another small one. There is no doubt in my mind but what bob cats kill deer and even goats.

L AST summer I had been out to the coast for a while. Upon returning home, I noticed some buzzards upon a snag about a quarter of a mile from the house. Soon as I got things unloaded I got the dogs and up we go to find out what was dead. We found a goat that had been killed about four days before. The evidence showed that a cat had been the first one there. The goat had been entirely covered with fern, and later a bear had come along and drug it down the hill where it was then. The dogs couldn't smell anything but bear then. Next morning nothing had been around. That evening about 4 o'clock I went back. Away go the dogs —a running track. About ten minutes and I hear them bark treed. I fully expected to see a cougar. Can you imagine my surprise to see a bob cat. Well, there he was, a large cat but very thin, weighed 18 pounds. I watched there for days and no other cats came around, so I am sure I got the guilty one.

The winter of 1932 and 1933 was a bad one in Oregon. The snow was deep and stayed late in the spring. The cats sure done their stuff while things were in their favor. I found one big buck a bob cat had killed in the deep snow that I am sure he could not have downed otherwise.

I am enclosing a picture of my dogs, myself, one old cougar, three small ones and six bob cats. Note the spots on the little cougar in the center of picture. I have had cats get out of traps lots of times, but I have never had one fail to go up a tree when a dog gets after it. Yet all the cats I have ever run treed in a few minutes after they jumped up, with the exception of one, and the dog was so slow the cat out-walked it. I suppose Mr. Lynch will say, "Oregon Short Legs", now or some such name. Well, call them what you want, Friend Lynch, that is everybody's privilege. Our cats will still be here and I will be out after them every chance I get. Maybe some more of the boys will be ready to talk bob cat by the time this gets a show. Well, come on. I would like to, if there is any place else besides Maine where cats weigh 50 pounds. So if any of you fellows know anything about cats let's hear from you. Maybe some of the old timers can learn something yet. I am not so old myself.

———o———

CROWS GOOD RIDDANCE

I HAVE been noticing in every sporting magazine, H-T-T included, articles about game conservation, which I advocate to the letter. Here in our part of the state I know what is keeping the game from increasing. Nothing but crows, timber cats and large owls. The crows are here by the countless thousands and as more timber and weeds are removed every year, it makes it just that much easier for the crow to search out the nesting place of quail, all song birds and rabbits as well. You can very easily see why that is true. When I am out with a gun I never fail to try and kill the above mentioned creatures and I feel as though I had rid the country of one more pest. Now what I would advocate would be for the state to put a bounty of say ten cents on adult crows and five cents on each egg or young crow before it leaves the nest. You would be surprised what the boys of a community would do to the crows. Take the bounty out of the hunting license fund. It could not be used to any better advantage.

Stray cats are the next menace. A quail will set for a cat just exastly as it will for a bird dog and consequently you know what happens to the quail. I saw that illustrated while out hunting. They flush them first and they just scatter and hide. Then they just pick them up at will. One

cat will put a whole covey out of commission in just about thirty days. I made up my mind after witnessing that, that all cats caught away from home should never get home again. That is, if I had a gun with me.

Four or five years ago ringnecks were shipped in this part of the state and liberated. The second year one could see quite a few of them, showing an increase. Now you very seldom hear of one. The crows got next to a new supply of food and are destroying the nests. I truly wish that all sporting magazines would start advocating some kind of a bounty on crows.
E. G. RITTLER,
Henry County, Iowa.

COON HIDE STRETCHING

FOR many years I have been reading H-T-T and I especially like trapping stories, especially trapping for foxes. In the pictures of coon hides I seldom see one properly square stretched. If you care to print this, I will tell the readers what I know about coon hide stretching.

Stretching a coon hide. — First cut around all four feet, then split down the hind legs to the root of the tail. Next lay the coon on his back and split down the center of the belly, beginning at the chin. Now step on one front foot and hold the other in your hand and split straight across. Then you are ready to take off the pelt. Skin out the hind legs and tail, then hang it up by the hind legs and finish. This method keeps the meat clean.

Now, to square stretch it, take an old door or a square frame of board. Drive one nail in the nose of the coon hide. Spread the head each way from that nail. Then put a nail between the outside and the center nail. Now come down the sides of the head a little way, bringing the front legs up even with the nose. Spread the legs out and nail. Now nail down the sides of the head and the sides of the leg, keeping them straight. Nail down the outsides of the front legs to the flank. Don't work too hard trying to keep this straight. Take hold of the tail and pull it down and nail at the root of the tail. Now, go straight from this nail each way even with

the width at the top. Now, go up across the hind legs pulling up and out with your nails until you have filled out the flank.

Always stretch both sides as you go. Then trim off the surplus from the hind legs and you have a square fur.
RUSSEL N. PITMAN,
Menard County, Ill.

TRAPPING IN ILLINOIS

YOU boys that don't live around our territory are sure lucky. Game is not exactly plentiful around here, but trap-lifters are. At the first of the season you have to set at night and pick them up about five in the morning, or you won't have your traps.

Muskrats are about the most plentiful around here and are easy to catch. My favorite set is the parsnip seat, which is made by sticking a parsnip about twelve inches above the trap, which is staked out in deep water. This season my partner

and I got one leg between us and that was on account of shallow water. That shows you that it pays to drown them. Make these sets in out-of-the-way places so as not to show the trap-lifter your set.

Skunks are not even known around here. The only ones I ever heard of was caught by a friend of mine three years ago.

The opossum is quite plentiful, due to the fact that no one traps them. My best set is to make a pen out of bark and in the back put sardines, stake the trap on a drop, as coons are sometimes caught and put up a big fight. Mink are scarce due to heavy trapping. The way to get them is to set at their dens.

Next year I will have to find new trapping grounds because the largest zoo in the world is going to be opened here and also due to the fact that the CWA ruins the woods here, but what can you expect here? I live only thirteen miles from Chicago.
LEONARD FANNING,
Cook County, Illinois.

THE VALUE OF SCENTS

(*Continued from page 7*)

a splendid scent for muskrat during the mating season. When a muskrat is caught and skinned remove the glands and at a set squeeze out a drop or so on some object a foot or so from the trap. A stick stuck in the ground near the set and scent rubbed from the muskrat gland is usually effective in attracting other muskrats.

Those of the dog family appear to relish their meat when it is in a spoiled and loud-smelling condition, therefore rotted flesh is valuable in calling the fox and coyote. Trappers chop up bits of cat or other flesh and bottle it up in the early fall. It is usually used in connection with fresher bait, the ill-smelling portion luring the animal to the set, and the larger bait keeping him there until he is caught.

A good scent for the coyote or wolf is as follows: If a female coyote can be caught while in heat cut out the uterus, and also the urine. Put in a pint bottle that has been thoroughly cleaned. Fill the bottle most full of water, put in a small pinch of assafetida about the size of a

large pea. Add three drops of the oil of anise, hang this out until it decays. Use only a few drops at each set, and it should be used only during the mating season; as it will be most attractive at that time.

Here is a mighty good scent for the raccoon which would pay anyone the trouble in getting the ingredients and mixing it. Take a half-pint of fish-oil, put in one-quarter of a beaver castor, and one-half of a beaver's oil-sack if it can be obtained. Add a little honey and fifteen drops of oil of anise. If this is prepared according to instructions you will have a scent that no 'coon will ever pass up. In using this scent only use what scent will stick to a small twig stuck into the bottle.

A scent for the cat family can be made as follows: Take one-half pint of fish oil, and add one-fourth beaver castor, one beaver oil sack, six muskrat musk bags taken from the rat in the spring. And add ten drops of oil of catnip. Anything that resembles a cat will stop and take notice.

A SCENT for the fox can be made as follows: Take an ordinary house cat or bobcat and cut the meat of the cat in small inch square pieces, and fill a two-quart fruit jar two-thirds full. Put the top on without the rubber ring so as not to make it air-tight. Then set in the sun until it thoroughly rots. This makes a pretty good scent. Every time you catch a female fox take the urine from her and put it into the scent until you have used the urine from at least half a dozen. This will prove an excellent scent for early fall.

Trappers to be very successful must know something of the habits of the animals they wish to catch. A meat, fish or flesh bait at a certain season may be best, while during the mating season scents will have great attracting value. No bait or natural food, neither scent, will perform wonders, yet either when rightly used is a great help in many instances in

Part of 1933 season's catch of coon by Francis Nichols and Gaylord Bevins, Fillmore County, Nebraska. Dogs are Bob, Western Ranger, Friend Jerry and Rock.

catching the animals. The observing trapper will learn many things that will help to increase his catch whether using bait or scents at sets or not. Although scent and bait when properly used have much value, neither is of assistance unless the traps are properly set. Make all sets skillfully so that when trap is set and covered to appearances there is no trap set.

If you tried scents during the fall with little success, make another attempt in the spring. There is no better time to appeal to hungry and sex instinct than when the fur-bearers are leaving their dens after hibernation and beginning to "run."

The best time to prepare lures is during the summer or early fall, before trapping operations start and while it is an easy matter to decompose fish for fish-oil; and the far-sighted trapper will have saved musk and other ingredients from last winter's catch to be used now in making up his supply of scent for next season.

—o—

GUN QUESTIONS AND ANSWERS

(Continued from page 39)

do better shooting, especially after mid-day when he would be tired, with a .25-20 or .32-20 Winchester Model 65, the Remington pump action .25-20 or .32-20 Model 25A which weighs but 5½ pounds—no more than his .22, or one of the Savage Sporters in these calibers—a 6 pound proposition. These latter have exceptionally good fitting stocks and are bolt action, which you seem to prefer.

The difference between a 5½ to 6 pound, and a 7 pound rifle he will likely find very great, especially if you will expect the boy to do some driving, and to take his place with a deer crew—instead of merely to stand on a stump or a rock ledge and watch a runway.

I prefer the Savage lever action to the .250 bolt action of that make for a hunting rifle for brush shooting. The trigger pull is better and the rifle carries far better in the hand or on the shoulder.

The Model 54 Winchester .250-3000 in either rifle or carbine style and the Remington bolt action in .25 rimless or .30 rimless would be other good selections but better for an older boy than yours. They are not nearly as light and handy on the shoulder or in the hand as a lever or slide action. Also the boy may have more trouble with the bolt handle working up and blocking him when he wants to fire. Safety may seem more complicated to him than pulling back a hammer or moving the simpler safety of the Model 99 or Remington pump action.

Matter of fact such a boy might do better with a .25-20 or .32-20 carbine fitted with jack sights than anything heavier and larger in either rifle or cartridge.

Remember that 80% of his shots will likely be within 50 to 100 yards in the brush, and he would not be liable to kill a deer on a hill to hill shot, no matter what he used, therefore fitting him up with a light rifle that he can carry comfortably and aim with reasonable certainty is a good deal more important than knock down and keep down ballistics.

Help him sight in his rifle at 50 to 75 yards —no need to worry about the long shots just yet, and impress that what he is looking for is Horns—great big horns—not Ears and that he must look things over carefully before shooting. $100.00 and costs if he makes a mistake.

Such a boy will want to eat every 3 or 4 hours, so a lunch in his coat is more important than the caliber of rifle. He will be certain to insist on shooting at something, every half hour or so. I have a boy who went through that age period (and so did I and you), and you might just as well plan that what that boy needs is an arm he can get sensible use out of at other times—and you still remain solvent on the ammunition purchases.

If he gets a buck—that's fine. If he doesn't, well, what of it? If he is a real boy, he'll get five times the kick out of it you will, will see three times as many deer as you, having younger and better eyes, and will imagine he is a combination of Buffalo Bill and Daniel Boone and that there is a bear in every thicket.

The ten years between 12 and 22 are worth forty years thereafter, in enjoyment—so I am betting on the boy. Be sure his rifle is properly sighted in. Gun & Ammunition Editor.

FUR FARMING
Game Breeding
and Plant Culture

Silver Fox Farming

By MRS. CHARLES D. DEGNAN

Pinehurst Fox Farm

A FEW years ago my husband and I were confronted with the problem of finding a new way to make a living. We had a country home that was too far from any town to make communication desirable so we centered our thoughts on our location and possible opportunities.

Since we knew that our vicinity was inhabited by wild foxes having fine pelts we decided to raise silver foxes. We then investigated and bought splendid foundation stock.

When we began caring for our foxes we became very much attached to them and are now more than ever thrilled by their cunning and clever antics.

I have "lived with" the foxes so to speak and know their dispositions as though they were my friends. (I really feel that they *are* my friends.)

I have named them all and am sure that some have learned theirs as a dog does. Hector was the first to make this noticeable. Since the ranch is near the house I often have occasion to pass near Hector's pen. I began always speaking to him and soon found that he would

come out to see me. Sometimes he gets out of his pen but if I go into the ranch and call "Hector" he will come to me as a dog would. I let him have a run, then take some meat to his pen, open the door, and in he jumps.

I think my experiences with one little pup might be of interest to some one. When she was but two weeks old my husband found her wet and chilled one rainy morning. At first he thought she was dead, but when he saw she was still living he brought her into the house. I put her on a blanket near the stove. As soon as she was warm and dry she seemed well and gave evidence of being really ugly.

Presently we noticed that the father and mother fox were looking for the lost "child." We were somewhat puzzled whether to put her back or give her to a cat, but decided to try her with the fox. All went well for a while.

From the start she had been very small and when about nine weeks old was still so small that she could crawl through the open spaces of two-inch mesh wire.

It seems that I was always looking for Midget, as she was a lively little thing and delighted in making explorations.

She was her father's pet, too. Hercules would care for her as tenderly as would the best of females.

When about ten weeks of age she was sick and we expected to lose her, bu great care brought her through very nicely. A diet of tender lettuce ground and mixed with choice meat put her on her feet.

Hercules was so lonesome for his little "daughter" that he chewed his way from his pen, crossed the ranch and endeavored to free her.

Then one night I found her hung in the wire as she had attempted to make another exploration but I was just in time to save her. My first thought was to cut the wire, but this I was unable to do. As a last resort I got inside the pen and held her up to keep her from choking to death. This made it possible for her to pull her head back and all was well once again.

My son sat by Midget's pen by the hour to make sure that she was not harming herself. At night she had to be shut in her little house, but we were careful to see that she had plenty of fresh air.

She is a full-grown fox now and people say that she is a beauty.

Not so many days ago I was watching the fox ranch from the lookout. Billy had a lame foot, as he had hurt it a bit in some way. Betty, his mate, washed it for him. Then he put his nose on her face as though he were kissing her kindly.

This winter we have had a great deal of snow and there were times when it was necessary to shovel snow from the feed boxes. As I did so the foxes would dig a tunnel on the inside. They seemed to enjoy themselves and I felt that they wished to help me.

I believe that the fox and fur business is destined to become of great importance and that many far-sighted people living in climates appropriate for the industry will establish ranches of their own. This can be done on a small scale at first as the lady of the house can easily take charge of feeding a few foxes.

Mrs. Degnan and Hector

Mr. Degnan and Billy

I find it a pleasure to take pans of food to the dear little creatures that run to the feeding places and look at me with truly grateful eyes. (All but three of our foxes do this and one of them—Juno—comes out to eat as soon as I close the ranch door. I can see her watching me from her spout.)

My enthusiasm in the fox business is not promoted by a fortune already made. For that matter I never expect a fortune—all I ask is a modest living.

———o———

MINK QUESTIONS ANSWERED
By W. E. KANE.

Ques. "What are the most important points to remember in starting a mink ranch?" (N. Dak.)

Ans. Several points of almost equal importance must be considered. I understand you mean to start a large operation which differs from a small or medium ranch as to requirements. For a large ranch a good location should be selected, if possible on a well traveled road, first, a certain amount of free advertising can be had, good advertising if you keep a neat place and bad if you do not; another thing you are always assured a good, well kept road, open winter and summer, which is highly necessary in the heavy snow country when supplies must be kept coming in regularly.

Second. Nearness to a source of cheap, dependable, year-round supply of food; you must make sure of this, some ranches are restricted as to the number of animals they can produce on account of a limited food supply.

Third, Good equipment, ample pens to house your increase without crowding and, of course, the finest breeding stock money can buy.

Fourth. Any well drained site is okeh; you don't need expensive land or expensive buildings, either; build for permanence and comfort rather than style, be thrifty as to outlay, but don't balk at paying a fair price to secure fine stock.

Ques. "Will a female accept and raise another's kits?" (Oregon).

Ans. Some will and some won't. Several years ago I lost a female when her litter was 10 days' old; two of these kits I placed with a female that raised them as well as her own; two were given a female with a litter of four; she kept them two days, then killed them both; why she waited that long before making away with them is a question. The remaining two were placed with a very gentle old female that I thought sure would accept them. The

writer was very careful in introducing these kits into the litter, keeping the female shut out of the nest box until I thought their strange odor would be lost in mixing with the other young in the nest, however, as soon as I let the female return she picked out the little strangers and very gently carried them outside and left them. Finally I found a home for them.

Ques. "What is your idea of crossing Yukon and central mink to improve color, size and fur texture? Please explain fully. (Iowa).

Ans. Central mink as I know them are a rather light colored, coarse furred animal with light brown or buff underfur; they are, however, usually of good size, even larger than standard type Yukon, being longer in body with a more pointed nose and larger tails; they are not a profitable subspecies to raise, owing to their comparatively low pelt value.

Crossing these large mink with good extra dark Yukons will work a wonderful improvement, fining and darkening the fur to a marked extent; the writer has seen one generation crosses with a pelt value of several dollars above average Central mink; surely, that is convincing enough. Good crosses are fine mink if selectively bred and bring prices comparing favorably with pure blood stock.

At accredited shows you will find these crosses classified as standard mink and some very remarkable specimens are shown. This field offers a great opportunity for study and experimentation.

At a future date the writer will continue these questions and answers, always with the hope that they may prove of value to someone.

———o———

SILVER FOX SALE

THE Hudson's Bay Company's fifth Silver Fox Sale of the season was held in their Fur Trade Sale Room, London, on May 14th.

The collection consisted of 9,823 skins and although buyers for the home trade were not present in their usual numbers, there was steady competition throughout for all grades.

Good color skins, valued at approximately sixty dollars and upwards, were in excellent demand and realized substantial increases in price; this was offset, however, by a decline in the poorer colors which, as is usual at this time of year, comprised the majority of the collection. The final average showed a decline of 5%, fully 70% of the offering being sold.

Low grades were again in good demand.

Considering the numerous difficulties of international trading at the present time, the result may be considered highly satisfactory and encouraging. The renewed evidence of the steady demand for Silver Fox is an indication of its continued popularity.

On the whole there are very few declines to be recorded, it being generally felt that there are good times ahead for the Fur Trade, and we have every reason to anticipate a strong demand during the Summer and Autumn seasons, particularly for all fine furs.

The best price was obtained by the three-quarter silvers bringing approximately $45.00 average. The top price was $153.00.

Selecting Pups as to Age

By CARL E. SMITH

IN selling a good many pups each year, it always surprises me the number of folks who will choose the younger ones just because they are a bit cheaper in initial cost. To be sure, the breeder can easily afford to sell pups considerably cheaper right out of the weaning pen than he can after he has boarded them some weeks or months or longer. But the difference in cost price between the little pups and those of older age and more maturity is usually not very large, and indeed it usually figures quite cheap board for the difference in age, when figured by the week or month. So the older pup may be much the cheaper pup of the two, even though he may cost you twice as much as a weanling pup of the same grade. But think of the time the older pup has been boarded, the risky age he has been kept past, and the losses or chances for loss taken by the kennel which has raised him past his more tender weeks into a more husky and rugged age.

Especially do amateurs take a greater risk in purchasing a younger pup, for it necessarily takes more skill, more care, more scientific feeding, and more frequent attention to raise a pup that is taken at six or eight weeks old than it does a pup of six or eight months old. A pup of the younger age, just weaned, must be fed about four times a day, of careful feeding, well prepared. A pup the same number of months old, as the little one is weeks old, can do on about half that frequent feedings, and can eat a wider diet successfully. Also, a pup that is six, eight or ten months old has been carried by most of the puppy dangers, except distemper, and even with that the greater the age and strength the greater chance of pulling through it, other conditions being equal.

So I often wonder why so many folks will pay the price they do for a pup just weaned, or just old enough to ship, when oftentimes a price one and one-half times as great will buy a pup twice or three times as old, ready to train at once, and perhaps started some in field work. It is an eternal mystery, only partly explained by the well known fact that more folks *have* the smaller price.

I have also been surprised in the near-autumn and near-hunting season how many will select the younger pups too young to use that fall's season, just because they can get such cheaper, when for not so many dollars more they can buy something which can be put to use at once. When you consider that the little pup will have to be wintered over and fed a whole year, before any hunting returns can be realized from him, and with all the risks attendant to this wintering over, not to speak of ex-

An all star litter of eight Pups

pense, it is hard to see why so many balk at a few dollars extra outlay when that small extra expenditure would secure immediate chances for value, save a whole year's time, save a lot of expense, and a lot of risk.

We realize the value of training your own, if possible, and advocate same whenever possible, and we know the value of having a puppy, yours from puppyhood. But the pups of the older ages mentioned are still pups, will make up quickly with any owner who will handle them properly, and are likely to be hardly more than beginners, at best, if trained much at all, at those ages.

It frequently happens that someone has to suddenly give up some young dog, practically grown, due to some change in plans which necessitate disposal; an animal still in the formative state for training, and quite young enough to train (if not already started), or finish training if it has been already started. Yet few will pay much if any, difference more for such an individual, than they would pay for a little pup. That, too, is somewhat difficult to

understand, when one considers what has been put into the older youngster, but I have seen some very attractive values in youngsters of that sort almost go begging at cheap prices, comparatively.

If you are well fixed for raising a little pup, have the time, like to do it, will take the risk, and are in no hurry—and have cheap feed available, you may be able to save a little by buying a younger pup. Otherwise, the time and board and risk saved in putting a few more dollars into an older pup, ready to start to do something *now*, usually shows those few extra dollars well spent.

---o---

TRYING OUT STRANGE DOGS

By CLYDE BLEVINS

A great deal of misunderstanding between our purchasers and dealers has resulted from hunters not knowing how to satisfactorily handle a strange dog when hunting upon strange hunting grounds.

A great many well trained coon hounds have been returned to me and the customer sorely disappointed in my ability to make satisfactory selection for his hunting grounds, he gave the dog what he considered a fair trial and all reasonable chances to make good, wherein if he had known just how to handle the dog and had used more time he would have been well pleased with the dog and its ability as a coon hound.

Some will want to know how I am so sure this particular dog would have done good work as I was not on the grounds and do not know how the dog worked for this customer, it is natural for a well trained dog to do good work if given the time and opportunity. I gave this dog a fair test upon hunting grounds similar to the grounds this man wanted to hunt the dog over, before shipment was made; upon dog's return I gave him another trial, found the dog satisfactory and shipped to another hunter. This second man knew how to handle strange dogs, gave the dog time and a chance and writes me that dog is all any hunter could desire—that the dog is improving with each trip out.

One particular instance the past season with a female coon hound I received the dog back within ten days from shipping date; at least four days of this time was taken in enroute and upon return; customer writes a very bitter letter stating dog was worthless. She left him in the woods the first night and he found her at a farm house; on another night she failed to run a coon's trail when showed its track; he failed to state how old the track was as he found the imprint in the mud; she would not hunt, seldom got out of lantern light, and was otherwise a worthless type of dog. Upon her return she was given another trial and did excellent work. I again shipped her and within 20 days from shipping date and before her trial time expired I received a letter stating that dog was satisfactory as he had taken nine coons so far and she was improving.

We must bear in mind that strange dogs will not work well for a strange master and over strange hunting grounds. The long confinement in a crate also has its effect upon a dog, it requires several days for a dog to rest up and get over his trip. Too many hunters are too anxious to see the new dog work, so as soon as the dog arrives, it may be just two hours before dark, they uncrate, feed a large meal and then throw the dog in a car and drive to their hunting grounds expecting the dog to do his "stuff", while in fact the dog is worn out, the heavy meal and the car ride have had their effect, the dog is car sick, sick from his long journey, does not know his new master from Adam's off ox, does not know where to call home, and when put out of the car, if he has life enough to move, he is as likely to go to the nearest farm house and pile up in the hay as to go back to the car. Such handling is the cause of so much complaint.

THE greater percent of our dogs are trained in the backwoods, have not been car broke, know nothing of hunting from a car, are used to one master only; they will not take the change so quickly as dogs that have been traded repeatedly from master to master.

Upon receipt of dog he should be allowed several days to get rested up and over his trip; allowed time to get himself settled and used to the changes in his environments. He should be taught to know his new master, should be taken over your hunting grounds a few times in order that he may know them. It is good policy to squirrel hunt the dog over the grounds you will later wish to coon hunt over. After he becomes acquainted he will feel free to range out wide, stay out longer and will not have the fear of becoming lost; it will not be necessary for him to come in so often and see where you are.

A strange dog cannot handle a trail as successfully at first as he will after he has treed a few coons, first the change in climate affects his scenting powers; he is not acquainted with the runs and habits of your coons; this he must learn before he is as fast or as successful as he will later become. Coons do not run alike on all hunting grounds; the only reason that

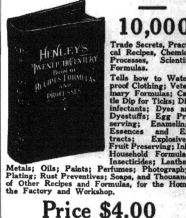

we have coons in our hunting grounds today is that by their cunning nature and tricks they have learned to outwit the hunter and his dogs. The coon learns where his safety places are located and when chased he will make for them. The dog also learns the tricks of the coon; after a few races the dog learns what to expect from the coon, he can take advantage of his tricks, he can match his skill against that of Mr. Coon, but until he learns this the dog is working at a disadvantage and will allow many coons to get away.

Many times a strange dog will take an off trail, if he is allowed his own way he will not likely hold it long, but if yelled to or hissed will run it, as it is his desire to do the will of his master; for this reason never yell or hiss a strange dog unless you are sure of what he is trailing. Many dogs that were fox-proof have been sadly spoiled by this method and had to be broken off fox again.

He may make several strikes that he will be unable to tree and many hunters will say he cannot tree, he does not know enough to hunt the tree or will not bark up; no dog can tree every trail he starts. He may have a fair trail where he starts it, it may lead to difficult grounds where no dog can work it out, it is not the fault of the dog—the trailing conditions were such that he could not handle.

TOO many hunters spoil good dogs by trying to show them how they should work. Allow a dog to work as he has been accustomed to working until you are better acquainted with him and his habits.

When the dog is trying to tree by examining trees where his trail plays out do not start shining trees all around him, this will cause the dog to think you have found the game and he may quit his efforts and start looking up the trees your light is on; he will settle down and show you which tree if given time.

Do not hunt your dog at random; first locate where coons are using. You might hunt the best dog to be found an entire season and never take one coon, because there were no coons where you were hunting. It is an easy matter to locate where coons are feeding and watering, any successful coon hunter can tell you where coon are using. They are successful because they know there are coons over the grounds they are hunting.

I could relate many incidents and could write several pages from my experience in testing strange dogs but to boil them down the few points listed below will help you to successfully test a strange dog.

First allow the dog at least ten days to get acquainted with you before you attempt to try him.

Second, be sure there are coons to be found where you try him.

Third, do not expect him to tree each time you go out; he cannot do his best work until he is used to your hunting grounds; he cannot do good work until acclimated.

Fourth, do not try to show the dog what he must do; allow the dog to hunt

in his accustomed way. It sometimes happens that the dog knows a great deal more about coon hunting than the majority of the coon hunters, so let him do his own hunting—you simply follow the dog and you will have better results.

Nowhere can we find a dog that will have all the good points and no faults, they are not made to order and are hard to remodel.

---o---

A REAL POINTER

The picture accompanying this story is that of a photograph of a pointer bitch owned by James P. McKain, a real sportsman and a wonderful dog handler as well.

One afternoon Jim was showing me how she performed some of her tricks, such as carrying an egg in her mouth without breaking it. Retrieving, posing in any way he asked her to do. "Well," I said, "if she were mine I would put her in the Dog Show April 20-21, Marion County Branch." He didn't think she could do any good but after some encouragement on my part he entered her in the show. There was plenty of stiff competition but when Poli Negra came walking out carrying her leash in her mouth just like a lady in the ring, cool, and unafraid, everybody

"Poli Negra," prize-winning pointer bitch owned by Jas. P. McKain

looked. She was a perfect picture. "Show," said Jim, and up went the head and there was a picture for any dog lover. She took first prize for bitches. Then came all of the pointers, quite a number of them, and it wasn't hard to see that Mr. Darby, the judge, thought Negra the best and he wasn't long giving her the prize. Everyone was satisfied with the decision because there she was, the living beauty.

I walked back to Jim and found him stroking her down the back. "Now what do you think?" I asked. He looked up and smiled but was unable to speak for a moment. "What will you take for her, Jim?" I asked and the quick reply was, "She is not for sale." "No, I should say not," I only hope she is with us this fall.

I have hunted with Jim and Negra, she works in the field just as nice as she does on the bench. She will retrieve anything you kill, and Jim doesn't fool her either because when he shoots, something falls.

Jim told me he once owned a dandy Irish setter, "Mischievous Pat," but he sold him. The next time he heard of him was when he won second place at the Madison Square Garden Dog Show. Right then he says

he made up his mind that the next one he raised that had brains and beauty combined, he would keep it for Jim.

H. B. SQUIRES,
Fairmont, W. Va.

---o---

INTERNATIONAL BEAGLE FEDERATION

A beagle is a derby until the second January 1 following his birth, after which he is eligible only in all age classes.

Derby classes are divided by height only. (Those 13" or under and those above 13" and under 15".) This measurement being taken at the shoulder blade with the dog in a normally erect position. All age classes are again subdivided by sex.

The International Beagle Federation is composed of four Associations, Ohio, Eastern, Tri-State and Western, which embraces the Canadian clubs. These associations are composed of 34 clubs who this year came to bat with a total of 668 starters in spring derbies alone, not to mention the Futurity stake with another 84 starters. A total of 752 starters this spring.

The Ohio Association will be used in this description to explain my point, probably giving it a little unequal publicity over the other associations but it becomes necessary to confine myself to limits with which I am familiar. Being a member of the Olentangy Club at Mt. Gilead, Ohio, this becomes the most familiar ground.

In Ohio are nine clubs belonging to the Association.

Buckeye at New Philadephia.
Northern Ohio at Chippewa Lake.
Muskingum Valley at Zanesville.
Trumbull-Mahoning at Warren.
Highland at Greenfield.
Stark at Waynesburg.
Olentangy at Mt. Gilead.
Summit at Akron.
Ottawa River at Toledo.

Each of these clubs, some time during March or early April hold a spring derby field trial resulting in the awarding of first, second, third and fourth places and a reserve, in each of the two classes.

These winners now go to the Ohio Championship stake and run it off with the winners of the other eight clubs.

These four winners in each class now compete with the winners of the other three associations in the International Championship Stake.

This is the picture over the United States and Canada in the spring. Each individual busily breaking and training his pups to compete in the home club stake. Then carrying his winner to the association stake to which his club belongs, backed by the rooters of his local club. Then to the International providing he be fortunate enough to place and competing with the best derbies in the country as one of the representatives of his home association.

This stake is always held in Ohio and on the running grounds of one of the Ohio clubs who act as hosts and see that their grounds are plentifully stocked with game.

In these trials the entries are drawn and run in braces. Outstanding hounds are called back, rebraced and rerun in a second series, every effort being made to allow the dog to show his ability and demonstrate his superiority if he can. Each brace is run for at least 30 minutes.

Fall trials in Ohio begin in September, each club running six classes divided as to size, sex and age. Trials in other states are similarly handled and many are held as late as November and December, although October has always wound up the Ohio season.

A copy of the Federation's annual year book giving Constitution, By-Laws, General, Spring Derby and Futurity running rules may be obtained free from the Secretary, G. G. Black, Medina, Ohio, R. 3.

* * *

The last International Championship stake was held at Greenfield, Ohio, April 14-15, with Eddie Ponzi and Dale Sutton as judges. The results follow.

Am also enclosing the results of the 1934 futurity stake held at the same place on the four days following with Ponzi and Dr. Snyder judging.

DR. G. V. MILLARD.

* * *

INTERNATIONAL SPRING DERBY CHAMPIONSHIP STAKE OF THE I. B. F.

15″ Dogs and Bitches
13 Starters

Judges: E. Ponzi, West Frankfort, Ill., and Dale Sutton, Pewee Valley, Ky.
First—Collins' Driver. Owned by Theo. W. Collins, Ripley, Ohio.
Second—Orangedale Sunny Ted. Owned by W. J. Sulcebarger, Greenfield, Ohio.
Third—Heck's Queen. Owned by Walter E. Heck, St. Louis, Mo.
Fourth—Bardstown Famous. Owned by G. P. Muhs, Louisville, Ky.
Res.—Mill-Gan Molly. Owned by A. D. Milligan, Struthers, Ohio.

13″ Dogs and Bitches
16 Starters

Judges: E. Ponzi, West Frankfort, Ill., and Dale Sutton, Pewee Valley, Ky.
First—Gaysong Polly. Owned by Jewell Williams, West Frankfort, Ill.
Second—Porter's Blue Comet. Owned by Charles E. Porter, Imperial, Penna.
Third—Dunbarton Della. Owned by John Waters Parrish, Pikesville, Md.
Fourth—Sheik's Lady. Owned by J. L. Meyers, Pittsburgh, Penna.
Res.—White Art Jerry. Owned by Harry M. Curtis, Springfield, Ohio.

FIRST ANNUAL FUTURITY STAKE FOR BEAGLES

13″ Bitches
37 Starters

Judges: E. Ponzi, West Frankfort, Ill., and Dr. T. B. Snyder, Phoenixville, Penna.
First—Shawanoo Bess II. Owned by Shawanoo Beagles, Forest, Ont., Canada.
Second—Sutton's Tiny Girl. Owned by Mr. and Mrs. Dale Sutton, Pewee Valley, Ky.
Third—Marietta Empress. Owned by Dr. E. L. Cornman, Marietta, Penna.
Fourth—Helen Hicks. Owned by Mrs. W. C. Edmiston, Ralston, Nebr.
Res.—Blackfork Girlie. Owned by L. H. DeCamp, Mansfield, Ohio.

13″ Dogs
19 Starters
Same Judges

First—Pastime Pal. Owned by Harvey L. Low, Wallkill, N. Y.
Second—Kiantone Honey Boy. Owned by R. Paul Akin, Jamestown, N. Y.
Third—Blueray Squawker. Owned by Dr. D. H. Long, Zanesville, Ohio.
Fourth—High Hill Stubby. Owned by Edwin L. Wells, Maybrook, N. Y.
Res.—Milldale Rusty. Owned by H. F. McCoppin, Hillsboro, Ohio.

15″ Bitches
12 Starters
Same Judges

First—Schaefer's Trujean. Owned by C. G. Schaefer, Springfield, Ohio.
Second—Blueray Careful. Owned by Dr. D. H. Long, Zanesville, Ohio.
Third—Watatic Queen May. Owned by Joseph R. Phillips, Imperial, Penna.
Fourth—Rider's Nell. Owned by H. D. Yeager, Volant, Penna.
Res.—Marless Mix-Up. Owned by Kickapoo Beagles, Medina, Ohio.

15″ DOGS
16 Starters
Same Judges

First—Haig's Traveler. Owned by Haig's Beagles, Preston, Ont., Canada.
Second—Mill-Gan Skipper. Owned by A. D. Milligan, Struthers, Ohio.
Third—Blueray Bouncer. Owned by Dr. D. H. Long, Zanesville, Ohio.
Fourth—Tecumseh's Finder. Owned by Homer W. Ballinger, Springfield, Ohio.
Res.—Jambar Zane. Owned by R. A. Bierdeman, Youngstown, Ohio.

———o———

BI-CARBONATE OF SODA, A KENNEL AID

By CARL E. SMITH

ONE of the kennel difficulties, especially in winter, is the coming on of an acid condition of stomach and bowels; particularly if the feeding in winter be a bit heavy, the exercising light, and a preponderance of starchy and "heating" foods given, as so often is the case. In summer, the greater exercising, sunning, and the occasionally chewing of grasses, etc., tends to help correct the system; in winter these helps are partially or wholly cut off, so the correction must be made artificially.

Bi-carbonate of soda, (ordinary baking soda) is the same good corrective for the dog that it is for man. Sometimes the acid condition becomes acute and you have the early stages of running fits, where the dog develops a sharp pain apparently caused by the sudden rise of gas and the feel of food taken in upon the irritated membrane; so the dog stops eating, looks wildly about and starts the well known wild howling and trying to run over anything in sight, to get out of the way. In these early stages, I have found some baking soda, dusted and stirred into the food, a very effective corrective; (usually it is well to cleanse the system first with a dose of castor oil, though I also sometimes mix in some soda and warm water, shake it up with the castor oil, and give the physic that way—thus getting a mild purge and physic, and an alkaline corrective and soothing mixture, at the same dose). When feeding the food and soda mixed, after the physic, a couple of drops of essence of peppermint, also stirred in and administered with the soda, into the food mixture, also aids in passing the gas off quickly and in allaying the sudden colic that seems to arise in such cases; at least we have used these means very successfully, both with pups, and with older dogs. The use of baking soda, or milk of magnesia, is also useful in soothing the after irritation which sometimes follows the use of harsh vermifuges.

The soda not only helps to "sweeten up" the digestive system, but it also helps to sooth irritated mouth membranes, and is a mild antiseptic in cleansing and stopping, to a certain extent, decay.

FULTON COUNTY MEET

THE first of a series of Coon Dog Field Trials, sponsored by Fulton County Sportsman's Association, was held May 6th at Fountain Valley Tourist Camp, four miles east of Fayette, Ohio, on U. S. 20 N.

There was an extra large attendance and the seats were well filled.

The results of the finals were as follows:
"Indian Runner," owned by Relue Bros., Fort Wayne, Ind., first tree and second line.
"Will of the Wisp," owned by F. J. Drongenyor, Ft. Wayne, Ind., won second tree.
"Little Bob," owned by Clifford Hess, McClue, Ohio, won first line.

Fulton Co. Sportsmen Assn.,
J. H. Gamber, Secretary,
Fulton County, Ohio.

———o———

TROTTERS TRIALS

THE following is the result of one coon chase on May 6th: First tree was won by a hound owned by Voiers and Smith, Harveyburg, Ohio, and the entry of Noble Pace, Xenia, Ohio, took second tree. First line money went to Albert Bender's hound from Portsmouth, Ohio, and second line was won by a hound owned by H. May, Blue Creek Ohio.

This was our first attempt at staging a field trial and we were somewhat green at the job. We expect to put on a bigger and better trial our next attempt. Watch H-T-T for announcement of future meet The advertisement of our last trial in H-T-T brought us results.

Trotters County Club,
Adams County, Ohio.

———o———

TORRINGTON RESULTS

THE Torrington Fish & Game Association, Inc., held their seventh annual coon dog field trial, May 5th, at the State Rifle Range, Torrington, Conn. There were 78 dogs entered from Vermont, New Hampshire, Massachusetts, New York, New Jersey, Pennsylvania Maryland, Delaware and Connecticut. The committee headed by Charles Dupont deserves much credit for the fine manner in which the trial was run. The boys laying the trails had a tough day, trailing through swamps, woods and over ledges with the mercury up to summer heat.

The results of the finals were as follows: First tree "Ring", C. J. Edwards, Matamoras, Pa.; second tree "Ted", L. Bemis, West Springfield, Mass. First line "Rowdy", Charles Corsa, Cannondale, Conn.

In the special "Free for All" race both tree and line were won by "Pete" belonging to Ralph Pomeroy, Westfield Coon Club, Westfield, Mass.

In the "Pot Race," "Hillbilly," owned by Castle & Cole, Rhinebeck, N. Y., led the pack at the finish.

The Torrington Fish and Game Ass'n,
FREDERICK L. DOUGAL, JR. Sec'y.

———o———

CRESTLINE TRIALS

THE second of a series of Coon Dog Field Trials was held May 13th at Crestline Walton Lake Grounds, Crestline, Ohio. The event was very successful, and eighty hounds were entered with the following results:

First Tree Dog, $40.00—winner, Dayton Danger—owned by Dayton Kennel Club, Dayton, Ohio.
Second Tree Dog, $20.00—winner, Black Boy—owned by Wildwood Kennel, Akron, Ohio.
First Line Dog, $25.00—winner, Breezy Sam—owned by F. E. Dagenhart, Springfield, Ohio.
Second Line Dog, $15.00—winner, Lindy—owned by Cowell & Peterson, Perrysville, Ohio.

A $2.00 prize was awarded winner of tree and line dogs of each heat.

A large crowd turned out to watch the field trials. Many of the dog owners and spectators brought their families and enjoyed picnic dinners on the grounds.

The next meet will be July 15th.

A. G. HOLCKER,
Sec. Crestline Walton Lake Club,
Crestline, Ohio.

———o———

EASTERN SHORE TRIAL

THE Eastern Shore Coon Hunters' Club are sponsoring a field trial for coonhounds near Millington, twenty miles south of Elkton, Maryland. A purse of three hundred dollars is guaranteed. Date is Sept. 15.

Frederick Hasselberg,
Millington, Md.

———o———

[Editor's Note—We will gladly publish all field trials when held, if the secretaries of the various field trials will send them in.]

A REAL SERVICE

THOUSANDS of readers of H-T-T will take motor trips on their fishing and hunting expeditions this year. In planning these trips many of these parties overlook the important feature of getting the best route, from the standpoint of distance and convenience, and simply start out "blind", confident that they know the way. Oftentimes the shortest route is not the best or the quickest route by any means, and no one can tell this by simply looking at a map and adding up the mileage figures. One mean detour will take the "pep" out of an otherwise enjoyable auto trip.

A service designed to eliminate just such bug-bears as this is offered by The Conoco Travel Bureau, Dept. 82, Denver, Colorado.

If you intend taking a trip by auto either in U. S., Canada or Mexico, write them at the address above telling about when and where you want to go. They will send you free of charge road maps of each state through which you will travel, marked with the best route. They will also send illustrated booklets of interesting vacation and historic spots, camps and hotel directories along the way. You will also receive a passport which introduces you to 18,000 Conoco stations and provides a space to record the expense of your trip. This is a real service, which will surely save you money and grief and you should take advantage of the opportunity offered.

———o———

LICENSE FEES

IN the June issue of the Hunter-Trader-Trapper appears an editorial commenting on the new plan of the Ohio Conservation Division in the issuance of licenses.

I wish to call your attention to the second paragraph thereof particularly the latter part which goes on to say in part:

"The issuing fees being set aside for the restoration of game and fish, instead of having the county clerks collect and retain such issuance fees".

I wish to say that I am heartily in favor of sportsmen's organizations taking charge of the issuance of licenses but I don't like the idea of inferring that the county clerks retain such fees for themselves. They do of course retain the fees but at the end of each month they are accountable to their respective county treasuries for such fees collected.

J. S PALMER,
Clerk of Courts.

———o———

THREE-DAY LICENSE

TO enable week-ending anglers to fish Ontario's water, the Ontario government has decided to issue a special three-day non-resident fishing license at a total cost of $1.00. A. O. Seymour, general tourist agent of the Canadian Pacific Railway, states that by this means the Deputy Minister of Game and Fisheries hopes to encourage sportsmen to try for themselves the facilities which the province provides for catching trout, bass, "muskies", wall-eyed pike, great northern pike and all the other species of fish which abound in Ontario's cold, clear waters.

———o———

FOXES ABUNDANT

I ESPECIALLY enjoy the coon-hunting stories and would like to see more of them. Our game is scarce around here, especially raccoon but we have an abundance of foxes.

I wonder if some of the old timers could come through with some dope on how to break a dog from running foxes. It is a hard matter to break a dog where the foxes are more plentiful than other game, except the skunk; we have plenty of them here. Never having seen anything about the best methods of breaking a dog from this habit, I sure would like to hear some of the old timers' advice.

J. N. Brothers (Augusta),
Bracken County, Ky.

Q. I am planning a canoe trip down the Mississippi from Lake Itasca to New Orleans.
2. Where can I obtain maps?
3. What information should I particularly need?
4. What is the best time to start?
John J. Foucault, Minnesota.
A. A wonderful trip to make. No other in the country is more desirable I have been nearly half the distance and vouch for the interest, adventure, education in it.
2. The Mississippi River Commission, Secretary, St Louis, Mo., publishes the full set of inch to the mile maps from source to the Passes. Have these all bound in cover like a book—half sheet size.
3 A man named Glazier wrote the story of the trip—a very unreliable book, but gives ideas of interest and some value. When you reach St. Paul (you have to carry around the Falls there) I'd suggest you shift into an 18-foot skiff with canvas over whole length, at night to sleep on board. Or into a 20-foot long cabin boat, 30-inch deep hull and equipped with a 6-horse-power outboard motor, or even 12-horse. The book, Shantyboat, by the Uightys, published by the Century Publishing Co, of New York City (Order through any book store) gives fullness of what you may expect. My own book, Driftwood, printed by Century Co., also, is a complete description in fiction of a Mississippi river flood. I should suggest you get Horace Kephart's books on camping and cooking, and have a camp gasoline stove in your boat, also suggest "River Trapper," from H-T-T office, $1.00. You'll need mosquito dope before October 1st.
4. I should say for Upper River, June 1st or so; and for lower river, after Oct. 1st—below St. Louis. For full trip, start on Upper River, say, in July or August.

Q. Could I shoot foxes ahead of slow-trailing hound?
2. Would this be a successful method?
3. How could I trap foxes in Ozarks of Missouri?
4. Would scent baits be good?
5. How is scent bait used for mink?
6. What is a good fox scent bait?
7. What good bait for mink?
Edwin Roy Summers, Mo.
A. No better sport than this
2. You have to know fox habits, where they have their runways, where they feed, play, sleep, whether they run nights or days or both, whether they sleep in burrows in day time, or on the ground. You have probably both eastern and Florida grey foxes; kit foxes; and red foxes. And occasional coyotes which may fool you into thinking they are foxes, though you should be able to recognize all kinds of habits, tracks, hair in the brush, etc.
2. You'll need all the tricks of trapping found in H-T-T and other books about catching foxes. "Traplines and Trails" contains the scope needed. If you go through H-T-T for three or four years and study all the fox, wolf and coyote sets described, you'll be grounded in the topic. A few weeks' trapping will then give you practical experience. There are probably 200 to 500 sets you can use, as described in the books.
4. Scent is good if it is according to the locality. A scent good in the hills may be suspicious in the swamps. A strange scent if it is also mixed with human scent, tracks, steel, etc., often frightens animals, especiallily those as sly as foxes. There are fine scents advertised in H-T-T. One of the boys tells me that E. J. Dailey, Ogdensburg, N. Y., sent him some scent mighty good in the Ozarks for foxes, another kind for mink. I expect to try the fox scent in Mexico this winter. Anise oil is a good all-around fox scent. Three or four drops at a trap.
5. Many different ways. On a twig above trap, on bait, on both sides of the trap in a runway, and wherever the mink passes by.

6. For convenience I use several divisions in listing scents; sex, hunger, curiosity, memory, fear, affection (play etc.), news, etc. Each is a science in reality the foi example a fear scent where foxes run along a trail. A fear-scent will drive the fox off the path to go around into a trap. Anise and other sweets are "appetite" scents, etc. Fish for mink, and for foxes along fish streams. Meat back in the high country. Also fruit, nuts, and other vegetation have their place. Such things usually have to be worked out for regions and individual animals.
7. Mink are a kind of weasel, living mostly on fish, crabs, mussels, snails, occasionally snakes. Then they eat small animals along their streams and runways, mice, rats, up to muskrat size, and some birds. They are strong for sex lure—but should not be trapped, nor should any animal be trapped in the courting season, as this spoils trapping for the next year; there are many mink sets in H-T-T—copy them out into a notebook and use where they are fitted.

———

Q. What counties in Penna. have the best general hunting and state game?
2. How are trapping conditions in some of the northern counties?
3. Are there any professional trappers?
4. What do you think of forestry as an occupation?
5. How are conditions in Penna. as to raising fur?
J. C. A., Pa.
A. Wayne, Pike, Potter, and Juniata counties are among the leaders for the larger game such as deer, bear, turkey, fox, partridge, rabbits, squirrels, bob-cats, 'coon, and various other fur-bearers.
2. Plenty of trappers but still some uncovered territory for the kind of trapper who is willing to prospect to locate it. The easier places are mainly taken, but where there are no motor roads, territory is still not overworked. This prospecting should be done in early fall, but not in summer before the young animals are raised, otherwise the mother may move her young to other locations if molested.
3. Numerous trappers do nothing each season but trap for the fur animals.
4. Forestry is well worth learning, however at present there are many graduates of Forestry colleges who are unable to locate a position.
5. Study any fur price list of various sections of the United States and you will get an idea how Pennsylvania fur ranks with more Northern or Southern sections. Altitudes, selective breeding and food play a part in the quality of ranched fur. You should get the book: "Practical Fur Ranching," price $2, from H-T-T office.

———

Q. Will buckshot, heavy shot, copperized shot in any way injure the choke or spread the choke of a gun?
2. Will brush or scatter loads injure the bore of shotguns?
3. I have a double German gun made by J. P. Sauer and Sons Co. Can it be serviced by any one in America?
4. This is a 12 ga., 28 inch barrel, and 6¼ lbs. Is it considered a good gun?
Geo. Rehman, Ohio.
A. If the heavy shot jam at the muzzle, they sometimes open up the barrel, injuring it badly. Shot should always be chambered in the choke and it is advisable to insert card collars inside the shells to insure against the lead jamming. Hard shot as small as BBs sometimes make trouble in light guns.
2. No.
3. Any gunsmith will be able to take care of it for you.
4. Yes. There are several grades in this make.

Q. Are goats profitable to keep?

2. Where can I obtain data on cost of feeding and making returns?

3. What are the best breeds?

4. Where are good markets for goat products?

5. I have five acres at edge of town, wooded, high and a stream on it. I'll be glad to have information.

Burdge Ashton, Michigan.

A. Goats are very profitable, if one knows how to handle them. Whole tribes of people have subsisted on them for thousands of years. Few animals have a more consistent record of supporting their owners, if the owners know their job. And no form of domestic stock has a more attractive interest.

2. Dept. of Agriculture, Washington, D. C., prints many documents on this subject. You'd need to study encyclopedias, and the subject of Mohair (the textiles made of goat hair) use of goat skins, etc. Get all the books and articles on goats you can, and consult your librarian in the public library on books that tell about goats—the Bible has many references of value.

3. Depends on territory. Goats are adapted to certain terrain—and whether you raised for hides, hair, meat, milk, breeding stock, would all depend on your pasturage, and the slant of your approach. Each kind of profit requires a certain breed—and you'd find it would pay to study all angles first. Fifty or a hundred pounds of literature on the subject can be had. Your own State Dept. of Agriculture should supply you with valuable suggestions in reports and through your county agricultural agent.

4. For milk, cheese, etc., special customers often in hospitals or foreign quarters. Hides for leather, hair for weavers of cloth, etc. Meat through butchers, etc.

5. I don't know how much you can handle per acre. You'd have to feed and you'd have to figure close on so small a tract. Navajo Indians have flocks of several hundred and they pasture large areas—thousands of acres.

Q. How can I tan a cowhide so it will be pliable enough to make mocassins from?

2. Where can I obtain borax to tan skins with?

3. How can I take the hair from a cowhide?

4. Are J. Glynn & Sons, Phila., Pa., good people to buy guinea pigs from?

E. B. S., Me.

A. Home-tanned skins are not usually pliable enough for mocassins unless you used sheep or deer skins which are thinner than cowhide. It takes professional equipment to produce soft leather from cow-hide. You can tan a hide as follows: Remove all fat and flesh and place in solution made by dissolving 7 lbs. caustic lime in five gallons of water until hair slips off readily. Should be in warm place. Takes 8 or 10 days. Then wash thoroughly and place in a barrel in which a solution of 12 pounds alum and 15 gallons water, to which is added 3 lbs. washing soda, six pounds common salt and five gallons cold water. At the end of a week, remove and wash thoroughly for at least a quarter of an hour. Dry slowly and work backward and forward over a pole in the meantime. May be sandpapered to the thickness desired.

2. Borax is mainly used in cleaning and preparing skins and can be obtained cheaply at any drug store.

3. See answer to Question 1.

4. We believe so and suggest you always favor H-T-T advertisers as we make effort to list only those considered reliable, and thus you are offered that protection.

Q. Is there any more wild ginseng and golden seal found in northern Minnesota?

2. Does any firm buy red squirrel skins so numerous here?

3. Is it true that many people pan gold in the Sierra Nevada Mountains?

4. Can the unemployed make a living there, as said, 50 cents to $5 a day?

5. Could a Northerner get in?

6. What time of year is best?

7. Where could individuals find gold that way?

8. Please tell me how would I go about panning gold?

9. Are motorcycles as cheap in California as in the East?

10. Do lynx cats have regular trails?

William H. Stassen, Minn.

A. Diggers have skinned the roots so close that hardly any wild sang survives. This is, of course, a general statement. There are probably many beds undiscovered in unsuspected places.

2. The mid-winter skins are very beautiful, tough and could be made into a fine coat, waistcoat, cape and other linings. A good many of the boys are handling their own skins, learning to tan, cut, trim, sew and make them up, as regards these furs the buyers refuse to take.

A few garments could readily be sold in most communities, if they were gracefully designed, and properly handled.

3. A great many people worked the streams last summer. Some of them made a living. Many managed to eke by.

4. Not unless one has had experience and knows how.

5. The false glory of California has been the idea anybody could make a living there, could find gold anywhere, could spend the days basking in the sun. The chambers of publicity are now trying to get other people to support the thousands their advertising lured with cheap promises to come live in California. They even poison off the game and fur which would be mighty useful to hungry people if it was plenty.

6. Summer season—but don't think you could live on California gold. All the gold in California never paid day wages to the vast throngs who wasted their lives, part of their best years, trying to find the stuff.

7. Write to the U. S. Geological Survey, Washington, D. C., for pamphlets on panning gold and prospecting outfits.

8. As above. Prospecting for Gold, by Dr. L. Stolfa, 2401 Gunderson Ave., Berwyn, Illinois, tells about this.

9. About the same.

10. They follow edges of timber, they skirt certain rock ledges, and they often circle the shores of lakes, following streams. Occasionally, though, they go far from home, leave their usual haunts and perhaps go scores of miles into distant places. I don't believe any one has given these cats and cougars their due study — peculiar, canny, wonderful beasts that they are.

Q. Please send me a list of best books on Deep Sea Fishing.

2. What books about duck hunting?

E. J. Hofheinz, Texas.

A. There are a good many books about deep sea fishing, some narratives, some helpful handbooks, such just cheery sporting stuff. Holder's Big Game Fishes of the U. S., Book of the Tarpon, Dimock, Fishing from the Earliest Times, Tales of Fishes, (Zane Grey) Tales of Fishing Virgin Seas (Grey), are among the suggestions. Outdoor Life Bookshop, Mount Morris, Ill., will send you a list of Fish and Fishing books for selection. Also duck hunting book list.

2. I suppose Grinnell's American Duck Shooting is the best. Then there is Shooting Over Decoys by Hamilton. Wildfowl Tales by Hazelton is another. I should suggest, too, that you include books on shotguns, including the catalogues of gun companies who make shotguns, whose advertisements you find in Hunter-Trader-Trapper. I know of no more interesting books of information than the catalogues of companies making sporting goods—and no collection harder to make than keeping up with new guns, tackle, etc.

Q. I would like to know where I could get books on raccoon hunting, where to go, what nights and other information?

2. Would American Pit Bull Terriers be suitable for coon hunting?

3. Could I keep 10 or 12 squirrels in a big cage and could I make the nest boxes?

W. Mc., N. J.

A. You could do no better than to purchase "The Coonhound" and "Cooning With Cooners," both published by Hunter-Trader-Trapper and sold for $1 each.

2. If you intend to take the sport seriously I suggest a good hound rather than the breed you inquire about.

3. If they had ample room they would undoubtedly live peaceably, but confined closely the males would undoubtedly fight. Full descriptions of various nest boxes for animals will be found in the H-T-T book, "Practical Fur Ranching," $2.00 postpaid.

Q. Please give me the details on how to make a successful and proven deep snow fox set, including how to fasten, size of trap, bait and scent, etc.

P. T., Mich.

A. Following is one method: Take a rabbit or other small, unskinned animal and place some lure of the natural variety on the fur and bury this about six or eight inches deep in fox section. Watch this from a distance until you note foxes have located it. They may circle it a few nights and will then dig a little just over the bait. Now is the time to place a number 2 trap that has been parafined, just over the bait, filling in space by brushing snow with evergreen bough, also brush out all tracks. If the foxes take the bait, place more in same place and conceal trap just above it so the digging fox will dig upon the trap. A trap that has a large pan and operates high is best for this particular set. Such traps are made by The Animal Trap Co. of America at Lititz, Pa. A drag and about five feet of chain is used for fastening. It is a good plan to make the sets when it is snowing lightly. This is a simple set that has to its credit very many foxes.

58 Hunter-Trader-Trapper—July 1934

CLASSIFIED DEPARTMENT

Advertisements under this heading will be inserted for 10c per word cash with order. Name and address count as part of the ad. No advertisement will be printed in which only the box number appears; full name and address must be given. No advertisement taken for less than $1.00. All advertising must be in our hands not later than the 1st of the preceding month. Rate on display advertising will be sent on application. No display advertising however will be inserted in classified columns. We reserve the right to refuse any advertising. All articles having any appeal to sportsmen will find a ready sale through these columns. Make use of them. The number of classified ads that appear in each issue is a silent testimonial of results. Advertisements appearing in these columns are not guaranteed.

BEAVER

LAKE SUPERIOR STOCK BEAVER; BOOK for six cents. Union Fur Farms, Wadena, Minnesota. (6-8)

FITCH

ORDERS TAKEN FOR DARK GERMAN UN-related fitch kits. Phillippe Putnam, Hillsboro, Oregon.
GERMAN FITCH, FINE DARK BREEDERS, booking orders for 1934 kittens, reasonable prices. Krause, 210 Evergreen, Woodlynne, New Jersey.
YOUNG GERMAN HARTZ FITCH FROM IM-ported stock. Satisfaction guaranteed. Prompt delivery. Geo. White, Route 1, Hollidaysburg, Pennsylvania. (7-8)
GERMAN FITCH EACH $7.00, TRIOS $18.00. Will exchange for mink. Lesley Wiles, Route 2, Box 72K, Fresno, Calif.

FOXES

CROSS FOXES—DIVERSIFY. ADD CROSSES and profits now. Free booklet. Foxy's Fox Farm, Greenfield, Ohio. (**)
FOR SALE—RED, CROSS AND SILVER black foxes. Arthur Quist, Two Harbors, Minnesota. (**)
SELL CHEAP, FOXES AND HOME ON Lake Michigan. D. Sawyer. Pentwater, Mich.
SILVER FOX PUPPIES FROM REGISTERED stock. Very reasonable. Ralph Jones, Box 395, Springfield, N. J. (7-8)
SILVER FOXES FREE—HAVE A PAIR IN breeding. Raise the "Aristocrat of Furs." Anyone can—we tell you how. Enormous demand throughout the world for Silver Fox Pelts. Prices going up. Up! Astonishing offer for a short time. Two pair Silver Foxes for the price of one pair. Terms. Write today. Kelmoor Fur Farm, Thompson, Ohio.
FOR SALE—LIVE WILD RED FOXES FOR restocking, chasing and breeding purposes. Henry Hainline, Creston, Iowa.

MINK

BUY ADACKS — GENUINE NEAR BLACK, registered breeders. The finest, silkiest mink you can buy. Pelts not as good, but better than wild. Booklet, feeding and breeding instructions. 50c. Adirondack Ranch, 4-A, Onchiota, N. Y. (5-7)
LEARN ABOUT THE "LDIA" STRAIN OF Alaskan mink. Write for free booklet. Book "Minks and Mink Raising," $2.00. Lomman's Fur Farm, Barnesboro, Pa. (7-10)
PIONEER BREEDERS OF EASTERN MINK. Davis Fur Farms, St. Johnsbury, Vt. (**)
EASTERN MINK OF REAL PELT VALUE. Silver and cross foxes. Leonard Chisholm, Saugus, Mass. (2-7)
MINK—PURCHASE YOUR FOUNDATION stock from one of the oldest ranches producing selected Eastern mink. Hillside Spring Fur Farm, Eden, Wisconsin. (3-8)
A-1 MINKS, TWENTY YEARS RANCHING. Stanstead Fur Farms, Stanstead, Que. (5-2-35)
EASTERN MINK—RECEIVED TOP PRICE for Eastern ranch pelts at New York auction. Vermont Fur Farm, Middlebury, Vermont. (5-10)
EASTERN MINK—SHIPPED ON APPROVAL —low prices. I. Bloomberg, Lynn Center, Ill. (5-10)
EXPERIENCE, PELT VALUE AND AMERI-can National show winnings are proof to you our Yukon territory mink are right for foundation stock, or to improve quality of your herd. Yukon Fur Farms, Box 65, Petersburg, Alaska. (**)
FINE DARK EASTERN MINK AT REASON-able prices. Harry Comerford, Pine St., Clinton, Mass. (7-12)
FOR SALE—JAMES VALLEY MINK, LIVE delivery guaranteed. Art Inman, Hecla, So. Dakota.
INTERIOR ALASKAN MINK, BOOKING OR-ders for 1934 young, filling orders for Black Diamond mink food. Black Diamond Fur Farm, DuBois, Pa.

IMPORTANT

Advertisements appearing in the classified columns are not guaranteed, however every precaution is taken to bar those of undesirable nature. The Publishers of Hunter-Trader-Trapper are glad to hold purchaser's money order or certified check made payable to the seller until the article advertised is found to be satisfactory.

DARK EASTERN MINK PRICED RIGHT. A. J. Plummer, 37 Highland St., Winchendon, Massachusetts. (7-8)
500 DARK EASTERN MINK. LET US show you this stock before you buy. Brattleboro Mink Ranch, Western Ave., Brattleboro, Vermont. (7-11)
WANTED TO BUY. YOUNG MINK, STATE price. Geo. Truskauskas, R. D. No. 2, Torrington, Conn.
EXTRA FINE DARK EASTERN MINK. Deers Horn Minkery, Lancaster, Mass. (7-12)

PHEASANTS & GAME BIRDS

PHEASANTS, BANTAMS, PIGEONS, PETS. Priced reasonable. Harry Swinburne, Delhi, Iowa. (**)
BIG MONEY RAISING PHEASANTS. RAISE 95%; large illustrated book tells how, $1.00. Lux Game Farm, Hopkinton, Iowa. (**)
TURKEN EGGS—HALF TURKEY, HALF chicken. The coming breed, $3.00 for 13, delivered. C. H. Rue, Minerva, Ohio. (5-7)
EGGS — STOCK P H E A S A N T S, QUAIL, Silkies. Low prices. Paramount Farm, Martinsville, Ind. (5-7)
BLACK DUCK, GREY AND WHITE MAL-lard eggs, Pearl white and Lavendar guinea eggs, $1.25 setting, up. Seabrights, Minorca and Brahmas. Cyril Menges, Turbotville, Pa. (6-11)
LOOK! BANTAMS, PHEASANTS, EGGS, extra dark German fitch, cheap. Askea Farms, Washington, Iowa.
PHEASANTS, BANTAMS, WILD DUCKS. Immediate delivery. Highland Pheasantry, Troy, Ohio.

RACCOON

FOR SALE—A BALANCED FEED FOR raccoon. This feed gives wonderful results in producing young. Price $3.50 in hundred pound lots and $3.00 in five bag lots. Circular on breeding and care 25c. L. S. Russell, Cardington, Ohio. (**)
FOR SALE—WIRE NET FOR HANDLING raccoon and other fur bearing animals. Price $3.50 postpaid. Circular on breeding and care of raccoon, 25c. L. S. Russell, Cardington, Ohio. (**)
GENUINE BLACK RACCOON, YOUNG, OLD, reasonable. Addison Verbsky, Euclid Ave., Euclid, Ohio. (5-10)
WANTED—RACCOON CUBS, WILL PAY $2 00 at 4 months old. Ray Brown, Morganville, N. J.
SELECT YOUR RACCOON PUPS FROM OL-son's famous large, dark, northern stock. Prices reasonable. Clifford Olson. Odessa, Minn
A SPECIAL PRICE ON 1934 GENUINE black raccoon for early fall delivery. I also have grey raccoon for pets and a few half blood whites. Circular on breeding and care 25c. L. S. Russell, Cardington, Ohio. (**)
WHITE COON—TEN WEEKS OLD, YEAR-ling and two year olds for sale at reasonable prices. For information write E. C. Sheen, Jr., 383 N. Lincoln Ave., Salem, Ohio.
FOR SALE—RACCOONS, FANCY PETS, leaders, breeders, dark restocking, satisfaction guaranteed. Lowest prices write, James McKinley, Georgetown, Ohio.

PURE ALBINO BABY RACCOON, EIGHT-een dollars. Acil Underwood, Fowler, Mich.
GENUINE BLACK AND NORTHERN RAC-coon at depression prices. Home Lake Game Farm, Claremont, Minn.

FUR RABBITS

FREE SAMPLE COPY, "WIEDEMAN'S RAB-bit Farmer," 1616 Redfield, La Crosse, Wis. Contains valuable rabbit information. (**)
BELGIAN HARES—A VERY INTERESTING and instructive book on raising Belgian hares and other rabbits. It tells how to select the stock; how to make the hutches and pens; how, when and what to feed them; how to prepare for the young; number of young; weaning, marketing, killing, their ailments and everything the beginner should know; price only 50c postpaid, worth double. W. J. Gibson, 101 North Powell Ave., Columbus, Ohio. (**)

COTTONTAIL RABBITS

WILD RABBITS — JACKS AND COTTON-tails. Can furnish any number in season for restocking and coursing. My prices will interest you. Live delivery. Earl Johnson, Rago, Kansas. (**)

MISCELLANEOUS ANIMALS AND BIRDS

SNOW WHITE SQUIRRELS, $50.00 PAIR. W. C. Koon, Monongah, West Virginia. (4-3-35)
CASH PAID FOR BUTTERFLIES, IN-sects. See Sinclair advertisement on page 31. (1-8)
GET A PAIR OF FLYING SQUIRRELS free. Send only two yearly subscriptions to H-T-T at $2 00 per year each, or one subscription for 2 years at $4.00 and we will send you a pair of these cute little petts with a booklet on their care. Shipment will be made by express and safe delivery is guaranteed. Mail your order both for the subscription and the flying squirrels to the address given below. We will forward the subscription to the publishers of this magazine promptly, and will send the squirrels direct to you. Wildwoods Fur Farm, Woodville, Texas. (**)
BABY BEARS — SELLING $5.00 PAIR lower than any recognized dealer. Wait, write Crowe, Wayne, N. J. Also supplying all animals and birds. State wants. Season lists 10c. (**)
ANIMALS—BIRDS AND REPTILES, ETC. at bargain prices. Armadillos, dollar fifty each, Chamelons ninety cents dozen, Bob-whites and blue scaled quail, $3.90 per pair; tame white tail Virginia deer only forty dollars each. We guarantee full live arrival on everything we ship. Stamp for new illustrated folders; all kinds, parrots, game, animals, birds, reptiles, etc. Big bargains. American-Mexican Bird & Animal Co., P. O. Box 705, Laredo, Texas. (6-12)
BEARS—BABY BEARS VERY TAME, BRED extra dark female fitch $8.00. Rabbits. Reasbeck, Vankleek Hill, Ont., Canada.
FOR SALE—FISHER, MARTEN, MINK AND raccoon. I. W. Robins, Box 275, Ingersoll, Ont., Canada.
AN AMAZING OFFER — "SILVERTRIPT" black silver foxes, cross foxes, Alaskan and cross-bred mink, the finest money can buy, are now for sale on a time payment plan to suit your pocket book. Now you can start in this profitable business. We teach you everything, market your pelts, in our cooperative association and help you build up a profitable business. Our guarantee is your protection. Moose Lake Fur & Animal Farm, One North La Salle St., Chicago, Illinois. (6-11)
FOR SALE—RACCOONS, FOXES, SKUNKS, squirrels, rabbits, mink muskrats, pigeons. Junior Wilbke, Caledonia, Minn. (6-8)
FOR SALE — MINKS, SQUIRRELS, RAC-coons, foxes, ferrets, muskrats, rabbis, skunks, wolf pups, opossum. B. Tippman, Caledonia, Minnesota.
FOR SALE—RED FOX PUPS $6.00; YOUNG coons $4.00. G. G. Link, Maitland, Mo.

FOR SALE—WILD CAUGHT NORTHERN red fox pups, silver foxes, cross foxes, dark mink kits, wolves, silver tip badgers, priced right. Medicine Lake Fur Farms, Florence, So. Dak.

YELLOW HEAD PARROTS WITH CAGE $10.00 each. Talking $20.00. Tame Spider monkeys $18.00; Ocelots $25.00; Orange squirrels $4.50 each. National Products Co., Laredo, Tex.

WANTED—MOUNTAIN LION CUBS, WILD cat kittens, red fox, coons, squirrels. Consider adults. Sam Orleans, General Delivery, Newport News, Va.

PINE WOODS FUR FARM, OF RATHdrum, Idaho, offers finest minks, fitch, silver foxes, martens, fishers, etc. at lowest prices. Square deal assured.   (7-12)

BOATS AND MOTORS

BUILD COLLAPSIBLE BOAT FOR $5.00. Photograph and complete instructions. 25c; or sectional Wood Row Boat plans 50c. E-Z Mfg. Co., East Dedham, Mass.

HOUSEBOAT WANTED—GOOD CONDITION, suitable for including outboard motor or sail. Cabin at least 8 x 12, on Ohio or Mississippi tributaries. Exchange very fine old violin, German make, cash difference. A. C. Gilman, 7808 Whitethorn Ave., Cleveland, Ohio.

PARROTS AND CAGE BIRDS

PARROTS—YOUNG HAND RAISED YELlow heads, eating by themselves, choice birds, $10.00 each, two for $16.00. Laredo Zoological, Laredo, Tex.

BUSINESS OPPORTUNITIES

LIFELONG INCOME! MAKE MASTER REMedies from common herbs! 128-page illustrated book, 30c. Bluegrass Bureau, Newport, Ky.   (**)

ATTENTION! $27.00 WEEKLY OPERATING newspaper clipping bureau. Complete instructions 25c cash. Fireside, Royal Oak, Mich.   (**)

250 UNUSUALLY SUCCESSFUL MONEYmaking ideas; many new; from Government records. Only 35c coin or stamps. Enterprise Bureau, Tower HT, Syracuse, N. Y.

CAMERAS & PHOTO FINISHING

ROLLS DEVELOPED. TWO BEAUTIFUL double-weight professional enlargements and 8 guaranteed Never Fade Perfect Tone Prints. 25c coin. Ray's Photo Service, La Crosse, Wis.   (2-7-34)

FELLOW SPORTSMEN: WE DEVELOP and print any size kodak film and make you one 5 x 7 enlargement of the best negative for only 25c (coin). Reprints 3c each. Glossy enlargements 5 x 7, 10c each or three for 25c. Good work, prompt service. La Crosse Film Service, La Crosse, Wisc.   (**)

FILMS DEVELOPED 5c PER ROLL; PRINTS 3c each. Ask for Special Bargain List. Roanoke Photo Finishing Company, 164 Bell Avenue, Roanoke, Va.   (**)

FILMS FINISHED 25c COIN. ENLARGEment. Coupons. Crawford's Photos. Humboldt, Iowa.   (4-9)

8 x 10 ENLARGEMENT 25c (SEND NEGative). Developing and printing roll films 25c; 10 Kodak size negatives; reprinted 25c. Cardinal Photographers, Summit, N. J.

21 REPRINTS 25c. FILM DEVELOPED, 2 sets prints 25c. Reliable Finishers, Albany, Wisconsin.

DUCKS, DECOYS AND EGGS

FOLDING DUCK, OWL, CROW, DECOYS. Cheap! Write, Reynolds Decoy Factory, Forest Park, Ills.   (6-9)

CANADA GEESE LARGE TYPE, $7.00 PER pair. Wesley Paul, Davis, N. C.

WILD GEESE FOR SALE. CANADAS, Hutchins, blues, snows, whitefronts, Egyptians, Pintail ducks. Japanese Silkie Bantams, Guineas. Audley Russell, Tekamah, Nebr.

DUCK AND FISH ATTRACTIONS

MINNESOTA WILD RICE SEED—WRITE for special prices. Prompt delivery. MacGregor-Dennerly, Aitkin, Minnesota.   (3-8)

DUCK! FISH! MUSKRAT! FOODS! PLANT Now! Results next fall. Write Terrell, Naturalist, 255R, Oshkosh, Wisc.

PLANT NATURAL DUCK, FISH, GAME Foods now, for better hunting, fishing. Booklet free. Wild Life Nurseries, Box 71J7, Oshkosh, Wisconsin.

HUNTING DOGS

AIREDALES

OORANG AIREDALE PUPPIES AND trained dogs bred from oldest and best known strain in America. Safe delivery and satisfaction guaranteed. Sportsmen's Club Service, LaRue, Ohio.

REGISTERED AIREDALE PUPPIES. HUNTers, watch-dogs and pals. $15.00 to $25.00 each. Satisfaction, safe delivery guaranteed. Lawrence Gartner, Lexington, Ohio.

MIFFLIN LAKES KENNELS, ASHLAND, Ohio, sell choice Airedale puppies, reasonable.

BASSET HOUNDS

HUNTERS, PUPS. DIME BRINGS ILLUStrated descriptive folder and price list. Thirty Basset pictures, list, 25c. Smith Basset Hound Kennels, Spring Valley, Ohio.   (**)

BEAGLES

REGISTERED BEAGLE PUPPIES. BROKE dogs. Reasonable. Thurston Ensor, Westminster, Maryland.   (7-8)

CHOICE A. K. C. LITTER REGISTERED English Beagle puppies for sale. Leo Cline, Gouverneur, N. Y.   (5-10)

HOUNDS AND HUNTING, MONTHLY MAGazine. Most beagle and rabbit hunting stories. Yearly $1.50, sample 20c. 7½-page beagle standard illustrated 50c. Hounds and Hunting, Decatur, Illinois.   (**)

NOTICE

The express company will hold your money during the trial of any dog for a period of six days only. This of course applies to C. O. D. shipments on trial. However, most dog men will not ship a dog under these conditions during the open season.

BEAGLES FOR SALE—FINEST AMERICA; dime brings literature. Masterly Beagles, Johnson Creek, Wisconsin.   (**)

BEAGLES, RABBITHOUNDS, BROKE. Beagle pups, any age. Guy Werner, Hanover Junction, Pa.   (2-7)

CHOICE PEDIGREED ENGLISH BEAGLE pups, 4 to 10 months, 19 champions in pedigree, also matured stock. D. J. Miller, Route 2, Shreve, Ohio.

BEAGLES—SIX MONTHS OLD. ANDREW Freund, Bagley Road, Berea, Ohio.

NICELY STARTED BEAGLES 12 MONTHS old, farm raised, $15.00 each. No papers. James Nissley, Pemberton, Ohio.

FOR SALE—WE ARE BOOKING ORDERS for spring puppies. A few yearlings for sale. Also Castell's Place Masterman at stud. Castell's Place Kennels, Nashville, Ohio.

A. K. C. BEAGLES—ALL AGES. WRITE your needs. Art Bevins, Stelzer Road, Columbus, Ohio.

BEAGLES — BROKEN FEMALES $6.00, males $8.00. On trial, pups cheap. Harold Purdy, West Union, Ohio.

REGISTERED PUPPIES AND BROKEN dogs. Reasonable. Brierwood Beagles. S. Sharkey, Westminster, Md.   (7-12)

TWO THOROUGHLY AND TWO PARTLY trained beagles. H. L. Miller, Enola, Pa.

FARM RAISED BEAGLES — FEMALE bred, puppies, trained yearlings. Argonaut Beagles, Box 726, East Akron, Ohio.   (716-35)

WANTED—RABBIT HOUNDS FOR TRAINing. For field trials or shooting dogs. Excellent references. Harold Seidel, Route 2, Danville, Pa.

BEAGLES—65 READY TO START, BLACK blanket, tan head, white trimming; shipped C. O. D. for inspection. Return express paid if not pleased. Reasonable. Julius Reysen, Campbellsport, Wis.

BEAGLE PUPS A. K. C. REGISTERED, $7.50. Irvin Bankson, Rossburg, Ohio.

BEAGLES PEDIGREED, S T A R T E D, youngsters and puppies. Horace Mitten, Millersburg, Ohio

BEAGLE PUPPIES REGISTERABLE A. K. C. Field and Show bred, black blankets $15.00 each. M. E. Wilkerson, 1836 Koehne St., Indianapolis, Ind.

SPORTSMEN—YOU WILL NEVER REGRET, trying one of my real broke beagles or rabbithounds. Trial. Guy Werner, Hanover Junction, Pa.   (7-1-35)

BEAGLES, BROKEN, STARTED, PUPS, pedigreed. D. Hamme, Seven Valleys, Pa.

FORTY BEAGLES, BROKEN PUPPIES, coonhounds, trial. M. Baublitz, Seven Valleys, Pennsylvania.   (7-12)

BLOODHOUNDS

ENGLISH BLOODHOUNDS, MAN TRAILERS and puppies from imported stock. Enclose dime for answer. Barrett's Bloodhound Kennels, Morristown, Tenn.   (7-12)

FOR SALE—BLOODHOUNDS, ONE STUD dog, one brood bitch, three litters of pups. Willard Evans, Douglas, Ariz.

BLOODHOUNDS — REGISTERED BLOODhound pups. Booklet training bloodhounds 25c. Crossbred bloodhound and foxhound, bloodhound and Airedale pups. German shepherd guaranteed watch dog $10.00. Reasbeck, Vankleek Hill, Ont., Canada.

BIG GAME DOGS

ARIZONA LION, CAT AND BEAR HOUNDS. Trained, partly trained and pups. Photos and descriptions, ten cents. The Lee Brothers, Paradise, Ariz.

SPANIELS

COCKER SPANIELS—HUNTING STOCK. Mrs. Chas. Grey, 6600 Mariemont, Cincinnati, Ohio.   (3-7)

FANCY SPRINGERS $10.00 UP. INTERNAtional champion bloodlines — Best for less. Hanks Springer Kennels, Ellensburg, Washington.   (**)

IRISH WATER SPANIELS — GENUINE curly coated, rat-tails. Registered stock from working strains. Puppies, youngsters, trained dogs always on hand. Percy K. Swan, Chico, California.   (**)

REGISTERED SPRINGER SPANIELS FOUR months old. Wilber Wright, Swanton, Ohio.

REGISTERED SPRINGER SPANIEL AT stud. Eligible pups, prices right. Donald Batdorf, Swanton, Ohio.

SPRINGER PUPS, GOOD BREEDING, LITter registered $7.50. John H. Miller, Berlin Star E., Millersburg, Ohio.

REGISTRED IRISH WATER SPANIELS, genuine curly coated, top-knot, rat-tails; imported stock. Also several thoroughly trained males. Minnesota Kennels, Rush City, Minn.

COCKER SPANIEL PUPPIES A. K. C. LITter registered. Wesley Coomer, Ashley, Ohio.

SPANIELS — PEDIGREED SPRINGERS 4 months, $5.00 to $10.00. Orley Dawley, Mexico, N. Y.

ELIGIBLE SPRINGER PUPS, 3 MONTHS old. Paul Yoder, Smithville, Ohio.

CHESAPEAKES

CHESAPEAKE RETRIEVER PUPS, THREE months old. Jim Hollingshead, 212 W. Paterson St., Flint, Mich.

COLLIES

COLLIE PUPS REGISTERED, $10.00. Caleb Hobbs, Columbus, Ohio, Route 1.

PEDIGREED COLLIE PUPS. MALES $15.00-$20.00; Embden Geese $6.00. Maple Syrup, 5 gallons $10.00. Coolspring, Mercer, Pa.   (7-8)

COONHOUNDS

OAK GROVE KENNELS, INA, ILLINOIS, offers for sale high class coon, skunk and opossum hounds, either open or silent trailers, fox hounds, rabbit hounds, beagle hounds. Pointers and setters. Young dogs and puppies. All shipped for trial; satisfaction guaranteed. Prices reasonable. Catalogue 10c.   (**)

$200.00 BUYS A COON DOG THAT MUST please you. H. L. Low, Walkill, New York.   (9-8-34)

NOTICE 50% REDUCTION ON COON AND opossum hounds, setters and pointers, fox and cat hounds, bear and lion hounds, varmint and rabbit hounds. Shipped on trial, catalog 10 cents. Blue Grass Farm Kennels, Berry, Kentucky.   (**)

FOR SALE—COONHOUNDS, OPEN AND silent trailers. None better, also combination dogs. Trial. Harry Thompson, Pekin, Ind.   (4-9)

REGISTERED P U P S, B L U E STREAK strain, Miss Youngstown, Redbone strain, $25, male or female. Elmer W. Warner, New Middletown, Ohio.   (**)

KENTUCKY COONHOUNDS, TWO-YEARold. 15 days' trial. Purchase money back guarantee. $15.00. Bury Miller, Lynn Grove, Ky.   (5-1-35)

REBUILDING KENNEL. FIFTY NIGHT hounds ½ price. Sam Levers, Wooster, Ohio.   (6-7)

$50.00 BUYS A TENNESSEE PRIZE COONhound. Money deposited in bank for trial. Bruce Huff, Martin, Tenn.

HOUND PUPS, 4 MONTHS, GOOD ONES. Guaranteed O. K. Suitable for either night game or rabbits. Males $5.00, females $3.00. Order from this ad. Chas. Fisher, Route 1, Sonora, Ohio.

THE GREATEST DEGREE OF COMPEN-
sation in hound ownership is realized in the
possession of specimens displaying individual
excellence bred for a specific purpose. Our fa-
mous coonbred old time long eared black and
tans fill that need. Catalog 10c. Hermosa
Vista Farm, Bannock, Ohio.   (6-11)
FOR SALE—REGISTERED ENGLISH FOX
and coonhound pups. Field trial prospects.
Roscoe Williams, Greggton, Tex.   (6-7)
BLACK, TAN, BLUETICK COONHOUNDS.
Cheap, two years. Earl Aufrance, Nashville,
Ohio.   (6-7)
FOR SALE—EIGHT OLD FASHIONED
long eared black and tan coonhound pups. Geo.
Pettygrove, Oxford, Nebr.
SALE—WELL TRAINED KENTUCKY RED-
bone coonhound; also good on fox and mink.
Z. T. Hodges, Jackson, Mich., Route 7.
EIGHT TRAINED COON DOGS. SOME
nicely started, registered, young fellows, sired
by Pay Day and Blue Streak. Pair setters.
Write me. R. J. Wells, 506 W. Evergreen,
Youngstown, Ohio.
COONHOUNDS, COMBINATION HUNTERS
and pups. Trial. Ruby Souder, Pekin, Ind.
ONE FIVE YEAR OLD MALE COONHOUND,
open trailer, true tree barker, priced right.
Guarantee to please. Marshall Steele, Route 3,
Waterbury, Conn.

DIXIE IS ONLY FEMALE LIVING OUT OF
The Original Black Belle and Tennessee Bill.
She has puppies sired by old Bones. Lady
Ebony (full sister to Flying Ebony) has puppies sired by Black Belle Bones. All puppies
registered and these will be shipped express
prepaid for regular price of $25.00. Leon
Robinson, Dunkirk, Ohio.
DEATH FORCES ME TO SELL FOR CASH
trained and partly trained coonhounds. Must
sell. Craig Carmany, Route 2, Clinton, Ohio.
MALE AND FEMALE COONHOUNDS, 2 TO
3, best breeding, fine lookers, grand voices,
nearly finished $20.00 and $25.00 each. Some
good good old cooners $20.00. Some high class
cooners, trial here. Will trade real coon getter
for good 22 Colt Auto. Will buy one or two cub
bears. Roscoe Enzor, Greenwich, Ohio.

NOTICE—50% REDUCTION ON SETTERS
and pointers, fox and cat hounds, wolf and deer
hounds, coon and opossum hounds, bear and
lion hounds, varmint and rabbit hoends.
Shipped on trial. Catalog 10 cents. Blue Grass
Farm Kennels. Berry, Kentucky.   (**)

FOX TERRIERS, ETC.

GREAT DANES

IRISH TERRIERS

POINTERS AND SETTERS

FOUR ENGLISH SETTER PUPS TEN AND twelve dollars. John Woodward, Lima, Pa.

IRISH SETTER PUPPIES, CHAMPION SIRE. Good individuals. Eligible $25.00. A. L. Queen, Lexington, Ohio.

FOR SALE—THOROUGHBRED POINTER pups, two months old. Males $12.00; females $8.00. Clifford La Fountain, Lower Warren St., Glens Falls, N. Y.

IRISH SETTER PUPS, ELIGIBLE $10.00 and $15.00. Vern Waite, Waverly, Iowa.

FOR SALE—REGISTERED ENGLISH SETter puppies, 2 months old, priced reasonable. K. R. Lindsay, Route 1, Manawa, Wis.

WANTED—BIRD DOGS FOR TRAINING, 34 years' experience developing shooting dogs. Grouse, pheasant, quail. Excellent references. A. E. Seidel, Danville, Pa.

ENGLISH SETTER PUPS, WHITE AND black, registered, "American Field." L. D. Blair, Indiana, Pa.

POINTERS — SETTERS — HOUNDS — Pets. Free list. Ernst Kennels, Washington, Missouri.

BIRD DOG FANCIERS—TAKE NOTICE—I offer two of the best looking, most perfect broken bench show winners and field dogs to be had. Three years old, real style, looks and bird sense all combined; farm raised dogs with plenty experience both North and South. Steady to wing and shot, perfect retrievers. The kind to give real pleasure in field and at home for the man who cares. On trial, $35 each. Shelby Loan Co., Raleigh, Tenn.

TWO FARM RAISED, LOVELY LOOKING, all day hunting bird dogs 3 years old, perfectly broken, steady to shot and wing, good retrievers and all day hunters, male and female, female bred and guaranteed safe in whelp. These dogs for the man who cares. $25 each on trial. Frazier, Box No. 53, Bickford Sta., Memphis, Tennessee.

RABBIT DOGS

FOUR HALF-WALKER AND HALF BEAGLE pups. $10.00 each. Registered female beagle $20.00. Lawson Barrett, 721 Riverside Ave., Jacksonville, Fla.

RABBIT HOUNDS ON TRIAL; YOUNG started dogs and puppies on inspection. James Nissley, Pemberton, Ohio.

SMALL RABBITHOUNDS $5.00 AND $7.00. Trial. Harold Purdy, West Union, Ohio.

NOTICE—50% REDUCTION ON SETTERS deer hounds, coon and opossum hounds, bear and lion hounds, varmint and rabbit hounds. Shipped on trial; catalog 10c. Blue Grass Farm and pointers, fox and cat hounds, wolf and Kennels, Berry, Kentucky. (°°)

BASSETS FOR RABBITS. ILLUSTRATED folder and list, 10c. Smith Basset Hound Kennels, Spring Valley, Ohio. (°°)

FOR SALE—PAIR MALE AND FEMALE rabbit hounds, Kentucky-English Red bone breeding, medium size, two years old, extra good voices, long ears, raised and trained together but no relation. Know how to hunt brush, briars and swamps. Will stay until rabbit shot or holed. Hole barkers. Never gun or man shy. Pair $18.00, ten days' trial. Bank reference. Money back guarantee. J. N. Ryan, Murray, Ky.

FOR SALE—MALE RABBIT HOUND, TWO years old, medium size, bluetick Redbone breeding, long ears, good voice, fast and snappy. He knows how to start rabbit—will stay until rabbit shot or holed. Hole barker. Never shy of man or gun. Ten dollars ($10.00), fifteen days' trial. Money back guarantee. J. M. Erwin, Murray, Ky.

FOR SALE—ONE SMALL MALE RABBIT hound, two years old; he has an extra good musical voice, good router and steady on the trail; neither man or gun-shy. Over 200 rabbits to his credit this past winter. Price $12.50 on 15 days' try out. Ray Moody, Paris, Tenn.

FARM RAISED AND TRAINED RABBIT hounds. $20.00 a pair. 30 days' trial. D. Scott, Martin, Tenn.

TRAINED RABBIT HOUNDS—PAIR, MALE and female, 2½ years old, medium size, long eared, extra good voices. Blue Tick and Redbone breed. Raised and trained together. Will start a rabbit anywhere and stay with it until holed or shot. Good hole barkers. Brush, briar, swamp hunters. Neither man or gun shy. Pair $20.00, either $10.00 C. O. D., 10 days' trial. Money back guarantee. Bank references. Odell Kennel, Murray, Ky.

ST. BERNARDS

BEAUTIFUL REGISTERED ST. BERNARD puppies. Herbert Hoban, Jr., Waldron, Ind.

SCOTTISH TERRIERS

SCOTTISH TERRIERS, ARISTOCRATIC companions for house or car. Ideal hunters for small game. Quality puppies from trained stock, $25.00 up. Also fine young stud, reasonable fee. Evergreen Farm Kennels, Columbus Junction, Iowa. (°°)

SCOTTISH TERRIER PUPPIES, SIRED BY son of Champion. Pearl Elkins, Kokomo, Indiana, Route 3. (°°)

SCOTTIES—BLACKS, BRINDLES, WHEATens. Excellent bloodlines, quality stock. Healthy registered puppies. $20.00 up. Colonial Kennels, What Cheer, Iowa. (1-12)

MISCELLANEOUS DOGS

BEAGLES, SETTERS, POINTERS, FOXhounds, Springer spaniels. Grown stock and puppies, ready to ship and train. Stud dogs at public stud. Brood and show stock a specialty. Photos 6c in stamps. Stanford Kennels, Bangall, New York. (°°)

A LARGE WATCH DOG, ONE-HALF AIREdale; one-half German Shepherd, 10 months old, $10.00, inspection. A real pal. James Nissley, Pemberton, Ohio.

"KENNEL BUILDING AND PLANS"—THE only book on the subject; will fill a need for complete and reliable dope on kenneling; applicable to any breed and to one or a hundred dogs. Written plainly and is very interesting. Fully illustrated by photos and drawings. The book is bound in red paper with cardboard reinforcing, cloth backbone and printed on heavy enamel paper, a very durable and attractive binding. Price only $1.00. Hunter-Trader-Trapper, Columbus, Ohio. (°°)

HIGH CLASS COONHOUNDS AND RABBIT dogs. Trial. Grisham's Kennels, Baldwin, Mississippi.

HOUNDS, BIRD DOGS, BEAGLES AT ONEhalf their real value; must dispose of them. Write for full particulars. Wm. Phillips, Snover, Mich.

FOR SALE—COONDOGS, TWO MALES, ONE extra tree dog, two hound pups 7-11 months, four "22-championship registered" beagles 11 months. $8.00 to $12.00. Ed Shipley, Gulf Road, Elyria, Ohio.

FOR SALE—COON, FOX RABBIT HOUNDS, spaniels and pups. C. Chandler, Sharon Center, Ohio.

THE ROOKWOOD KENNELS, BOX 83, Lexington, Ky., offers for sale pure-bred English bloodhounds, Walker foxhounds, coon, deer and rabbit hounds. (7-8)

FOR SALE—COONHOUND AND BEAGLE puppies, depression prices. W. Porter, Orrville, Ohio.

HOUNDS, COON, FOX, BEAGLES $8-$10-$15. Tree, hole, vermin dogs, hound crossed, for coon, squirrel, possum, $5.00, terriers $4.00. All running 1-6 years. Dawson, Tuckerton, New Jersey.

REAL MALE COONER. HEALTHY, CLASSY coon, foxhound puppies, Walker, July, Redbone, males $5.00, females $3.00 each. Also female cocker, smooth fox terrier. Erwin Kopp, Johnson Creek, Wisc.

DOG REMEDIES AND SUPPLIES

MANGE CURED ONE APPLICATION, DOG or other animals. Guaranteed. Price $2.00. Kirk White, Cooperstown, New York. (11-10-34)

EZ FED WORM CAPSULES—EZ FED BEcause contents are simply sprinkled on egg or milk, not forced down throat; 50c and $1.00 sizes. EZ Fed Chemical Co., 233 W. Lakeview, Columbus, Ohio.

MAKE YOUR OWN DOG AND PUPPY cakes—summer and winter ration; know what your dog eats; recipes and full directions 25c. Running fits, their causes and riddance; folder 25c. Make your own dog carriers for running board, trunk rack or bumper. Neat, light, strong, curtained; inexpensive. Haul your dogs comfortably outside and save inside upholstery soiling and clothes; 25c brings full directions; illustrated. Special offer limited time, all 3 folders, 50c postpaid. Smith Basset Hound Kennels, Spring Valley, Ohio. Illustrated Basset folder and price list, 10c. Thirty Basset pictures, list, 25c. (°°)

STOP SKIN TROUBLE ON DOGS—DISCUSsion of causes, riddance, prevention, corrective diet, sanitation, care, conditioning, and three tried and proven recipes for external treatment with directions for use. All for 50c. Smith Basset Hound Kennels, Spring Valley, Ohio. (°°)

MANGE CURED OR MONEY REFUNDED. Stainless. Postpaid $1.00. Geer, Fifth St., East Liverpool, Ohio.

DOG COLLAR PLATES—GOLD INLAID lettering (very attractive) 50c. 3 for $1.00. Brass nameplates 20c, 3 for 40c. Rivets free. Metal Stamp Co., Fitchburg, Mass.

"THE CARE OF DOGS" BY A. F. HOCHwalt. How to Select, Train, Feed and House your Dogs to Keep them happy and healthy. Contains 25 pages of indispensable information for dog owners—prospective and otherwise. Hunter-Trader-Trapper, 386 So. 4th St., Columbus, Ohio. Only 10 cents. (°°)

DOGS TRAINED AND BOARDED

COONHOUNDS TRAINED TO TRAIL AND tree in two months. $10.00 per month. Extra good squirrel dogs and coondogs for sale. Good rabbit and fox dogs cheap. Theo. DuBois, Farmington, Ills.

START YOUR PUP THE ROBINSON AND Warner way. If you expect to hunt coon, cats, bear or lions, price $1.00. Leon Robinson, Dunkirk, Ohio.

DOGS WANTED

WANTED—ONE COON, SKUNK, MINK DOG, 20 days' trial. Money deposited with H-T-T. Robt. Iseler, Port Hope, Mich.

WANTED—TO GET IN COMMUNICATION with kennel having Scottish Deerhound bitch. Edward Cooper, Bramwell, W. Va.

FERRETS

FERRETS—RAT KILLERS $2.50 EACH. Deposit with order. B. & B. Fur Farms, Port Clinton, Ohio. (°°)

FERRETS—MALES $2.50, PAIRS $5.00. Yearling females, special ratters $3.00, ship C. O. D. Alfred Jones, New London, Ohio.

BOOKS AND PUBLICATIONS

"MORE FUR BEARING ANIMALS" BY Hardison Patton. Just published. Gives all necessary instructions for raising the Angora Rabbit, Nutria, Fitch and Fisher successfully. It includes revisions on raising the Silver Fox, Mink and Muskrat. Cloth, 6x9, $3.00 postpaid. Clement V. Ritter, Publisher, 58 East Washington St., Chicago, Ills.

WILL BUY OR EXCHANGE NICKEL NOVels such as "Liberty Boys," "Tip Top," "Work and Win," "Nick Carter," etc. Arthur Neetz, Box 214, Emaus, Pa.

"THE USE OF RIFLES FOR GAME AND Target," by C. S. Landis. A splendid guide for Sportsmen on the selection, sighting and shooting of rifles. Illustrated. 42 pages of useful rifle information.

"DOG OWNER'S TEXT BOOK," BY A. F. Hochwalt. A splendid guide for Dog Owners on the proper training, feeding and care of Dogs. Illustrated. 48 pages, including "Don'ts" that the dog owner should know.

"THE CARE OF DOGS" BY A. F. HOCHwalt. How to select, train, feed and house your dogs to keep them happy and healthy. Contains 25 pages of indispensable information for dog owners—prospective and otherwise. Only 10 cents each. If all three ordered at one time, will send them for 25 cents, postpaid. Hunter-Trader-Trapper, 386 So. 4th St., Columbus, Ohio. (°°)

FIREARMS

GUNS, RIFLES, REVOLVERS, FISHING tackle. I will trade, buy or sell all makes. Write for special cash prices on new guns. Send stamps for big bargain list. The "Reliable Gun Man" will save you money and give you prompt service. Emil C. Novotny, 324 Jackson St., St. Paul, Minnesota. (2-7)

RIFLE TELESCOPE SIGHTS, GUNS, AMmunition. (List 3c.) Knight, Box 294, Seneca Falls, N. Y. (8-7-34)

RIFLE TELESCOPES FOR HUNTING AND target; send for catalog, showing our latest improved mountings. Malcolm Rifle Telescope Co., Auburn, N. Y. (5-10)

PERMABLUE GUARANTEES FACTORY reblue; non-paint. Gunsmith's favorite, 50c. Easy instructions. Permablue Co., 2902 W. Sheridan, Des Moines, Iowa.

GENUINE U. S. ARMY LEATHER SLING straps, new 1¼" postpaid 85c each. Hudson, H-52 Warren St., New York.

A-1 USED ARMY LEATHER GUN SLINGS 35c postpaid. Swivels, set 50c. New 22 high standard automatic $16.50. Stevens No. 056 bolt action 22 repeater with peep sights $9.75, single shot $3.95, peep sight attached, $4.95. Sedgley Springfield Sporter, caliber 30-06 (sample gun) $57.20. Sleeping bags, wool $7.45. Kapok $5.45. Bargain list free. Ammunition, sights, guns. J. Warshal & Sons, 1014 1st, Seattle, Wash.

EXPERT GUN RESTOCKING, PRICES REAsonable. J. C. Denham, Xenia, Ohio. (6-5-35)

WINCHESTER SINGLE SHOT HORNET; converted by Sedgley, brand new $17.95. Hudson, H-52 Warren St., New York, N. Y.

NEW RIFLE MUFFLER—MAKES 22 sound like air gun. Stops flinching, improves accuracy. Any size $3.50. Spencer Laboratories, Akron, Ohio.

REMINGTON 12 AUTO NEW $30.00 OR trade even for Parker, Ithaca, Winchester 12 double cylinder improved cylinder or quarter choke with auto ejectors, fine condition. Raymond M. Reese, Lovington, Ill.

L. C. SMITH SINGLE TRAP GUN LIKE new $85.00; Parker D. H. single trigger $85.00; Parker V. H. single trigger $75.00; Parker D. H. trap gun $75.00; Parker V. H. $40.00; Parker G. H. $35.00; Parker V. H. 20 gauge $65.00; Fox A grade $45.00; Fox 16-gauge Sterlingworth; Baker 20-gauge; Marlin 20-gauge; Winchester 20-gauge; Rem 20-gauge Auto; Remington over and under; Rem Auto, Ventilated rib and poly choke; Remington auto 2 bbls.; Ithaca No. 4 single trap; beautiful 10-gauge hammer gun $25.00. Win. 30/06-model 54 with 48W and 17A sights, two others. 250, 300, 303, 30/30 Savages; 32/40, 38/40, 38/66, 30/30 Winchester; 35 Auto, 35 pump, 38/40 pump Remingtons; 25, 32, 380 Colt Pistols; K22 S & W; 32/20 Bisley; 30 Luger and case. Cocker pups, not registered, $25.00 pair. If you want a new gun, fish rod or what, name it, save you money. H. L. White Co., 11 Church St., Burlington, Vermont.

AMMUNITION SALE, SPECIAL PRICES $3.00 per hundred, metal case bullets. 25-30-32 and 35 Remington rimless, 25/35, 25/36, 22 Savage, 7 mm. Mauser, 30/06 Boatail, 303 British, 32/40, 32 Special, 401 Auto. Also 45/70 black powder, $2.50, 50/70, $2.75. 38 S & W short, $1.60. 32 S & W, $1.40. 32 short Colt, $1.20. Specially selected Government cartridges. 1017 revolver, $2.25; 1933 stock, $3.00; 30/06 Springfield, $2.25; 45 Colt D. A. $2.00. Hudson, H-52 Warren St., New York.

BINOCULAR—WIDE-ANGLE PRISM, 8x30. Unconditionally guaranteed. $32.00. Herbert J. Mayer, Plymouth, Wis.

BRAND NEW 10-GAUGE WINCHESTER repeater $28.00. Reuben R. Cross, Neversink, New York.

BRAND NEW COLT, NEW SERVICE, 45 caliber, 44/40 caliber, 5½"; also 38 W. C. F. 4½" at $19.85. Hudson, H-52 Warren St., New York.

PARKER GH, 10-BORE, PERFECT CONDItion, $50.00. H. B. Prindle, Andover, Mass.

12 ONLY! SMITH & WESSON NEW DEparture, 32 cal. 3" blue, new, never used, $18.75. Colt Army Special, 32/20, 4 and 6" blue, $21.85. Also 41 cal., latest improvements, 4" blue, $19.85. Hudson, H-52 Warren St., New York.

MILITARY MAUSER CARBINE AUTO Pistols, 9 mm. with wood holster, in good condition $21.00. Hudson, H-52 Warren St., New York.

OVERSTOCKED—30-06 CARTRIDGES $2.00 the 100, 30-06 expanding $3.00, Krag $3.00, Krag Rustless $4.00, 45 automatic $2.50, 303 British $2.50. D. O. Amstutz, Ransom, Kans.

8-GAUGE $55.00; GERMAN REPEATER $15.00; list 10c. Frayseth's, Willmar, Minn.

SPECIAL LIST OF 185,000 ASSORTED cartridges, to close out, send stamp. Hudson, H-52 Warren St., New York.

410 H. & R. HANDY GUN 12¼" BARREL as new $9.50; 410 shotguns rechambered for 3" shells, single barrel $1.50, double $2.50; 20-gauge model 12 Winchesters rechambered for 2¾" shell and action changed to handle same $3.50. F. R. Krause, Sleepy Eye, Minn.

WANTED AT ONCE. RIFFLES, SHOTguns, pistols. Will trade for new ones. J. Warshal & Sons, 1014 1st, Seattle, Wash.

HIGH GRADE DOUBLE BARREL HAMmer, 10-gauge shotguns, write for list. Hudson, H-52 Warren St., New York.

WANTED — REMINGTON 35-CALIBER slide action model 14 rifle. H. Klinkhamer, 1051 West 18th St., Erie, Pa.

"THE USE OF RIFLES FOR GAME AND target," by C. S. Landis. A splendid Guide for Sportsmen on the selection, sighting and shooting of rifles. Illustrated. 42 pages of useful rifle information. Only 10 cents. Hunter-Trader-Trapper, 386 So. 4th St., Columbus, Ohio. (**)

FOX HORNS

RAW STEER HORNS FOR MAKING BLOWing horns 16 to 18 inches $1.00 each. Beautifully finished, high tone, blowing horns for calling dogs 12 to 14 inches $2.00, 16 inches $2.50 each. Prepaid. National Products Co., Laredo, Tex.

FISHING SUPPLIES, ETC.

FISHERMEN—TRY STICKER BAITS. FORget the weeds. They are more weedless, lifelike than any bait used. Bait and fly-rod size.

TIE FLIES? YOU NEED OUR CATALOG. W. C. Dette, Roscoe, N. Y. (11-10-34)

SOUR CLAMS, 2 POUNDS $1.00. DOUGHbait (carp), 2 pounds $1.00. Angleworms, large supply, $1.00. Postpaid. Grigg, Hopkinton, Iowa. (4-9)

GLOWING NEW NIGHT FISHING BAIT. Make, use, sell! Instructions 20c (coin). International Agency, Cincinnati, Ohio. (**) Send for circular. Sticker Bait Co., Willoughby, Ohio. (4-7)

SHUREBITE SUCCESSFUL DISCOVERY IN fish lures. Write for our free folder. ShurEbite Bait Company, 216 E. 32nd St., Lorain, Ohio. (5-7)

ATTRACT FISH TO YOUR BAIT EASILY. Also, when to fish for successful catches. Both secrets only fifty cents. Money refunded if dissatisfied. Charles Mead, Box 11, Hillsboro, Oregon. (5-7)

SINKER MOLDS FOR MAKING YOUR OWN. Four popular sizes, easy to operate, lasts a lifetime, complete instructions with mold, $1.00. Dolph Manufacturing Co., Cedar Rapids, Iowa. (5-4-35)

"ALL ABOUT FISH," A NEW BOOK BY W. S. Berridge, presents many strange creatures that inhabit the deep. The book shows many illustrations made from photos taken by the author himself. It contains over 250 pages, neatly bound in cloth. Price $2.50 postpaid. Can also be had with a year's subscription to H-T-T for $4.00. Hunter-Trader-Trapper, Book Dept., 386 So. 4th St., Columbus, Ohio, U.S.A. (**)

LIVE BAIT, GUARANTEED ALIVE, PARcel post, quick service; worms, night crawlers, helgramites, soft crawfish, other kinds. Free price-list. R. & R. Bait Store, 46 East Rich St., Columbus, Ohio. (6-8)

SINKER MOLDS—DIPSY AND PYRAMID. Free folder. Reading Instrument Co., Box 78, Reading, Pa. (6-11)

LIVE HELGRAMITE FOR BLACK BASS $2.50 per hundred; $1.50 per fifty; 85c per twenty-five. Geo. O. Strong, Millheim, Pa.

SOMETHING DIFFERENT! SOMETHING better! "When to fish for successful catches." Remarkably accurate. Also, "How I Attract Fish to the Bait." Both secrets, fifty cents. Money refunded if dissatisfied. Charles Mead, Box 11, Hillsboro, Ore.

LIVE VIGOROUS HELGRAMITES $1.50 PER fifty, postpaid. C. Boyer, Penns Creek, Pa.

DOUBLE YOUR CATCH OF BULLHEADS or mud cats. No hooks required, don't waste time putting on bait or taking them off. Method 50c. Harned, Browns Valley, Calif.

LIVE HELGRAMITES, $2.75 PER HUNdred, $1.50 per fifty. Marvin Snyder, Middleburg, Pa. (7-10)

CAMPING

JOIN CAMPERS' CLUB—EXPERT ADVICE given by school man camper. Write Campers Club, 120 Greenacres Ave., White Plains, New York. (6-7)

HELP WANTED AND INSTRUCTION

USED CORRESPONDENCE COURSES AND educational books sold or rented. Inexpensive. Money back agreement. Catalog listing 3,000 bargains free. Courses bought. Lee Mountain, Pisgah, Alabama. (1-12)

FORESTRY JOBS AVAILABLE — $175.00 month, steady. Cabin, hunt, trap, patrol. Get details immediately. Rayson Service, W-16, Denver, Colorado. (6-11)

WANTED—FARMERS, HUNTERS, TRAPpers, qualify for steady government jobs; commence $105-$175 months. Write today for valuable free information. Instruction Bureau, 382, St. Louis, Mo. (6-7)

WANTED—NAMES OF MEN DESIRING steady outdoor jobs; $1700-$2400 year; patrol parks; protect game. Write Mokane Institute, M-26, Denver, Colorado.

WORK FOR "UNCLE SAM." START $105.00-$175.00 month. Men-women, 18-50. Many examinations coming. Steady. List positions and full particulars free. Write today sure. Franklin Institute, Dept. F-59, Rochester, N. Y.

LAKE PROPERTY HOMESTEADS AND LANDS

SELL YOUR PROPERTY QUICKLY FOR cash, no matter where located. Particulars free. Real Estate Salesmen Co., Dept. 5, Lincoln, Nebraska. (11-10-34)

LAKE FRONTAGE—PRIVATE LAKES, farm land, at lowest prices ever known. This may be your last chance. Government may stop sale of land. Write for list. Arthur Goff, Cable, Wis. (3-8)

FOR RENT OR LEASE BY WEEK: SOLItude! Log cabin in pines. Rent only building on 640 acres surrounding two lakes. Sandy beaches amid rolling hills timbered with pine, white birch and oaks. Lake is mile long. Fish for black bass, pike, smaller pan fish. Pick blueberries, blackberries, raspberries. Within hour's drive of 100 lakes and seven trout streams draining five directions. Lake Guthrie, highest body of water in lower peninsula of Michigan, 1400 feet above sea level, five miles from paved road US-27 near Gaylord, where are hospitals, movies, golf course. Forced to open to public my private lake. Rents for $30 a week, accommodates eight or ten. Make up party. Also lake and river lands for sale cheap. If you desire privacy telephone Dearborn 1171-W or write James Clyde Gilbert, 214 Meridan Avenue, Dearborn, Michigan. Making up schedule now. (**)

FREE HOMESTEADS — SOME IMPROVED; forfeited; 18 states. Maps, "700 Facts," 40c. Fisher, 386 So. 4th St., Columbus, Ohio.

25-ACRE HOMESTEAD RELINQUISHMENT, $500, on graveled road, school and postoffice one mile. Running water, 5-room cottage, game and fish close. Write for particulars. Bernard Denn, Camas Valley, Ore.

LOT 100x400 ON CUB LAKE, KALKASKA County, Mich. Water front, sell for $250.00. Gus Hofmann, 3107 Wilson Ave., Chicago, Ills.

FOR SALE—FENCED AND LICENSED Beaver Farm in heart of National Forest. 110 acres with private lake full of game fish, surrounded by virgin forest. Fred Irish, Sidnaw, Mich.

HUNTING CAMP SITE IN GOOD BEAR AND Dear country. Near trout stream. Oscar H. Nick, Erie, Pa.

LOT 50x250 ON BEAR LAKE, KALKASKA County, Mich., adjoining State Forest preserve, sell for $150.00. Gus Hofmann, 3107 Wilson Ave., Chicago, Ills.

WANTED—LOG CABIN IN NORTHERN woods for two weeks, July or August in exchange for use of comfortably furnished 8-room house, 30 minuutes drive from Chicago's World Fair. References exchanged. Reply by letter So. Hoyne Ave., Chicago, Ills.

$5.00 DOWN; $5.00 MONTHLY — 5 ACRE fruit, poultry, fur location, river front; Ozarks; $125.00. Hunting, fishing, trapping. Hubbard, 250 Grossman Bldg., Kansas City, Kans. (7-12)

INSECTS WANTED

CASH PAID FOR BUTTERFLIES, INsects. See Sinclair advertisement on page 31. (1-8)

INDIAN GOODS AND BEAD WORK

SEND 5c FOR LIST INDIAN ELICS, ANtique firearms. F. E. Ellis, Webster Grove, Missouri. (oo)

INDIAN RELICS, BEADWORK, COINS, curios. Catalog and arrowhead, 6c. Vernon Lemley, Northbranch, Kansas. (**)

MEDICINAL ROOTS & HERBS

WANTED—COMMON WEEDS BY STEADY buyers! Details 10c coin. International Agency Cincinnati. (oo)

WILD GINSENG, WORTH $7.00 PER LB. How, when, where to dig, etc. Full instructions. Ginseng plant and root, $1 00 postpaid. Grigg, Hopkinton, Iowa. (4-9)

GINSENG AND GOLDEN SEAL WILL PAY highest market price. J. A. Jackson, Bellefontaine, Ohio. (6-7)

MEDICAL

PILE SUFFERERS—THE HORRIBLE DIScomfort of hemorrhoids can now be relieved with our home treatment. Send fifty cents for complete dollar course. Complete satisfaction or money back. Arrow Laboratories, R. Fairhaven, Mass. (F-10)

TAROZ OINTMENT FOR LACERATIONS, abrasions, antiseptic dressing for boils, etc. Try a box, 25 cents, postpaid. McGruder Medical Co., Goshen, Ind.

SICK PEOPLE. GOLDEN RAIN HERB IS a miraculous herb that positively helps Diabetes $1.00 package. Medicinal Products Co., Laredo, Texas.

MEN—INTRODUCTORY: $1.50 BOX PHOSphide Tonic Tablets. Ironized. Only 50c. Limit 3. Eleven gigantic medical discovery prescription formulas Free. Golden Laboratories, Box No. 321-T, Evanston, Ill.

OLD COINS

$5 TO $500 EACH PAID FOR OLD COINS. Keep all. Many very valuable. Get posted. Send 10 cents for illustrated coin value book, 4 x 6. Guaranteed prices. Coin Exchange, Box 38, LeRoy, N. Y. (4-9)

PATENTS

PATENT - SENSE — VALUABLE BOOK (Free) for inventors seeking largest deserved profits. Lacey & Lacey, 635 F Street, N. W., Dept. HTT-7, Washington, D. C. Established 1869. (**)

PATENTS—LOW COST. BOOK AND INformation free. L. F. Randolph, Dept. 379, Washington, D. C. (5-10)

PRINTING

CIRCULARS, STATIONERY, CUTS MADE from photographs. Free samples. Fancier's Press, Batavia, Ohio. (7-12)

SALE OR EXCHANGE

FOR SALE OR EXCHANGE—SEVERAL trained foxhounds including one registered five year old Goodman bitch, has everything for gun dogs. One litter foxhound pups, Walker Maryland cross out of cold trailing, hard driving gun dogs. One litter of eligible A. K. C. English beagles, championship bloodlines. Priced to sell or trade for small trained rabbit hounds; could use good shotgun or high power rifle. G. K. Holbert and M. K. Laroe, Sugar Loaf, N. Y.

POINTER BIRD DOG FOR COONHOUND. Ray Brown, Matawan, N. J., Route 2.

FINEST FLY FISHING OUTIT, COMPLETE, never used, for what? Diadul, 4209 N. Kedvale, Chicago, Ills.

PAIR IRISH SETTERS. TRADE FOR GUNS. Robt. Roney, Troy, Ohio.

FOR SALE OR TRADE—PEDIGREED FOX and coon hound pups. Also 3 old tree dogs. Want guns or? Steve Zellinski, Redgranite, Wisconsin.

FOR SALE OR TRADE—ONE MALE LEAD coon and two females. Everett Miller, 2746 Fifth Ave., Huntington, W. Va.

WILL TRADE SAXOPHONE, GOOD MAKE and condition for a good coonhound that is a good squirrel dog. S. A. Malcomson, Clayton, Illinois.

TRADE—SAXOPHONE FOR 351 WINCHESter, 32 Remington rifle, 16 Browning Automatic, 20 Winchester repeater or typewriter. Wm. Wintlyn, Nekoosa, Wisc.

TRADE—NO. 5 OLIVER VISIBLE TYPEwriter and case, fine. Want Colts .22 revolver, cylinder type, high speed. Clarence Schleich, Freeport, Ill.

SALE OR EXCHANGE—COONHOUND PUPpies cheap, parents straight cooners, beauties; one broke hound $25.00 bargain, want mink offers. Chet Hoke, Elk Creek, Nebr.

SALE OR EXCHANGE—TWO "PR" REGistered American coonhounds $25.00 or good deer rifl. Truman Chaplewsky, Melvina, Wis.

EVERYBODY SEND ME YOUR TRADE OR sale list and I will send you my list. Herman Deshman, Corona, New Mex.

FOR SALE OR TRADE—A-1 COONHOUND well broke; want good guns. John Cox, Bruceville, Ind.

GOOD COONHOUND PUPS; COONHOUND. George Galser, Pippin Rd., Mt. Healthy, Ohio.

SALE OR EXCHANGE—TRAINED RAT dogs $5.00, pistol, binoculars. Carl Montgomery, Memphis, Mo.

BLACK AND GRAY RACCOONS. HENRY Sheppard, Stanley, N. Y.

FOR SALE OR TRADE—ENGLISH SETTER puppies. One unbroken rabbit dog. Frank Welsch, R. D. No. 1, Brookville, Pa.

TAXIDERMY

TAXIDERMISTS', FURRIERS' SUPPLIES—Illustrated catalog. P. E. Miller, Cambridge. Ohio. (3-2-35)

GLASS EYES, PANELS, HEADFORMS, AND all taxidermists' and furriers' supplies. Largest stocks in the world. Lowest prices. Big new catalog free. Write today. Rex Eye Co., 901-D Wrigley Bldg., Chicago, Ill. (**)

MAKING CHOKERS, FOX, COYOTE, $6.00 complete. Stranges Taxidermy. Clarkston. Washington. (2-7)

EXPERT TAXIDERMY—CHOKERS MADE, tanning anything. Ralph Feld, Edison, Ohio. (3-2-35)

CASH PAID FOR BUTTERLIES, INsects. See Sinclair advertisement on page 31 (1-8)

TAXIDERMIST SUPPLIES — THE BEST paper game head forms on the market. Illustrated catalogue 15c. Money refunded with first order. L. Loew & Son, Colville, Wash. (6-11)

USE "AMERICAN BEAUTY" PANELS. Beautiful designs. Highest quality. Lowest prices. Catalogue free. Nippon Panel Co., Williamsport, Penna. (**)

FURS — FOXES MADE INTO CHOKERS $6.00; taxidermy. Prices reasonable for A-1 work. Mohr, Route 9, Box 111A, Seattle. Wash. (6-11)

GLASS EYES, BIRD BODIES, HEAD forms, panels. Special 30-pair glass eye assortment $1.00. Learn Taxidermy, book complete $1.00. Supply catalog free. Schoepfer-Eyes, 134 West 32nd St., New York, N. Y. (**)

WHOLESALE PRICES ON EYES, HEADforms, beautiful mounting shields, all taxidermy supplies. Write today. Taxidermic Manufacturers, Memphis, Tenn.

BEAUTIFULLY MOUNTED ELK HEADS $20 each. Coyote heads $5.00. Stranges Taxidermy, Clarkston, Wash. (7-9)

TAXIDERMIST 5-PLY FIR SHIELDS $0.90 each. Oak and walnut $1.20. Paper deer forms. Keystone Pattern Works, So. Williamsport, Pa.

TAXIDERMY TAUGHT FIVE COURSES. Blue Beaver Taxidermy School, Lemont, Ills.

TRAPS

SNARES — FAMOUS KLEFLOCK STEEL animal snares. Choice of expert trappers. No. 0—Skunk, rabbit, jack rabbit, 3 for 50c, $1.60 dozen. No. 1—fox, lynx, 45c each, $3.75 dozen. No. 2—Coyote, badger, beaver, 50c each, $4.00 dozen. No. 3—All wolves, mountain lion, small bear, 65c each, $5.00 dozen. No. 4—Large bear, 5/32 inch cable, 11 feet length, $1.25 each. Kleflock killer trap—light, compact, powerful, bait, trail and water sets, for muskrat, mink, marten, 60c each, $6.50 dozen. We pay the postage on all orders. Setting instructions with each first order. Kleffman Lock Snare Co., Dept. B, Hibbing, Minn. (**)

TRAPPERS

OLD TRAPPERS KNOW THERE ARE more Victor, Newhouse and Oneida Jump guaranteed steel traps set every year than all other brands combined. Try the new No. 33 Victor, price 50c each. Reduces the number of "wringoffs." No. 0 Victors, 18c each; No. 1's, 20c each; No. 1½'s, 33c each; No. 2's double spring, 48c each; No. 0 Oneida Jumps, 20c each; No. 1 Jumps, 24c each; No. 1½ Jumps, 37c each; No. 2 Jumps, 58c each; No. 3 Jumps, 76c each; No. 4 Jumps, 91c each; Victor Gopher Traps, 24c each; Newhouse Gopher Traps 26c each; No. 44 California Gopher 25c each; and out-o-sight mole traps $1.00. Non-rusting copper trap tags, 15 for 50c; 25 for 75c; 40 for $1.00; 60 for $1.50; 100 for $2.00. Buy from your local hardware dealer or order direct. Prices postpaid. Prices for Newhouse Traps sent on request. Animal Trap Company, World's Oldest and Largest Manufacturers of Animal Traps, Lititz, Pa. (**)

Are You Going Through Another Season Without a Good Coonhound

FOUR SKUNKS AND ONE COON

MY boy you see in the picture is a great lover of all outdoor sports and is the first one to look the good old H-T-T over every month. In the picture with him is "Lark" and a one night's catch of four skunks and one coon. "Lark" is a real coon dog for his age and your book "The Coonhound," was a great help in his training.

James Wells, Wells Co., Ind.

CONTENTS

Supposed Origin.
Proper Breeding.
Inbreeding.
Crossbreeding.
Selecting a Puppy.
Training with an old Dog.
With a Lead Raccoon.
Random Training.
Rabbit Proofing.
Ailments and Remedies.
Glossary, Etc.

You don't have to. It's entirely up to you. Read these letters and you'll find the way out. A well-bred pup plus proper training is the answer.

CAUGHT MORE COON THAN ANY OTHER DOG IN THE SOUTHWEST

I am enclosing a picture of "Lead" and part of last winter's catch. These eight coon were caught in five night's hunting. This dog caught more coon last winter than any other dog in the southwest. I trained this dog without an old one by reading "The Coonhound" by Robert Legare.

Bryan Faulkner, Hodgeman Co., Kans.

TRAIN YOUR OWN

TRAINING your own coonhound is not difficult. You can do as well as others have. A pup from coon hunting parents is half the battle. Many of them are advertised in H-T-T. Then get a copy of "The Coonhound" and train him yourself. A hound you train will do better work for you than one trained by someone else because he's YOUR DOG.

- - - - - - - USE THE COUPON - - - - - - -

HUNTER-TRADER-TRAPPER

386 So. 4th St.   Columbus, Ohio.

Gentlemen—Here is $1.00. Please send me my copy of "The Coonhound" by postage prepaid.

Name ....

Address ....

TRAPPERS INTERESTED IN THE world's most efficient traps are invited to write for catalog and prices of the new Gibbs-Triumph consolidated lines showing the largest range of pelt getters made by any one manufacturer. Get posted on Triumph Stretchers that produce fine, shapely skins which command high prices. We are headquarters for Copper Address Tags, stamped with name and address, legal in all states. For trapping Muskrats, Mink, Marten, no trap has ever beaten Gibbs Two Trigger. Write today, postcard will do. W. A. Gibbs & Son, Inc., Oneida, N. Y., Chester, Penna., Toronto, Ont.   (**)

PERSONAL FOX TRAPPING LESSONS AT my Adirondack Camp, low rates. Write E. J. Dailey, Ogdensburg, N. Y.

TOBACCO

"GOLDEN HEART" TENNESSEE'S FINEST Mellow Natural Leaf. 10 pounds Smoking or Chewing, $1.00. Box of Twists Free. Farmers Sales Co., Paris, Tenn.

PROSPECTORS

MINERAL RODS ON MONEY BACK GUARantee. If not satisfied after using them 3 days, send them back to us and we will refund your purchase price. Map of hidden treasures with each mineral rod. T. D. Robinson, Dept. 17, Box 68, Elgin, Texas.   (7-8)

MISCELLANEOUS

FOR SALE—SKIM MILK POWDER. THE best most handy feed, prompt shipment, low prices, write Michigan Dairy Farms Company, Homer, Mich.   (4-9)

THE SHEPHERD OR POLICE DOG, BY Enno Meyer. Tells of the breeding, rearing, training, care and all pointers necessary to raise the shepherd or police dog. Illustrated. Price 50 cents. Hunter-Trader-Trapper, Columbus, Ohio.   (**)

SELL—QUALITY TIRES REBUILT LIKE new. Goodyear, Firestone, and nationally advertised brands—98 cents up. Rubber Products Co., Ft. Worth, Texas.   (**)

BARTENDER'S GUIDE FOR HOMES AND stores, 128 pages, 429 recipes, price 35c prepaid. William Gibson, 101 N. Powell, Columbus, Ohio.   (4-7)

OLD AGE PENSION INFORMATION. ENclose stamp. Judge Lehman, Humboldt, Kans.   (5-10)

ULTRA-LENS POCKET MICROSCOPE, 500X magnification (250,000 areas) 50c, postpaid. 250X, 30c. Phliegor Laboratories, Miltin, Pa.   (**)

RUBBER GOODS OF EVERY DESCRIPTION mailed in plain wrapper, postpaid by us. Write for mail-order catalog, saving 50%. N-R Mfg. Co., 11 Chatham St., Hamilton, Ont.   (6-11)

TARANTULAS! REAL LIVE SPECIMENS of the giant spiders shipped anywhere, upon receipt of price $1.00 each. Trapdoor spiders, the most remarkable of all web-spinning creatures, shipped for $1.50 each. Centipedes, Scorpions and horned lizards secured only on special order. Everything shipped carrying charges collect. Everything shipped alive. Address Raymond W. Thorp, 3517 Marmion Way, Los Angeles, Calif.

"FISHES, THEIR JOURNEYS AND MIGRAtions," by Louis Roule. The author is a well-known scientific student of fish, and he brings to this popular work a sound background of knowledge. This book contains 270 pages, with 54 illustrations, bound in cloth. Price $3.75 postpaid. Will be given with a year's subscription to Hunter-Trader-Trapper for $5.00. Hunter-Trader-Trapper, Book Dept., 386 So. 4th St., Columbus, Ohio, U. S. A.   (**)

JUMPING BEANS, NEW CROP, $1.00 HUNdred, $6.00 thousand. Cash with order. Hilario Cavazos, Laredo, Tex.

100 AIRPLANES, $80 UP, FLYAWAY, OWNer's price, name and address. Send 20c. Used Aircraft Directory, Athens, Ohio.

WHY BE DIVORCED——SAMPLE 25c. Moyer, Box 241, Milton, Pa.

WINES AND LIQUOR CHEAPLY MADE. Good whiskey (25c gallon) without a still. Particulars for stamp. G. O. Shaver, DeQueen, Arkansas.

TRAINING THE RABBIT HOUND, BY CARL E. Smith. A book on Beagles and Bassets with descriptive and historical sketches of each breed, their training, breeding, and kennel care. The training methods described in this book can be applied to any dog, even though it is not a beagle or basset. If you are interested in the grand old sport of rabbit hunting, you will want this book; if you have a young dog to train you can't afford to be without a copy. If you have any kind of a dog, the chapter on disease and home remedies is worth many times the price of the whole book. Cloth bound, nicely illustrated, and very attractive. Price only $1.00 or given with one new subscriber at $2.00 per year. Hunter-Trader-Trapper, Columbus, Ohio.

"Bound to Get Results"

That is not our own statement—it is the expression of an advertiser who voluntarily wrote us after advertising in Hunter-Trader-Trapper. Many others are received daily expressing satisfaction as to results.

Extra Money for You

You don't have to be in business to make money through H-T-T classified columns. Around the house you have many useful articles that you no longer use. Sell them through an H-T-T ad and get a few extra dollars to pay those bills that have a nasty habit of piling up in January. Or our "Sale or Exchange" column offers you an opportunity of trading something you don't want for something you need. Use an ad in H-T-T next month.

Your Ad Should Do As Well---Try It and See

Paste or write your ad in the space below.

Hunter-Trader-Trapper, Columbus, Ohio.

Here is $_____ Please insert the following advertisement in your magazine for _____ issue(s). In figuring the cost of the ad I have counted my name and address. It is my understanding that a copy of the magazine containing my ad will be sent free of charge.

RATE—10c PER WORD—10% Discount for cash with a 6-months order. In figuring number of words, name and address must also be counted.

Printed in the USA
CPSIA information can be obtained
at www.ICGtesting.com
LVHW081451160224
772051LV00036B/1171